# Project Management For Dummies

Cheat Sheet

## Avoiding the Most Common Project Pitfalls

- Vague project objectives
- Vague or missing assumptions
- Key commitments not in writing
- Key audiences overlooked
- Lack of team-member commitment
- Failure to hold people accountable
- Backing into project schedules
- Failure to define and sustain a team identity

- Insufficient monitoring
- No formal risk identification and management
- Poor communication
- No organized approach to evaluating and introducing requested changes
- Failure to improve your performance on the next project by incorporating the lessons gained on the last one

## Developing Meaningful Project Objectives

- Focus on outcomes rather than activities.
- Use clear language — no technical jargon or acronyms.
- Make sure that every objective has at least one measure.
- Make sure every measure has at least one performance target.

- Make sure every objective is time-specific.
- Make sure it's possible to achieve each objective.
- Check with all project drivers to be sure you've identified their expectations.

## Developing Achievable Schedules

- Identify all required activities.
- Break activities down into sufficient detail.
- Always consider both duration and interdependencies.
- Factor in resource availability.
- Recognize and record all assumptions.
- Reexamine your original schedule after your project is approved but before you start work on it.

- Keep in mind that a duration estimate is your best sense of how long an activity will take to perform, as opposed to how long people want the activity to take.
- Consider the impact of other projects and work activities that are going on at the same time as your project.
- Develop contingency plans for high-risk activities.

## For Dummies: Bestselling Book Series for Beginners

# Project Management For Dummies®

Cheat Sheet

## Improving Your Personnel Estimates

- Distinguish between person effort and duration.
- Describe clearly the work to be done on all activities.
- Specify personnel requirements by needed skills and knowledge.
- Revise your estimates, if necessary, after people have actually been assigned to your team.
- When estimating the work effort required, consult the people who'll be performing the activities.
- Consider your past experience with similar activities.
- Factor in productivity, availability, and efficiency.
- To support future estimates, record the work effort actually invested in activities.

## Eliciting and Sustaining Commitment

- Clarify how your project will benefit the organization and individual team members.
- Involve team members in the planning process.
- Demonstrate to people that the plan is feasible.
- Address issues, concerns, and questions promptly and openly.
- Provide frequent and meaningful feedback on project progress and people's performance.
- Recognize people's contributions.
- Encourage team members to get to know each other.
- Focus on people's strengths rather than their limitations.

## Communicating Effectively

- Keep project meetings to one hour or less.
- Always prepare and distribute minutes of meetings.
- Highlight important information on the first page of a report.
- Don't assume.
- Reinforce important messages by using different media.
- Always verify with people that they've received your communication and understand the message.
- Use meetings to brainstorm, explain important information, and reinforce relationships.

Copyright © 2001 Wiley Publishing, Inc. All rights reserved.

Item 5283-X

For more information about Wiley Publishing, call 1-800-762-2974.

Wiley, the Wiley Publishing logo, For Dummies, the Dummies Man logo, the For Dummies Bestselling Book Series logo and all related trade dress are trademarks or registered trademarks of Wiley Publishing, Inc. All other trademarks are property of their respective owners.

## For Dummies: Bestselling Book Series for Beginners

# Praise for Project Management For Dummies

"Everything you need to run a successful project is here in one appealing package — a must for all project teams. Stan Portny has the ability to put his finger on the real project-management challenges faced by real team members. I will be buying a copy of *Project Management For Dummies* for every member of our company. Stan Portny is the perfect choice to write *Project Management For Dummies*.

> — Richard Cutting, Director of Project Management,
> Melard Technologies, Inc.

"Appropriate material for *all* individuals responsible for managing a project large or small. Stan Portny is the *best* in the field — his teachings have contributed to the successful growth of management skills for numerous Air Force students."

> — Maggie Grace, Education and Training Administrator,
> U.S. Air Force

"Stan Portny has been teaching people how to manage successful projects for many years. His practical approach to project management and step-by-step methodology is sensible and easy to follow. Mr. Portny takes into consideration both the technical and interpersonal aspects that are essential for successful project management. I recommend this book for new project managers as well as for experienced mangers who want to refine and renew their skills."

> — Rhoda N. Cahan, Vice President, Training Division,
> Computer Generated Solutions, Inc.

"If you have been asked to manage a project and don't know where to turn, or want to avoid the problems you've seen others deal with, this is the book. In addition to helping you learn how to plan, organize and staff a project team, this book provides clear practical insight on the "soft side" of project management: how to identify key stake holders, get buy-in, and keep everyone informed. This book provides a step-by-step approach that can be used by virtually everyone."

> — Steven R. Smith, Manager, Human Resources, Novartis
> Pharmaceuticals Corporation

"*Project Management For Dummies* outlines the specifics of project management. From project management to all phases of planning and implementation, it outlines in clear, concise verbiage the entire process, including potential pitfalls and problems encountered during the lifespan of a project. Personally, I have found this book to be a great resource that I continue to refer back to."

— Gene Reichert, Manager of Corporate Field Services

"Stan Portny takes the sometimes overwhelming discipline of project management and, using real life experiences, presents it in an exciting and understandable fashion. For any new project manager, this book conveys the tools and techniques, and more importantly, the mindset needed to successfully deliver projects."

— John Halper, Vice President, Global Applications,
Seagram Universal

"The project-management tips and techniques in the book are right on target. If you live in a world of multiple priorities and high expectations, and need to get it right the first time, grab this book. It's an easy-to-read, surefire roadmap to success."

— Kathleen Zingaro, Vice President of Human Resources
at Just Born, Inc.

 TM

# References for the Rest of Us!®

## BESTSELLING BOOK SERIES

Do you find that traditional reference books are overloaded with technical details and advice you'll never use? Do you postpone important life decisions because you just don't want to deal with them? Then our *For Dummies®* business and general reference book series is for you.

For Dummies business and general reference books are written for those frustrated and hard-working souls who know they aren't dumb, but find that the myriad of personal and business issues and the accompanying horror stories make them feel helpless. *For Dummies* books use a lighthearted approach, a down-to-earth style, and even cartoons and humorous icons to dispel fears and build confidence. Lighthearted but not lightweight, these books are perfect survival guides to solve your everyday personal and business problems.

*"More than a publishing phenomenon, 'Dummies' is a sign of the times."*

— *The New York Times*

*"A world of detailed and authoritative information is packed into them…"*

— *U.S. News and World Report*

*"…you won't go wrong buying them."*

— *Walter Mossberg, Wall Street Journal, on For Dummies books*

Already, millions of satisfied readers agree. They have made For Dummies the #1 introductory level computer book series and a best-selling business book series. They have written asking for more. So, if you're looking for the best and easiest way to learn about business and other general reference topics, look to For Dummies to give you a helping hand.

Wiley Publishing, Inc.

5/09

# Project Management

## FOR

## DUMMIES®

# Project Management FOR DUMMIES®

by Stanley E. Portny

Wiley Publishing, Inc.

**Project Management For Dummies®**

Published by
**Wiley Publishing, Inc.**
111 River Street
Hoboken, NJ 07030
www.wiley.com

Copyright © 2001 by Wiley Publishing, Inc., Indianapolis, Indiana

Published by Wiley Publishing, Inc., Indianapolis, Indiana

Published simultaneously in Canada

No part of this publication may be reproduced, stored in a retrieval system, or transmitted in any form or by any means, electronic, mechanical, photocopying, recording, scanning, or otherwise, except as permitted under Sections 107 or 108 of the 1976 United States Copyright Act, without either the prior written permission of the Publisher, or authorization through payment of the appropriate per-copy fee to the Copyright Clearance Center, 222 Rosewood Drive, Danvers, MA 01923, 978-750-8400, fax 978-646-8700. Requests to the Publisher for permission should be addressed to the Legal Department, Wiley Publishing, Inc., 10475 Crosspoint Blvd., Indianapolis, IN 46256, 317-572-3447, fax 317-572-4447, or e-mail permcoordinator@wiley.com

**Trademarks:** Wiley, the Wiley Publishing logo, For Dummies, the Dummies Man logo, A Reference for the Rest of Us!, The Dummies Way, Dummies Daily, The Fun and Easy Way, Dummies.com, and related trade dress are trademarks or registered trademarks of John Wiley & Sons, Inc. and/or its affiliates in the United States and other countries and may not be used without written permission. All other trademarks are the property of their respective owners. Wiley Publishing, Inc., is not associated with any product or vendor mentioned in this book.

LIMIT OF LIABILITY/DISCLAIMER OF WARRANTY: WHILE THE PUBLISHER AND AUTHOR HAVE USED THEIR BEST EFFORTS IN PREPARING THIS BOOK, THEY MAKE NO REPRESENTATIONS OR WARRANTIES WITH RESPECT TO THE ACCURACY OR COMPLETENESS OF THE CONTENTS OF THIS BOOK AND SPECIFICALLY DISCLAIM ANY IMPLIED WARRANTIES OF MERCHANTABILITY OR FITNESS FOR A PARTICULAR PURPOSE. NO WARRANTY MAY BE CREATED OR EXTENDED BY SALES REPRESENTATIVES OR WRITTEN SALES MATERIALS. THE ADVICE AND STRATEGIES CONTAINED HEREIN MAY NOT BE SUITABLE FOR YOUR SITUATION. YOU SHOULD CONSULT WITH A PROFESSIONAL WHERE APPROPRIATE. NEITHER THE PUBLISHER NOR AUTHOR SHALL BE LIABLE FOR ANY LOSS OF PROFIT OR ANY OTHER COMMERCIAL DAMAGES, INCLUDING BUT NOT LIMITED TO SPECIAL, INCIDENTAL, CONSEQUENTIAL, OR OTHER DAMAGES.

For general information on our other products and services or to obtain technical support, please contact our Customer Care Department within the U.S. at 800-762-2974, outside the U.S. at 317-572-3993, or fax 317-572-4002.

Wiley also publishes its books in a variety of electronic formats. Some content that appears in print may not be available in electronic books.

*Library of Congress Cataloging-in-Publication Data:*

Library of Congress Control Number: 00-109389

ISBN: 0-7645-5283-X

Manufactured in the United States of America

15 14 13 12 11

1O/RQ/RQ/QU/IN

# *About the Author*

**Stan Portny**, president of Stanley E. Portny and Associates, LLC, is an internationally recognized expert in project management and project leadership. During the past 28 years, he has provided training and consultation to more than 100 public and private organizations in the fields of finance, consumer products, insurance, telecommunications, pharmaceuticals, information technology, defense, and health care. He has developed and conducted training programs for over 25,000 management and staff personnel in engineering, sales and marketing, research and development, information systems, manufacturing, operations, and support areas.

Stan combines an analyst's eye, an innate sense of order and balance, and a deep respect for one's personal potential to help people understand how they can take control of often chaotic environments and produce dramatic results, while achieving personal and professional satisfaction. Widely acclaimed for his dynamic presentations and his unusual ability to establish a close rapport with seminar participants, Stan specializes in tailoring his training programs to meet the special and unique needs of individual organizations. His clients have included ADP, ADT, American International Group, Burlington Northern Railroad, Hewlett Packard, Nabisco, Novartis Pharmaceuticals, Pitney Bowes, UPS, Vanguard Investment Companies, and the United States Navy and Air Force.

Stan, a Project Management Institute certified Project Management Professional (PMP), received his bachelor's degree in electrical engineering from the Polytechnic Institute of Brooklyn and both his master's degree in electrical engineering and the degree of electrical engineer from the Massachusetts Institute of Technology. He has also studied at the Alfred P. Sloan School of Management and the George Washington University National Law Center.

Stan provides on-site training in all aspects of project management, project team building and project leadership. He can also work with you to assess your organization's current project-management practices, develop planning and control systems and procedures, and review the progress of ongoing projects. Finally, Stan can serve as the keynote speaker at your organization or professional association meetings.

Please contact Stan through any of the following means to tell him how you liked this book or to discuss how he can work with you to enhance your organization's project-management skills and practices: Stanley E. Portny and Associates, LLC, 44 Dorison Drive, Short Hills, New Jersey 07078; Phone: (973) 376-8887; Fax: (973) 912-8386; Email: sportny@att.net; Web page: www.StanPortny.com.

# Dedication

To my wife, Donna, and my sons, Jonathan and Brian. May we always share life's joys together.

# Author's Acknowledgments

Writing and publishing this book was a team effort, and I would like to thank the many people who helped to make it possible. First, I want to thank Holly McGuire, my acquisitions editor, who first contacted me to discuss the possibility of my writing this book. Thanks to her for that phone call, for helping me to prepare the proposal, for helping get the project off to a smooth and timely start, for coordinating the publicity and sales, and for helping to bring all the pieces to a successful conclusion.

Thanks to Kathy Welton, vice president and publisher, for deciding that a *For Dummies* book should be written on this topic and that I should be the one to write it.

A special thanks to Tere Drenth, my project editor, for her guidance, support, professional insights, and the many hours she spent polishing the text into a smooth finished product. I appreciated her encouragement, her candor, and her perpetual positive attitude that endured despite all the pressures and deadlines.

Thanks also to the many people at Hungry Minds whom I haven't met directly, but without whose help this book never would have been completed. Among those people are Erica Bernheim and Tonya Morgan-Oden, acquisitions coordinators; Michelle Hacker, editorial administrator; Pam Mourouzis, editorial manager; and Amanda Foxworth and Emily Wichlinski, production coordinators.

Finally, thanks to my family for their continued help and inspiration. Thanks to Donna, who never doubted that this book would become a reality and who shared personal and stylistic comments as she reviewed the text countless times while always making it seem that she found it enjoyable and enlightening. Thanks to Jonathan and Brian, whose interest and excitement helped motivate me to see this book to its completion. And thanks to all three for putting up with my sometimes-tense behavior, as I labored to relate the lessons I learned from thousands of people over more than 25 years in the pages of this book.

## Publisher's Acknowledgments

We're proud of this book; please send us your comments through our online registration form located at www.dummies.com/register.

Some of the people who helped bring this book to market include the following:

*Acquisitions, Editorial, and Media Development*

**Project Editor:** Tere Drenth

**Senior Acquisitions Editor:** Holly McGuire

**Acquisitions Coordinators:** Erica Bernheim, Tonya Morgan-Oden

**General Reviewer:** John Stouffer

**Editorial Manager:** Pamela Mourouzis

**Editorial Administrator:** Michelle Hacker

**Cover Photo:** Corbis, © Steve Chenn

*Production*

**Project Coordinators:** Amanda Foxworth, Emily Wichlinski

**Layout and Graphics:** Amy Adrian, Karl Brandt, Jacque Schneider, Jeremey Unger, Erin Zeltner

**Proofreaders:** Laura Albert, Corey Bowen, Vickie Broyles, Betty Kish, Angel Perez, Charles Spencer

**Indexer:** Steve Rath

---

*Publishing and Editorial for Consumer Dummies*

**Diane Graves Steele,** Vice President and Publisher, Consumer Dummies
**Joyce Pepple,** Acquisitions Director, Consumer Dummies
**Kristin A. Cocks,** Product Development Director, Consumer Dummies
**Michael Spring,** Vice President and Publisher, Travel
**Brice Gosnell,** Publishing Director, Travel
**Suzanne Jannetta,** Editorial Director, Travel

*Publishing for Technology Dummies*

**Richard Swadley,** Vice President and Executive Group Publisher
**Andy Cummings,** Vice President and Publisher

*Composition Services*

**Gerry Fahey,** Vice President of Production Services
**Debbie Stailey,** Director of Composition Services

# Contents at a Glance

*Introduction* ..............................................................*1*

*Part I: Defining Your Project and Developing Your Game Plan* ..............................................*7*

Chapter 1: What Is Project Management? (And Do I Get Paid Extra to Do It?) ..........9
Chapter 2: Defining What You're Trying to Accomplish — and Why ......................27
Chapter 3: Getting from Here to There ..................................................49
Chapter 4: You Want This Done When? ....................................................71
Chapter 5: Estimating Resource Requirements ......................................105

*Part II: Organizing the Troops* ....................................*135*

Chapter 6: The Who and the How of Project Management ..................................137
Chapter 7: Involving the Right People in Your Project ................................149
Chapter 8: Defining Team Members' Roles and Responsibilities ......................165

*Part III: Steering the Ship* ........................................*185*

Chapter 9: Starting Off on the Right Foot ............................................187
Chapter 10: Tracking Progress and Maintaining Control ..............................203
Chapter 11: Keeping Everyone Informed ................................................229
Chapter 12: Encouraging Peak Performance ............................................239
Chapter 13: Bringing Your Project to a Close ........................................249

*Part IV: Getting Better and Better* ..............................*255*

Chapter 14: Dealing with Risk and Uncertainty ......................................257
Chapter 15: Using the Experience You've Gained ....................................273
Chapter 16: With All the Great New Technology, What's Left for You to Do? ........279

*Part V: The Part of Tens* ............................................*293*

Chapter 17: Ten Questions to Help You Plan Your Project ............................295
Chapter 18: Ten Ways to Hold People Accountable ....................................299
Chapter 19: Ten Steps to Getting Your Project Back on Track ........................303
Chapter 20: Ten Tips for Being a Better Project Manager ............................307

Appendix A: Glossary ...................................311

Appendix B: Earned Value Analysis ...........................319

Index ..............................................331

# Cartoons at a Glance

*By Rich Tennant*

page 7

page 255

page 135

page 185

page 293

**Fax:** 978-546-7747
**E-mail:** richtennant@the5thwave.com
**World Wide Web:** www.the5thwave.com

# Table of Contents

*Introduction* ........................................................... 1
About This Book ...................................................2
Foolish Assumptions .............................................2
How This Book Is Organized ..................................3
    Part I: Defining Your Project and Developing Your Game Plan ........3
    Part II: Organizing the Troops ...................................4
    Part III: Steering the Ship ........................................4
    Part IV: Getting Better and Better ..........................4
    Part V: The Part of Tens ...........................................4
    Appendixes ...............................................................4
Icons Used in This Book ..........................................4
Where to Go from Here ...........................................5

*Part I: Defining Your Project and Developing Your Game Plan* ................................. 7

### Chapter 1: What Is Project Management? (And Do I Get Paid Extra to Do It?) ........................9
What Exactly Is a Project? .......................................9
    Defining projects .....................................................10
    Defining project management ...............................12
    Reading the fine print in the assignment .............13
Considering the Life and Times of Your Project .....13
    The conceive phase: Starting with an idea ...........14
    The define phase: Establishing the plan ...............16
    The start phase: Getting ready, getting set ...........17
    The perform phase: Go! .........................................18
    The close phase: Stop! ...........................................18
    Anticipating the most common mistakes .............18
    Managing your project's life ..................................20
Detecting Potential Pitfalls Early ..........................20
Investigating the Project-Management Mindset .....22
    Taking a look at the project manager's role .........22
    Taking the first steps .............................................23
    Staving off potential excuses ................................23
    Eliminating false expectations .............................24
    Hearing the good news .........................................25

**Chapter 2: Defining What You're Trying
to Accomplish — and Why** ...................................27

Defining Your Project with a Statement of Work ......................27
Looking at the Big Picture ...................................................29
Figuring out why you're doing this project ......................29
Defining where your project starts and where it stops ...........37
Defining your approach to the work on the project ..............38
What exactly are you trying to achieve? .........................40
Defining the Boundaries .....................................................44
Identifying limitations ..............................................44
Determining needs ...................................................46
Dealing with Unknowns in the Planning Process ......................46
Developing a Statement of Work ..........................................47

**Chapter 3: Getting from Here to There** ..........................49

Dividing and Conquering ....................................................49
Thinking in detail ....................................................50
Thinking of hierarchy ...............................................51
Special situations ....................................................57
Creating and Displaying Your Work Breakdown Structure ...........59
Considering different approaches to detailing an activity ........59
Identifying your Work Breakdown Structure entries ...............61
Developing your Work Breakdown Structure .......................61
Displaying your Work Breakdown Structure
in different formats ...............................................63
Some tips and hints ..................................................65
Using templates ......................................................66
Identifying Risks While Detailing Your Activities ....................67
Defining What You Need to Know about Your Activities .............68
Taking Different Paths to the Same End ..................................69

**Chapter 4: You Want This Done When?** .........................71

Analyzing Schedule Possibilities ..........................................71
Drawing network diagrams .........................................72
Using one of two formats for network diagrams .................73
Analyzing your network diagram ..................................76
Fleshing out your diagram .........................................83
Using a network diagram to analyze a simple example .........85
Developing Your Project's Schedule .....................................91
Developing your initial schedule ..................................91
Avoiding the pitfall of "backing in" to your schedule ...........92
Meeting an established time constraint ...........................92
Reducing the required time ........................................93
Estimating Activity Duration ..............................................99
Describing what happens ...........................................100
Considering resource characteristics .............................100

Finding sources of supporting information ...................................101
Improving activity span time estimates ...............................101
Displaying Your Project's Schedule ...................................................102

**Chapter 5: Estimating Resource Requirements ....................105**

Establishing Whom You Need, How Much, and When ...........................106
Describing people's skills and knowledge .................................106
Estimating needed commitment ...........................................109
Juggling multiple commitments ...........................................118
Working in Everything Else .............................................................124
Estimating the Dollars ...................................................................126
Different types of project costs ...........................................126
Developing your project budget .............................................128

*Part II: Organizing the Troops .......................................135*

**Chapter 6: The Who and the How of Project Management ........137**

Defining the Organizational Environment ....................................137
Centralized structure ...................................................138
Functional structure ...................................................139
Matrix structure ......................................................141
Recognizing the Key Players in a Matrix Environment ..........................143
Project manager .......................................................143
Team members .........................................................144
Functional managers ...................................................145
Upper management .....................................................145
Working Successfully in a Matrix Environment ..............................146

**Chapter 7: Involving the Right People in Your Project ............149**

Understanding Your Project's Audience .....................................150
Using categories to create an audience list ...............................150
Improving the completeness and utility of your audience list ....154
Developing an audience list template .....................................156
Identifying the Drivers, Supporters, and Observers
in Your Audience .....................................................158
Deciding when to involve them .........................................159
Using different methods to keep them involved ..........................161
Getting People with Sufficient Authority ..................................162

**Chapter 8: Defining Team Members' Roles and Responsibilities ...165**

Defining the Key Concepts ...............................................165
Assigning Project Roles ...................................................167
Determining what you can and can't delegate .............................167
Delegating with confidence .............................................170
Sharing responsibility .................................................170
Holding people accountable when they don't report to you ......172

Illustrating the Relationships .........................................175
        Developing a Linear Responsibility Chart ...................178
        Improving the quality of your chart .........................179
    Dealing with Micromanagement ...................................181
        Figuring out why you're being micromanaged ..............181
        Helping a micromanager gain confidence in you ..........182
        Working with a micromanager .............................183

## *Part III: Steering the Ship* .............................*185*

### Chapter 9: Starting Off on the Right Foot .................187
    Finalizing Your Project's Participants .........................188
        Confirming your team members' participation ............188
        Assuring that others are on board .......................190
        Filling in the blanks ..................................191
    Reviewing the Approved Project Plan ............................192
    Developing Your Team ..........................................192
        Developing team and individual project goals ............194
        Defining team member roles .............................195
        Defining your team's operating processes ...............196
        Supporting the development of team member relationships ......196
        Helping your team to become a smooth-functioning unit ..........197
    Setting Up Your Tracking Systems ...............................198
    Setting Up Schedules for Reports and Meetings ..................199
    Setting Your Project's Baseline ................................199
    Announcing Your Project .......................................200
    Laying the Groundwork for Your Post-Project Evaluation ....................200

### Chapter 10: Tracking Progress and Maintaining Control ........203
    Controlling Your Project ......................................203
    Preventing Resource Expenditures from Exceeding Your Budgets ......206
    Establishing Project Management Information Systems .....................206
        Monitoring schedule performance .........................207
        Monitoring work effort expended ........................214
        Monitoring expenditures ................................218
    Pulling it All Together .......................................222
        Identifying possible causes of delays and variances ....................224
        Identifying possible corrective actions .................225
    Managing Change ...............................................226

### Chapter 11: Keeping Everyone Informed .....................229
    Choosing the Medium that Fits Your Needs ......................229
        Sharing information in writing ..........................231
        Sharing information through meetings ....................232

Preparing a Written Project-Progress Report ............................234
Holding Key Project Meetings ...............................................236
   Regularly scheduled team meetings ...............................236
   Ad hoc team meetings ...................................................237
   Upper-management progress reviews ..............................237

**Chapter 12: Encouraging Peak Performance** . . . . . . . . . . . . . . . . . . **239**
Practicing Both Management and Leadership ..........................239
Developing Personal Power and Influence ..............................240
   Looking at the reasons people will do what you ask ...........240
   Establishing the bases of your power .............................243
Creating and Sustaining Team-Member Motivation ...................243
   Clarifying your project's benefits ..................................244
   Demonstrating feasibility .............................................245
   Reporting progress .....................................................246
   Providing rewards ......................................................247

**Chapter 13: Bringing Your Project to a Close** . . . . . . . . . . . . . . . . . . **249**
Finishing the Work ............................................................250
   Plan for project termination in detail ..............................250
   Reestablish team identity and spirit ...............................251
   Finish smoothly .........................................................251
Handling the Administrative Issues .......................................252
Handling the People ..........................................................252
Using a Novel Approach to Announce Your Project's Closure .............253
Conducting a Post-Project Evaluation ....................................254

*Part IV: Getting Better and Better* .............................*255*

**Chapter 14: Dealing with Risk and Uncertainty** . . . . . . . . . . . . . . . **257**
Defining Risk and Risk Management ......................................257
Identifying Risks ..............................................................259
   Recognizing risk factors ..............................................259
   Identifying risks .........................................................263
Assessing the Potential Consequences of Risks ........................264
   Assessing the likelihood of a risk occurring ....................264
   Assessing the magnitude of the consequences .................267
Managing Risk .................................................................268
   Choosing the risks you want to manage ..........................268
   Developing a risk-management strategy ..........................269
   Communicating about risks ..........................................269
Preparing a Risk-Management Plan ........................................271

**Chapter 15: Using the Experience You've Gained** . . . . . . . . . . . . . .**273**

Preparing for a Post-Project Evaluation . . . . . . . . . . . . . . . . . . . . . . . . . .273
Preparing for the meeting throughout the project . . . . . . . . . . . . . . .274
Setting the stage for the post-project evaluation meeting . . . . . . . . . .275
Conducting the Post-Project Evaluation . . . . . . . . . . . . . . . . . . . . . . . . . .276
Following Up on the Post-Project Evaluation . . . . . . . . . . . . . . . . . . . . . . .277

**Chapter 16: With All the Great New Technology,
What's Left for You to Do?** . . . . . . . . . . . . . . . . . . . . . . . . . . . . .**279**

Using Computer Software Effectively . . . . . . . . . . . . . . . . . . . . . . . . . . . .280
How software can help . . . . . . . . . . . . . . . . . . . . . . . . . . . . . . . . . . . . . .281
Supporting your software . . . . . . . . . . . . . . . . . . . . . . . . . . . . . . . . . . .286
Introducing project-management software
into your operations . . . . . . . . . . . . . . . . . . . . . . . . . . . . . . . . . . . .288
Making Use of E-mail . . . . . . . . . . . . . . . . . . . . . . . . . . . . . . . . . . . . . . . . . .289
Using e-mail appropriately . . . . . . . . . . . . . . . . . . . . . . . . . . . . . . . . . .291
Getting the most out of your e-mail messages . . . . . . . . . . . . . . . . . .292

*Part V: The Part of Tens* . . . . . . . . . . . . . . . . . . . . . . . . . . . . *293*

**Chapter 17: Ten Questions to Help You Plan Your Project** . . . . . . .**295**

Why Is Your Project Being Done? . . . . . . . . . . . . . . . . . . . . . . . . . . . . . . . .295
Who Will You Need to Involve? . . . . . . . . . . . . . . . . . . . . . . . . . . . . . . . . . .296
What Results Will You Produce? . . . . . . . . . . . . . . . . . . . . . . . . . . . . . . . . .296
What Constraints Must You Satisfy? . . . . . . . . . . . . . . . . . . . . . . . . . . . . . .296
What Assumptions Are You Making? . . . . . . . . . . . . . . . . . . . . . . . . . . . . .297
What Work Must Be Done? . . . . . . . . . . . . . . . . . . . . . . . . . . . . . . . . . . . . . .297
When Will You Start and End Each Activity? . . . . . . . . . . . . . . . . . . . . . . .297
Who'll Perform the Project Work? . . . . . . . . . . . . . . . . . . . . . . . . . . . . . . . .298
What Other Resources Will You Need? . . . . . . . . . . . . . . . . . . . . . . . . . . . .298
What Could Go Wrong? . . . . . . . . . . . . . . . . . . . . . . . . . . . . . . . . . . . . . . . . .298

**Chapter 18: Ten Ways to Hold People Accountable** . . . . . . . . . . . . .**299**

Involve People Who Really Have Authority . . . . . . . . . . . . . . . . . . . . . . . .299
Be Specific Regarding End Results, Time Frames,
and Expected Levels of Effort . . . . . . . . . . . . . . . . . . . . . . . . . . . . . . .300
Get a Commitment! . . . . . . . . . . . . . . . . . . . . . . . . . . . . . . . . . . . . . . . . . . . .300
Put it in Writing . . . . . . . . . . . . . . . . . . . . . . . . . . . . . . . . . . . . . . . . . . . . . . .300
Emphasize the Urgency and Importance of the Assignment . . . . . . . . . . .301
Tell Others about the Person's Commitment . . . . . . . . . . . . . . . . . . . . . . .301
Agree on a Plan for Monitoring the Person's Work . . . . . . . . . . . . . . . . . .301
Monitor the Person's Work . . . . . . . . . . . . . . . . . . . . . . . . . . . . . . . . . . . . . .302
Always Acknowledge Good Performance . . . . . . . . . . . . . . . . . . . . . . . . . .302
Act As If You Have the Authority . . . . . . . . . . . . . . . . . . . . . . . . . . . . . . . . .302

**Chapter 19: Ten Steps to Getting Your Project Back on Track** . . . . .303

Determine Why Your Project Got Off Track ..............................303
Reaffirm Your Key Drivers .......................................................304
Reaffirm Your Project Objectives ..............................................304
Reaffirm the Activities Remaining to Be Done ........................304
Reaffirm Roles and Responsibilities .........................................304
Develop a Viable Schedule .......................................................305
Reaffirm Your Personnel Assignments .....................................305
Develop a Risk-Management Plan ............................................305
Hold a Midcourse Kickoff Session ...........................................305
Closely Monitor and Control Performance
   for the Remainder of the Project .........................................306

**Chapter 20: Ten Tips for Being a Better Project Manager** . . . . . . .307

Be a "Why" Person ..................................................................307
Be a "Can Do" Person ..............................................................307
Don't Assume .........................................................................308
Say What You Mean; Mean What You Say ...............................308
View People as Allies, Not Adversaries ....................................308
Respect Other People ..............................................................308
Think "Big Picture" .................................................................308
Think Detail ...........................................................................309
Acknowledge Good Performance .............................................309
Be Both a Manager and a Leader ............................................309

*Appendix A: Glossary* .................................*311*

*Appendix B: Earned Value Analysis* ..................*319*

Defining Earned Value Analysis ...............................................319
Determining the Reasons for Observed Variances ....................324
Looking at a Simple Example ..................................................325
Calculating Budgeted Cost of Work Performed ........................327

*Index* .................................................*331*

# Introduction

**P**rojects have been around since ancient times. Noah building the ark, Leonardo da Vinci painting the Mona Lisa, Edward Gibbon writing *The Decline and Fall of the Roman Empire,* Jonas Salk developing the polio vaccine — all projects. And, as you know, these and many other similar projects have been completed with masterful success. (Well, the products were a spectacular success, even if schedules and resource budgets were astonishingly overrun!)

Why, then, is the topic of project management suddenly of such great interest today? The answer is simple. The audience has changed and the stakes are higher.

Historically, projects were viewed as large, technically-complex undertakings. The first project to use more modern project management techniques, the development of the Polaris submarine in the early 1950s, was a technical and administrative nightmare. Teams of specialists were used to plan and track the myriad of research, development, and production activities. And mountains of paper were produced to document the intricate work. People came to think of project management as a highly technical discipline consisting of confusing charts and graphs. Its execution was inordinately time consuming. It was the purview of highly trained technical specialists.

Certainly you still see a vast array of complex and technically-challenging projects to be performed in the world today. And there's a growing need for people who understand how to plan and manage these efforts and who want to devote their careers to doing it. But over the past decade, projects have exploded into the workplace. Projects of all types and sizes are now the way that all organizations accomplish their work.

At the same time, a new breed of project manager has appeared. These people never set a career goal to become project managers; many don't really understand what a project manager is. But these project managers have learned that they must be able to complete projects successfully if they're going to move ahead in their careers. In other words, project management has become a needed skill rather than a career choice.

Gradually, these new project managers are realizing that a special set of skills and techniques are needed to thrive in the ever-changing and demanding world of projects. They want to learn and practice these skills and techniques, but are unwilling to devote large amounts of time to doing either. It's to this "silent majority" of project managers that this book is devoted.

# About This Book

This book helps you recognize that the basic tenets of managing projects successfully are simple. The most complex "analytical technique" used to plan projects of any size takes less than ten minutes to master! In this book, you're introduced to the types of information necessary to plan and manage projects, as well as important guidelines for how to develop and use this information easily and effectively. You discover that the real challenge to a successful project is dealing with the multitude of people who'll be affected by or needed to support the project. Plenty of tips, hints, and guidelines are presented for identifying key players and involving them throughout the process.

But successful project management isn't accomplished through knowledge; it's achieved through application. The theme of this book is that project-management skills and techniques aren't burdensome tasks to be performed because some process requires it. Instead, they're a way of thinking, a way of communicating, and a way of behaving. They're incorporated into the essence of how we approach all of our work every day.

To support this message, I've written the book to be direct and (relatively) easy to understand. But don't be misled — although its tone is conversational, this book explores all of the project-management tools and techniques available to guide your planning, scheduling, budgeting, organizing, and controlling.

The information is presented in a logical progression, the way that it should be practiced on the job. Examples and illustrations are plentiful, together with tips and hints. And humor is injected from time to time, to help it all seem doable.

My goal is that you'll finish this book with the feeling that good project management is definitely possible and with the determination to practice it!

# Foolish Assumptions

I'm assuming that a widely diverse group of people will read this book, including the following:

- Senior managers and junior assistants (the senior managers of tomorrow)
- Experienced project managers and people who've never been on a project team

    ✔ People who've had significant project management training and people who've had none

    ✔ People who've had years of real-world business and government experience and people who've just entered the workforce

However, I'm assuming that you have a desire to take control of your environment. I'm assuming that you'll read this book and wonder why all projects aren't well managed, because you'll think the techniques presented are logical, straightforward, and easy-to-use. And you'll be right. But I'm also assuming you'll recognize that there's a big difference between knowing what to do and doing it, and that you'll devote special effort trying to understand the forces that may try to prevent you from using these tools and techniques and trying to overcome them.

Finally, I assume you'll realize that you can read this book repeatedly and learn something new and different each time, thinking of this book as a friend or a comfortable resource that has more to share as you read between the lines and experience new situations.

# How This Book Is Organized

I've organized this book into five parts. The first three parts explore project-management planning, organizing, and control, respectively; the fourth suggests ways to use both your practical experience and technology to continually improve your project-management practices; and the fifth presents an array of quick hints and tips to help you perform some of the more common project-management tasks. The appendixes summarize common project-management technical terms and definitions and explain a technique used with increasing frequency today to monitor activities and expenditures on larger projects.

## Part I: Defining Your Project and Developing Your Game Plan

In this part, I discuss the special and unique characteristics of projects and key issues you may encounter when working in a project-oriented organization. I also show you how to clearly define the results you propose to accomplish through your project, the work you have to perform, the schedule you plan to achieve, and the resources you need.

## Part II: Organizing the Troops

In this part, I show you how to identify, organize, and deal with the people who'll play a part in your project's success.

## Part III: Steering the Ship

I show you how to begin your project, support it throughout its performance, and bring it to a successful closure.

## Part IV: Getting Better and Better

I show you how to manage the uncertainties surrounding your project, use lessons learned from previous projects to improve the way you handle future ones, and use available information technology to support project planning and performance.

## Part V: The Part of Tens

I share with you a collection of tips, hints, and suggestions about how to handle some of the more common situations you'll encounter as you work on your projects.

## Appendixes

Appendix A includes a comprehensive list of the most common project-management terms and definitions. Appendix B presents a technique to evaluate activity performance and resource expenditures on larger projects.

# Icons Used in This Book

Small icons are included in the left margins of the book to alert you to special information that's shared in the text. Here's what they mean:

Hints that'll help you apply the techniques or approaches discussed.

Project-management terms or issues that are a bit more technical.

Real-world and hypothetical situations illustrating techniques and issues presented in the text.

Potential pitfalls and danger spots.

Important information to keep in mind as you apply the techniques and approaches discussed.

# *Where to Go from Here*

You can read this book in many different ways, depending on your prior project-management knowledge and experience and your current information needs. However, I suggest you first take a minute to scan the Table of Contents and thumb through the different sections of the book to get a feeling for the different topics addressed.

If you're new to project management and are just beginning to form a plan for a project, first read Part I, which explains how to plan project outcomes, activities, schedules, and resources. If you're interested in finding out how to identify and organize the people and groups who'll be involved at some point in your project, start with Part II. If you're preparing to begin work or are in the midst of it, you might want to start with Part III. Or, jump back and forth to chapters that address topics that are of special interest to you.

I should offer you one word of caution. The discussion in Chapter 4 of how to use a network diagram to develop your project schedule is the most technically detailed presentation in the book. The technique itself really only takes about ten minutes to master, but the explanations and illustrations can appear somewhat overwhelming if you haven't used flowcharting before. If this is the first time you've seen this technique, I suggest you initially scan the entire chapter quickly and then read the different sections several times. The more you read the text, the more logical the explanations will seem. However, if you feel you're getting frustrated with the technical details, put the book away and come back to it at another time. You'll probably be surprised at how much more sense it'll make the second or third time you see it.

In any case, plan on reading each of the chapters of this book more than once. Often, the more you read a chapter, the more sense the approaches and techniques discussed make. And sometimes, a change in your job responsibilities creates a need for certain techniques that you have never used before.

# Part I

# Defining Your Project and Developing Your Game Plan

The 5th Wave          By Rich Tennant

YEAR 1 - GET RESCUED
YEAR 2 - GET RESCUED!
YEAR 3 - GET RESCUED!! NOW!!
(FOCUS MORE)
YEAR 4 - GET RESCUED
(SCREAM LOUDER!)
YEAR 5 - BUILD GOLF RESORT

"My project plan has changed a little this year."

# In this part . . .

**O**ften, the most difficult part of dealing with a new project assignment is deciding where to begin. Expectations are many, while time and resource restrictions are frequently severe.

In this first part, I identify how a project differs from other activities you perform and present a snapshot of the steps you take to plan, organize, and control a project. I offer you specific techniques and approaches to define clearly what you want your project to accomplish and who needs to be involved. I show you how to determine the work you'll have to do and how long it'll take to perform that work. Finally, I explain how you can estimate the resources you'll need to support your project work.

# Chapter 1

# What Is Project Management? (And Do I Get Paid Extra to Do It?)

*In This Chapter*

▶ Taking a look at the three basic elements of every project

▶ Understanding why projects fail

▶ Examining the requirements for project success

▶ Uncovering the project-management mindset

Successful organizations create projects that produce desired results in established timeframes with assigned resources. As a result, businesses are increasingly driven to find individuals who can excel in this project-oriented environment.

People wanting to move ahead in their careers appear to be getting the message. Growing numbers of people at all levels in organizations are looking for ways to get a better handle on their projects. A *Fortune* Magazine article recently identified "project manager" as the number-one career option. What the article didn't say is that the majority of people who are becoming project managers aren't doing so by choice. Instead, project management is often an unexpected but required progression in their chosen career paths.

Given that you're holding this book in your hands, you, too, have probably been thrust into a project-management role. As a new project manager, you need a new set of skills and techniques so that you can steer projects to successful completion. This chapter gets you started, helping you separate true projects from non-project assignments, understand why projects succeed and fail, and get into the project-management mindset.

## What Exactly Is a Project?

No matter what your job, you handle a myriad of assignments every day: Prepare a memo, hold a meeting, design a sales campaign, move to new offices. Or perhaps your day sounds more like this: Make the information systems more user-friendly, develop a research compound in the laboratory, improve the organization's public image. Not all of these assignments are projects. How can you tell which ones are?

## Defining projects

Large or small, a *project* always has the following ingredients:

- ✔ **Specific outcomes:** Products or results
- ✔ **Definite start and end dates:** Dates when project work begins and when it ends
- ✔ **Established budgets:** Required amounts of people, funds, equipment, facilities, and information

Figure 1-1 illustrates that each element affects the other two. Expanding desired outcomes may require more time (a later end date) or more resources. Moving up the end date may necessitate paring down the results to be accomplished or increasing project expenditures (exceeding the established budgets) by paying overtime to project staff. Within this three-part project definition, you perform work to achieve your desired results.

**Figure 1-1:**
Always define these three essential pieces of information for every project.

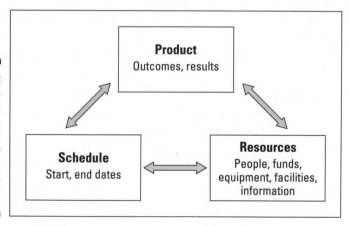

Projects come in a wide assortment of shapes and sizes.

- ✔ **Projects may be large or small.**

    - • Installing a new subway system, which may cost more than $1 billion and take 10 to 15 years to complete, is a project.

    - • Preparing a report of monthly sales figures, which may take you one day to complete, is a project.

🖝 **Projects may involve many people or just you.**

- Training all 10,000 of your organization's staff in a new affirmative-action policy is a project.

- Rearranging the furniture and equipment in your office is a project.

🖝 **Projects may be planned formally or informally.**

- Some projects are included in your organization's annual plan and require formal approval of all work to be performed, of all personnel assignments, and of all resource expenditures.

- Others are assigned to you in the course of a conversation, with no mention of budget or additional staff; it's expected you'll do whatever's necessary to complete them.

🖝 **Projects may be tracked formally or informally.**

- For some projects, all hours spent are faithfully recorded on time sheets and all dollars expended are separately identified in the organization's financial system.

- For others, no record of actual hours spent is ever kept and any expenditures are just considered as part of the organization's operating budget.

🖝 **Projects may be performed for external or internal clients and customers.**

- Repairing a piece of equipment that your company sold to a customer is a project.

- Writing an article for your organization's internal newsletter is a project.

🖝 **Projects may be defined by a legal contract or an informal agreement.**

- A signed contract between you and a customer requiring you to build a house defines a project.

- An informal promise you make to install a new software package on your colleague's computer defines a project.

🖝 **Projects may be business related or personal.**

- Conducting your organization's annual blood drive is a project.

- Having a dinner party for 15 people is a project.

No matter what the characteristics of your project, you define it by the same three ingredients: outcomes, start and end dates, and resources. The information you need to plan and manage your project is the same, although the ease and the time required to develop it may differ. The more thoroughly you plan and manage your projects, the more likely you are to succeed.

## Terms often confused with "project"

Two other terms are often confused with the term, "project":

✔ A *process* is a series of steps by which a particular function is routinely performed. A procurement process and a budget process are examples. A process is not a one-time activity that achieves a specific result; instead it defines how a particular function is to be done every time it's done. Processes, such as the activities performed to buy needed materials, are often included as parts of projects.

✔ A *program* is work performed towards achieving a long-range goal. A health-awareness program and an employee-morale program are examples. A program never completely achieves its goal (that is, the public will never be totally aware of all health issues); instead, one or more projects may be performed to accomplish specific results that are related to the program's goal (such as the conduct of a workshop on how to minimize the risk of heart disease). In this case, a program is comprised of a series of projects.

## Defining project management

*Project management* is the process of guiding your project from its beginning through its performance to its closure. Project management includes three basic operations:

✔ **Planning:**

- Specifying the results to be achieved
- Determining the schedules
- Estimating the resources required

✔ **Organizing:** Defining people's roles and responsibilities

✔ **Control:**

- Reconfirming people's expected performance
- Monitoring actions taken and results achieved
- Addressing problems encountered
- Sharing information with interested people

When project information is determined accurately and completely and shared effectively, you dramatically increase your chances of project success. When pieces of this information are vague, missing, or not shared effectively, you reduce your chances of success.

## Reading the fine print in the assignment

Projects are temporary; created to achieve particular results. So when the results are achieved, the project should end. This transitory nature of projects may create some challenges, such as the following:

✔ **Not the only assignment:** You may be asked to accept a new project in addition to — not in lieu of — existing assignments. You may not be asked how the new work will impact your existing work. It's just assumed that "you'll handle it." When conflicts arise over a person's need to spend time on his or her different assignments, guidelines or procedures to resolve them may not exist or may be inadequate.

✔ **People may not have worked together:** Even on small projects, you often seek the help of others. On larger efforts, one or more people may be formally assigned to a project team. However, you'll likely find that some of the people involved haven't worked together before. In fact, some may not even know each other. These unfamiliar relationships may slow the project down because team members may

- Have different operating and communicating styles

- Use different procedures for performing the same type of activity

- Not have had the time to develop a sense of mutual respect and trust for each other

✔ **No direct authority:** For most projects, the project manager and team members have no direct authority over each other. Therefore, you can't use the more common rewards of salary increases, superior performance appraisals, and job promotions to encourage top performance. And you can't settle conflicts over time commitments or technical direction with one, unilateral decision.

# Considering the Life and Times of Your Project

Figure 1-2 suggests that every project, whether large or small, passes through the five phases:

✔ **Conceive:** An idea is born.

✔ **Define:** A plan is developed.

✔ **Start:** A team is formed.

✔ **Perform:** The work is done.

✔ **Close:** The project is ended.

For small projects, this entire process can take a few days. For larger projects, it may take many years! No matter how simple or complex the project is, however, the process is the same.

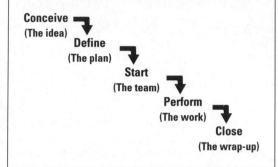

**Figure 1-2:**
Guide your project through the five phases of its life.

Conceive
(The idea)
Define
(The plan)
Start
(The team)
Perform
(The work)
Close
(The wrap-up)

# The conceive phase: Starting with an idea

All projects begin with an idea. Perhaps your organization's client identifies a need to be addressed, maybe your boss thinks of a new market to explore, or maybe you think of a way to refine your organization's procurement process. When an idea is formed, your project has entered the conceive phase.

Sometimes the concept phase is handled informally; for a small project it may just consist of a discussion and a verbal agreement. In other instances, especially for larger projects, proceeding with a project requires a formal review and decision.

### Answering two key questions

Consider the following two questions to decide whether to move ahead with your project:

- **Should you do it?** Are the benefits you expect to achieve worth the costs you expect to pay?

- **Can you do it?** Is your project technically feasible? Are the required resources available?

If your answer to both questions is "yes," you're ready to proceed to the define phase (see the following section) and develop your project plan. If your answer to either question is a definite, iron-clad "no," under no circumstances should you move on. You must consider whether you can redefine your project to make it feasible and desirable. If you can't, cancel it now. Doing anything else will guarantee wasted resources, lost opportunities, and frustrated staff.

Suppose you're in charge of the publications department in your organization. You've just received a request to have a 20,000 page document printed in ten minutes, which would require equipment that could reproduce at the rate of 2,000 pages per minute. You check with your staff, and you confirm that your document reproducing equipment has a top speed of 500 pages per minute. You check with your suppliers and find out that the fastest document reproducing equipment available today has a top speed of 1,000 pages per minute. Would you agree to plan and perform this project, when there is no conceivable way for you to successfully meet the request? Of course not.

Rather than promising something you know you can't achieve, consider asking your customer if it is possible to change the request. Can your customer accept the document in 20 minutes? Can you reproduce certain parts of the document in the first ten minutes and the rest later?

Sometimes you're convinced that it's impossible to meet a request or that the benefits you can realize won't be worth the cost to achieve them. But be sure to check with the people who developed or approved the request. They may know something you don't, or you may know something they don't.

Beware of assumptions that you or others make when assessing your project's potential value, cost, and feasibility. You may feel that the only way to complete your company move in a one week time period is to have all of the facilities staff work 12 hours a day from Monday through Sunday. However, your boss turned you down the last ten times you asked her to authorize overtime for the facilities staff. You conclude, therefore, that it's impossible to complete the move in one week. Of course, you're basing your conclusion on past experience. The only way you'll find out whether she'll authorize overtime for this project is to ask.

Most often, you can't be positive that the project will or won't be feasible and cost-beneficial, you can only be reasonably sure. Consider carefully what you don't know and how you will deal with this uncertainty. Chapter 14 discusses how to identify and plan for project risks.

### The cost-benefit analysis

A *cost-benefit analysis* is a comparative assessment of all costs that will be incurred to perform your project and to introduce and support changes resulting from it and all benefits anticipated from your project.

Some anticipated benefits can be expressed in monetary equivalents, such as reduced operating costs or increased revenue. For others, numerical measures can approximate some, but not all, of their aspects. If your project is to improve staff morale, for example, you may consider associated benefits to include reduced turnover, increased productivity, fewer absences, and fewer formal grievances.

The further into the future you look when estimating anticipated benefits, the less confident you can be that you'll actually realize them. For example, you may expect to reap benefits for years from the purchase of a new computer system, but changing technology may make your new system obsolete after one year.

Therefore, two key factors influence the outcome of a cost-benefit analysis:

✔ How far into the future you look to identify benefits

✔ The assumptions on which you base your analysis

While you may not want to go out and design a cost-benefit analysis by yourself, you definitely want to see if one has already been done and, if it has, what the specific results were.

## The define phase: Establishing the plan

When you know what you hope to accomplish and you believe it's possible, you need a detailed plan to describe how you and your team will make it happen.

Include the following in your project plan:

✔ An overview of the reasons for your project (Chapter 2 tells you what to include)

✔ A detailed description of results to be produced (Chapter 2 explains how to describe desired results)

✔ A listing of all work to be performed (Chapter 3 illustrates how to identify all required project work)

✔ The roles you and your team members will play (Chapter 8 explains how to describe roles and responsibilities)

✔ A detailed project schedule (Chapter 4 explains how to develop your schedule)

✔ Budgets for required personnel, funds, equipment, facilities, and information (Chapter 5 illustrates how to estimate resource needs)

✔ Assumptions (Chapter 2 discusses how to frame assumptions)

In addition, be sure to identify and describe how you plan to manage any significant risks and uncertainties. (Chapter 14 explains how to identify and plan for risks.)

Always put your plans in writing; it helps you to clarify details and reduces the chances that you'll forget something. Plans for large projects can take hundreds of pages; a plan for a small one can take a few lines on a single sheet.

The success of your project depends on how clear and accurate your plan is and whether people believe they can achieve it. Considering past experience helps to ensure reality, while involving people in the development helps to encourage their belief and commitment to achieving it.

Often the pressure to get results fast encourages people to skip over the planning and get right to the doing. This can create a lot of immediate activity, but can also create significant chances for waste and mistakes.

Be sure to have the plan reviewed and approved in writing before you begin your project. For a small effort, you may only need a brief e-mail and someone's initials.

## The start phase: Getting ready, getting set

Preparing to begin project work requires the following (see Chapter 9 for details):

- ✔ **Assigning people to all project roles:** Identify the individuals who'll perform the different project work and negotiate agreements to assure they'll be available to work on the project team.

- ✔ **Giving and explaining tasks to all team members:** Describe to each team member the work that he or she is to produce and how the team members will coordinate their efforts.

- ✔ **Defining how the team will perform the tasks necessary to complete assigned work:** Decide how the team will handle routine communications, make different project decisions, and resolve conflicts.

- ✔ **Setting up necessary financial, personnel, and tracking systems:** Decide which system(s) and accounts will be used to track the schedule, personnel information, and financial expenditures.

- ✔ **Announcing the project to the organization:** Let people know that your project exists, what it will produce, and when it will begin and end.

Suppose you don't join your project team until the start phase. Your first task is to revisit the thinking that led people to decide the project was possible and desirable during the conceive phase. At the least, you want to become familiar with all existing information. If people overlooked important issues, raise them now. When searching for the history that led to the decision to proceed with your project, check all minutes from meetings, memos, letters, e-mail messages, and technical reports. Then consult with all of the people who were involved in the decision.

## *The perform phase: Go!*

Finally, you get to perform the project work! Performing the work entails the following (see Chapters 10, 11, and 12 for more details):

- ✔ **Doing the tasks:** Perform the work that's laid out in your plan.

- ✔ **Continually comparing performance with plans:** Collect information on outcomes produced, schedule achievement, and resource expenditures; identify deviations from your plan; and formulate corrective action plans.

- ✔ **Fixing problems that arise:** Change tasks, schedules, or resources to bring project performance back on track with the existing plan or negotiate agreed-upon changes to the existing project plan.

- ✔ **Keeping everyone informed:** Tell people about scheduled achievements that are realized, problems encountered, and revisions to the established project plan.

## *The close phase: Stop!*

Finishing your assigned tasks is only part of bringing your project to a close. In addition, you must do the following:

- ✔ Get your clients' approvals of the final results.

- ✔ Close all project accounts (if you've been charging time and money to specially created project accounts).

- ✔ Help people move on to their next assignments.

- ✔ Hold a post-project evaluation to recognize project achievements and discuss lessons learned that can be applied to the next project (or at least informally make notes about lessons you learned and how you will use them in the future). See Chapter 15 for how to prepare for, design, and conduct a post-project evaluation.

## *Anticipating the most common mistakes*

The short-term pressures of your job may encourage you to act today in ways that will cause you to pay a price tomorrow. Especially with smaller, less formal projects, you may feel that there's no need for organized planning and performance.

Don't let the following temptations seduce you into taking seemingly easier shortcuts:

- **Jumping directly from the conceive phase to the perform phase:** You have an idea, and your project is on a short time schedule. Why not just start doing the work? Sounds good, but you haven't yet defined what activities you should do! Other variations on this include the following:

  - **Our project has been done many times before, why do I have to plan it out again?** Even though projects can be similar to ones done in the past, some things are always different. Perhaps you're working with some new people, using a new piece of equipment, and so on. Take a moment now to be sure your plan addresses the current situation.

  - **Our project is different from what we've done before, so what good is trying to plan?** This is the same as saying you're traveling in an area where you've never been, so why should you try to lay out your route on a road map? It's important to plan for a new project, because no one has taken this particular path before. While your initial plan will likely have to be revised during the project, it's critical for you and your team to have a clear statement of what your intended plan is.

- **Omitting the start phase completely:** Time pressure is often the culprit here. People don't appreciate the need to help the team define its procedures and relationships before jumping in to the actual project work. See Chapter 9 for a discussion of why this is so important — and get tips on how to do it.

- **Jumping right into the work when you join the project during the start phase:** The plan has already been developed, so why go back and revisit the conceive and define phases? Actually, you do this for two reasons:

  - To see if you can identify any issues that may have been overlooked

  - To understand the reasoning behind the plan and to decide if you feel the plan is achievable

- **Only partially completing the close phase:** At the end of one project, you often move right on to the next. Scarce resources and short deadlines encourage you to do this, and a new project is always more challenging than wrapping up an old one. You never really know how successful your project was, however, if you don't take the time to ensure that all tasks are completed to the satisfaction of your clients. And if you don't take positive steps to determine and reflect lessons learned from this project in the performance of future ones, you'll make the same mistakes over again and may fail to use those approaches in future projects that proved to be successful in this one.

## Managing your project's life

In a perfect world, you would perform all work in one phase of your project before you move on to the next one. That is, you would like to complete your project plan (in the define phase) before you prepare to begin work (in the start phase). And after you completed a phase, you would never return to it again.

But the world, of course, isn't perfect, and project success often requires a flexible approach that responds to the real situations you face.

✔ **You may have to work on two (or more) phases at the same time, if you hope to meet established deadlines.** Working on the next phase before you complete the current one increases the risk that you may have to redo tasks, which may cause you to miss deadlines and spend more resources than you planned. If you choose this strategy, be sure people understand the risks and associated costs. (See Chapter 14 for suggestions on how to assess and manage risks.)

✔ **Sometimes you learn by doing.** Even when you do your best to assess feasibility and develop detailed plans, sometimes you find out that you can't achieve what you thought. In these cases, you need to go back to the earlier phases of your project and rethink them in light of the new information you've learned.

✔ **Sometimes, things change.** Your assessments of feasibility and relative benefits were sound, and your plan was detailed and realistic. During the project, however, certain key people on whom you were counting left the organization. Or a new technology emerged that was more appropriate to use than what was in your original plans. Ignoring these occurrences could seriously jeopardize your project's success.

# Detecting Potential Pitfalls Early

Your project succeeds when you accomplish the desired outcomes on time and within budget. When success isn't achieved, time and again the same reasons are to blame. Recognizing and anticipating these situations allows you to ensure they won't sabotage your project.

Steer clear of the following situations that can cause project failure:

✔ **Not involving all key project audiences:** Failing to identify people who affect your success or not involving them in a timely and effective way

✔ **Vague objectives:** Lacking detailed performance targets to determine whether you've achieved your desired results

✔ **Vague or nonexistent role and responsibility definitions:** Not establishing a clear distinction between how different people on the same project team will work together to perform their tasks

✔ **Incomplete and inaccurate schedules and resource needs:** Missing activities; setting unrealistic estimates of task durations; failing to consider task interdependencies; not identifying needed skills; not estimating the person-hours in sufficient detail

✔ **Not identifying and sharing key project assumptions:** Failing to recognize that information you consider to be true may not be; believing that others know what you assume and don't need to be told

✔ **Not writing down key information:** Sharing important information and reaching agreements verbally and not confirming them in writing

✔ **Inaccurate and late progress monitoring:** Not recording personnel and financial expenditures and the dates on which activities are started and ended; not sharing this information with team members in a timely manner

✔ **Not holding people accountable for performance:** Having no rewards or consequences for meeting or missing project commitments

✔ **Not anticipating and planning for risks and uncertainties:** Not identifying what may go wrong; not developing contingency plans for anticipated problems; not sharing information about unanticipated occurrences

✔ **Poor team communications:** Purposely or inadvertently not sharing important information with all team members or sharing it late

✔ **Weak team leadership:** Not clearly articulating the project vision; neglecting to elicit people's commitments to achieve the desired results; failing to continually sustain individuals' motivation

✔ **Inconsistent upper-management support:** Failing to make sure assigned people stay with their projects; being unwilling to resolve time and resource conflicts; using inadequate systems and procedures to support project planning and control

✔ **Lack of commitment by all team members to the project's success:** Not making a personal commitment to achieve the promises made in the plan

The message is clear. To succeed in your projects, you must effectively manage

✔ **People:** Team members, organization management, and others who support or will be affected by your project

✔ **Processes:** Plan, organize, and control the work; make decisions and resolve conflicts

✔ **Systems:** Procedures and sources of information that affect how project activities are performed and how associated resources are assigned and tracked

You accomplish this by ensuring you have the following:

- **Accurate, timely, and complete information:** To support planning, ongoing performance monitoring, and assessment at completion
- **Clear and consistent communication:** Open and timely sharing of all information with all affected people
- **Commitment for success:** Personal promises by all team members to produce the agreed-upon results on time and within budget

# Investigating the Project-Management Mindset

The project manager's job is challenging. He or she must coordinate technically specialized professionals — who often have limited experience working together — to help them achieve a common goal. The project manager's own work experience is usually technical in nature, yet his or her success requires a keen ability to identify and resolve sensitive organizational and interpersonal issues.

Attitude and approach are critical to have the greatest chances for success.

## Taking a look at the project manager's role

The rules for performance in the traditional organization historically were simple. Your boss made assignments; you carried them out. Questioning your assignments was a sign of insubordination or incompetence.

The organizations' rules have changed. Today, the following is more likely:

- Your boss generates ideas; you must assess what it takes to implement them.
- Your boss tells you what he or she wants to achieve and the constraints for doing it. You must check to be sure the project meets the real need and then translate general expectations into specific results.
- You must determine the work to be done, schedules that can be met, and the resources required.
- You stay on top of the work performed and identify issues and concerns as they arise.

It doesn't make sense to do it any other way. If your boss did the detailed project planning, who would create visions and strategies? Your boss's assertion that something is possible doesn't automatically convince you that you can do it. You must be involved in developing the plans — it's your opportunity to understand the expectations and proposed approaches and raise any questions.

Here's the hard part, though: Most bosses, when assigning a project, don't remind you that you need to clarify the assignment, assess its feasibility, and so on. In fact, sometimes you're specifically directed not to spend time on further planning and analysis, but to start work at once in order to have any chance of meeting the aggressive time frames set.

Yet taking the initiative when planning and controlling a project is a necessity, whether or not you're asked to do this. Your boss wants you to successfully complete the assigned project. Approaching the assignment in this way gives you the greatest chance to meet that expectation.

## Taking the first steps

The key to project success is to be proactive. You don't wait for others to tell you what to do; you don't do it because the process requires it. You do it because you believe that it makes sense.

- ✔ You seek out information because you know you need it.
- ✔ You follow the process because you know it's the best way.
- ✔ You involve people whom you know are important for the project.
- ✔ You raise issues and risks and then analyze them and elicit support to address them.
- ✔ You share information with people you know should have it.
- ✔ You put all important information in writing.
- ✔ You commit to a project and then ask and expect others to do the same.

## Staving off potential excuses

Be prepared for others to fight your attempts to be proactive. Here are some of the more common reasons offered to justify being lax, along with your potential rebuttals:

✔ **Good project management is "nice to have" but not a necessity.**

**Response:** Good project managers often make it appear that they succeed while doing nothing special. As a result, others come to expect that project success can be achieved without using special tools and techniques. Unfortunately, experience overwhelmingly confirms that project failures can most often be traced back to the lack of appropriate planning, confused organization, poor tracking, and ineffective use of other aspects of the project-management process.

✔ **Your projects are all crises; you have no time to plan.**

**Response:** Unfortunately, this logic is exactly reversed! In a crisis, you can't afford not to plan. Why? Because you have a critical situation that has to be addressed with limited time and resources. You can't afford to make mistakes. And acting under pressure and emotion (the two characteristics of crises) practically guarantees that mistakes will occur.

✔ **Structured project management is only for large projects.**

**Response:** No matter what size the project, the information you need to perform it is the same. What are you to produce? What work has to be done? Who is going to do it? When will it be done? Have you met expectations?

For large projects, it could take many weeks or months to develop satisfactory answers to these questions. For a small project (a few days or less), it could take 15 minutes. But the questions still have to be answered.

✔ **Your projects require creativity and new development. They can't be predicted with any certainty.**

**Response:** Some projects are more predictable than others. However, people awaiting the outcomes still have expectations for what they will get and when. Therefore, it's especially important for someone managing projects with this sort of uncertainty to develop and share initial plans and to assess and share the impact of unexpected occurrences and changes.

## Eliminating false expectations

Beware of unrealistic expectations for what project management entails. The following are three common fallacies:

✔ **Project-management activities take no extra time to perform.**

**Response:** Speaking with people who are interested in and support your project, preparing a project plan, creating and sustaining a project team, and tracking and reporting on project progress all take time. But the time is more than saved in the long run, when potential problems are avoided and the results meet expectations.

✔ **Project management is just graphs and charts.**

**Response:** Graphs and charts support the analysis and display of project-management data. However, information alone doesn't ensure project success.

✔ **Project management is a software package.**

**Response**: Project-management software supports the recording, analysis, and storage of project data. But information alone doesn't ensure project success.

## *Hearing the good news*

Perhaps you're thinking: "I hear what you're saying about all this advance planning, but is it really worth it?" Trust me; it is. When you practice the principles of good project management, the following happens:

✔ You can do more.

✔ You can do it in less time.

✔ You can do it with fewer resources.

Sound too good to be true? It can happen because you do the following:

✔ Produce the correct outcomes to address the real needs.

✔ Don't waste time doing unnecessary activities or making up for something you forgot to do.

✔ Do activities in the right order at the right time, so people don't waste time waiting for results they need to proceed with their work.

✔ Ensure that people work only on needed activities and do them correctly the first time.

✔ Anticipate possible problems and either work to avoid them or are prepared to deal with them quickly and effectively, if they occur.

# Chapter 2

# Defining What You're Trying to Accomplish — and Why

*In This Chapter*

▶ Defining your project's Statement of Work

▶ Clarifying the need for the project

▶ Describing desired project outcomes

▶ Identifying project assumptions

**A**ll projects are created for a reason. Someone identifies a need and devises a project to address that need. How well the project ultimately addresses that need defines its success or failure.

This chapter helps you develop a mutual agreement between the project's requesters and the project team about what your project is to accomplish. It also helps you establish the conditions that will be necessary for you to perform the project work.

## Defining Your Project with a Statement of Work

A *Statement of Work* is a written confirmation of what your project will produce and the terms and conditions under which you will perform your work. Both the people who requested the project and the project team should agree to all terms in the Statement of Work, before actual project work is started.

# Other documents that are like a Statement of Work

Your organization may use a number of other documents that address issues similar to those in the Statement of Work. If you use these as sources of information to prepare or describe your project plan, be careful to note how they differ from your Statement of Work.

✔ **Market requirements document:** A formal request for a product to be developed or modified. The market requirements document, typically prepared by a member of your organization's sales and marketing group, may lead to the creation of a project. However, in its original form, it only reflects the desires of the person seeking a particular outcome and doesn't reflect any assessment of whether it's possible to meet the request or a commitment to meet it.

✔ **Business requirements document:** A description of the business needs to be addressed by a requested product, service, or system.

✔ **Project request:** A written request for the performance of a project by a group within the organization. The project request indicates a desire for a project, rather than a mutual agreement and commitment to perform it.

✔ **Project charter:** A document issued by upper management that spells out the project manager's authority to coordinate personnel in the performance of a project.

✔ **Project profile:** Highlights of key information about a project. Sometimes called a *project summary* or a *project abstract*.

✔ **Work order:** A written description of work to be performed by people or groups within your organization in support of your project. The signed work order focuses on work to be performed instead of on overall project outcomes to be achieved.

✔ **Contract:** A legal agreement for goods to be procured or services to be rendered from an external vendor or contractor. On occasion, the term *Statement of Work* is used to refer to the part of a contract that describes the goods and services to be procured from an outside source.

Your Statement of Work includes the following information:

> ✔ **Purpose:** How and why your project came to be, the scope of your project, and the general approach to be followed.
>
> ✔ **Objectives:** Specific outcomes you will produce.
>
> ✔ **Constraints:** Restrictions that will limit what you're to achieve, how and when you can do it, and for what cost.
>
> ✔ **Assumptions:** Statements about uncertain information you're taking as fact as you conceive, plan, and perform your project.

Think of your Statement of Work as a binding agreement. You and your team commit to producing certain results, and your project's requesters commit that they'll consider your project to be 100 percent successful if you produce these results. You and your team identify all restrictions regarding how you'll be allowed to approach your project work and what you'll need to support your work. Your project's requesters agree there are no restrictions other than the ones you have identified, and that they'll provide you the support you declare you'll need. You and your team identify all assumptions you made when agreeing to the terms of your Statement of Work.

Of course, it's impossible to predict the future. In fact, the further into the future you try to look, the less able you are to predict with certainty what'll happen. However, your Statement of Work represents your project commitments, based upon what you know today and expect to be true in the future. If and when situations change, you'll assess the impact of the changes on your Statement of Work and propose any corresponding changes to your project that you feel are necessary. Your project's requesters always have the option of accepting your proposed changes, allowing the project to continue as originally defined, or canceling your project.

# Looking at the Big Picture

Understanding the situation and thought processes that led up to your project helps ensure that your project addresses the true needs for which it's intended. Your project's *purpose statement,* should include the following information:

- ✔ **Background:** Why people authorized your project
- ✔ **Scope:** What work will be performed
- ✔ **Strategy:** How you will approach the major work of this project

# Figuring out why you're doing this project

When you're assigned a project or decide to take one on, why you're doing it may seem obvious — because your boss told you to or because your company needs the work. The real question, though, is not why you choose to accept the assignment but why your boss wants the project done in the first place. Work to develop a clear and concise description of your project's background.

### Identifying the initiator

As your first task, determine who had the original idea that led to the creation of your project. Project success requires that, at a minimum, you meet this person's needs and expectations.

Sometimes this is easy; the person who conceives your project is the one who assigns it directly to you. More likely, however, the person who assigns you your project is passing along an assignment received from someone else. If your project is passed along to several people before it reaches you, you may have difficultly determining who really initiated the idea. Further, the original intent may become blurred if every person in the chain purposely or inadvertently changes the assignment a little as they pass it on.

Take the following steps to determine who came up with the original idea for your project.

1. **Ask the person who assigns you the project if he or she originated the idea.**

2. **If it wasn't that person's idea, ask**

   • From whom the person received the assignment

   • Who, if anyone, was involved in passing the assignment to that person

   • Who had the original idea for the project

3. **Check with people you identified in Step 2 and ask them the questions in Step 2.**

4. **Check the following written records that may confirm who originally had the idea:**

   • Minutes from division-, department-, and organization-wide planning and budget sessions

   • Correspondence and e-mail referring to the project

   • Reports of planning or feasibility studies

A *feasibility study* is a formal investigation that's undertaken to determine the likely success of performing certain work or achieving certain results.

5. **Consult with people who appear to be potentially affected by or need to support your project; they may know who originated the idea.**

Identify your project initiator by name and position description: Not, "The sales department requested promotional literature for product Alpha" but, "Mary Smith, the sales representative for the northeast region, requested promotional literature for product Alpha."

Distinguish between drivers and supporters, as you seek to find your project initiator. (See Chapter 7 for information about how to define and identify drivers and supporters.)

 ✔ *Drivers* are the people who have some say when defining the results that your project is to achieve.

 ✔ *Supporters* are the people who help you perform your project.

Drivers tell you what you *should* do, supporters tell you what you *can* do. As an example, suppose the vice president of finance requests a project to upgrade the organization's financial information systems — he or she is a driver of the project. The manager of the computer center must provide staff and resources to upgrade the organization's information systems — he or she is a supporter of the project.

Sometimes, supporters claim to be drivers. When asked, for example, perhaps the manager of the computer center says she initiated the project. In reality, the manager authorized the people and funds to perform the project, but it was the vice president of finance who initiated it.

### Identifying others who may benefit from your project

Although they may not have initiated the idea, others may potentially benefit from your project when it's completed. Identify these people as soon as possible to determine their needs and interests and how you can appropriately address them. Those who may benefit from your project may include the following:

- ✔ People who already know it exists and have expressed an interest in it
- ✔ People who know it exists but don't realize it can benefit them
- ✔ People who are unaware of your project

Identify these additional audiences by

- ✔ Reviewing all written materials related to your project
- ✔ Consulting with people who you know will be driving or supporting your project
- ✔ Encouraging everyone with whom you speak to identify anyone else they think may benefit from your project

While you're working to identify people who could benefit from your project, also identify anyone who strongly opposes it.

- ✔ Figure out why they oppose your project and whether you can address their concerns.
- ✔ Determine whether they may be able to derive any benefits from your project and, if so, explain these benefits to them.
- ✔ If they continue to oppose your project, make note in your risk management plan of their opposition and how you plan to deal with it (see Chapter 14 for how to analyze and plan for project risks and uncertainties).

### Considering the project champion

A *project champion* is a person in a high position in the organization who strongly supports your project; advocates for your project in disputes, planning meetings, and review sessions; and takes whatever actions are necessary to help ensure that your project is successfully completed. (See Chapter 7 for more discussion about a project champion.)

Sometimes the best champion is one whose support you never have to use. Just knowing that this person supports your project helps others appreciate its importance and encourages them to work diligently to ensure its success.

Find out if your project already has a champion. If it doesn't, work hard to recruit one. Find people who can reap benefits from your project and who have sufficient power and influence to encourage serious, ongoing organizational commitment to your project. Explain to them why it's in their best interest for your project to succeed and how specifically you may need their help as your project progresses. Assess how interested they are in your project and how much help they're willing to provide.

### Considering people who'll implement the results of your project

Most projects create a product or service that'll be used to achieve a desired result. Often, however, the person who asks you to create the product or service isn't the one who'll actually use it to achieve the desired result.

Suppose your organization's director of sales and marketing wants to increase annual sales by ten percent in the next fiscal year. She decides that developing and introducing a new product, XYZ, will allow her to achieve this goal. However, she herself will not go to all of your organization's customers and sell them XYZ; her sales staff will. Even though they didn't come up with the idea to develop XYZ, the sales staff may have strong opinions about what characteristics it should have to meet sales expectations. So will the customer whom you hope will ultimately buy the product.

To identify the users of project products and services, try to do the following:

✔ Clarify the products and services that you anticipate producing during your project.

✔ Identify exactly how and by whom they will be used to achieve the desired end results.

### Defining needs to be addressed

The need(s) that your project addresses may not be obvious from looking at your project itself. Suppose, for example, that your organization decides to sponsor a blood drive. Is this project being undertaken to address the shortage of blood in the local hospital or to improve your organization's image in the local community?

When you clearly understand the needs, you can do the following, as necessary:

- ✔ Frame all project activities to be sure you accomplish the true desired results

- ✔ Monitor performance to ensure that the real needs are being met

- ✔ Realize when the project as assigned isn't the best way to meet the real need and suggest the project be modified or cancelled

Sure, it would be nice if, when given an assignment, you were told both the specific project outcomes you should achieve and the needs that your project is designed to address. However, usually you're just told what to produce (the outcomes) and not why it's to be done (the needs). It's up to you to figure out what the real needs are.

Consider the following, as you work to define the needs.

- ✔ **What needs do people want your project to address?** Don't worry at this point whether you feel your project actually can address these needs or whether it's the best way to address the needs. You're just trying to identify the hopes and expectations that led up to this project.

- ✔ **How do you know that the needs you identify are the real hopes and expectations that people have for your project?** Determining people's real thoughts and feelings can be difficult. Sometimes they don't want to share them; sometimes they don't know how to express them clearly.

A friend of mine received an assignment from his boss, who had just returned from an upper management retreat, to develop a new product. My friend knew that company sales had been dipping and that the retreat had been held to discuss possible approaches for reversing the trend. He also knew that the company's highly skilled market research department had been investigating new product ideas for the past six months. He assumed, therefore, that this project had been established by upper management, based upon the recommendations from the market research department, to increase sales in the coming year.

My friend's conclusion was reasonable but was, however, completely wrong. It turned out that, right before the retreat, the president of the company had received a call from his friend who asked if the company marketed a product like XYZ. Rather than admit that his company was not at the state-of-the-art, the president promised to provide his friend with the requested product. In fact, no one had any idea whether anyone other than the president's friend would ever buy the product that this person had been assigned to develop! When my friend found out the truth, he realized that this project's true measure of success would be how the president's friend reacted to XYZ and not the sales increase realized as a result of introducing XYZ into the company's product line.

So, when speaking with people, try the following:

- ✔ Encourage them to speak at length about their needs and expectations
- ✔ Listen carefully for anything that isn't clear or for any contradictions
- ✔ Encourage them to clarify anything that's vague
- ✔ Try to confirm your information from two or more sources

See if your organization performed a formal cost-benefit analysis to determine whether to proceed with your project. A *cost-benefit analysis* is a formal identification and assessment of all of the benefits that are anticipated from your project plus all of the costs for performing your project and using and supporting the products or services produced by your project. (See Chapter 1 for further details.)

The cost-benefit analysis documents the particular results that people were counting on when they made the decision to proceed with your project. It is, therefore, an important source of information about the real needs that your project is supposed to address.

### Confirming that your project will successfully address the identified needs

While needs may be thoroughly documented, you may have more difficulty determining with confidence whether your project can successfully address those needs. On occasion, extensive research is devoted to determining the chances that your project will successfully address a particular need. Along these lines, someone associated with the project may order a formal feasibility study to investigate and document these findings and conclusions.

Other times, however, your project may be the result of a brainstorming session or someone's creative "vision." In this case, you may have less confidence that your project will accomplish what they expect. Don't necessarily reject a project at this point, but aggressively determine the chances for success and how, if at all, you can increase these chances. If you can't find sufficient information to support your analysis, consider asking that a formal feasibility study be done.

If you feel the risk of project failure is too great, share your information with the key decision makers and explain why you recommend not proceeding with the project. See the discussion of risk management in Chapter 14 for more information.

### Identifying other activities related to your project

Determine whether other projects are ongoing or planned that

- ✔ Address issues similar to those your project will address
- ✔ Create products your project will need

✔ Need products generated by your project

✔ Use the same resources as your project

### Determining how important your project is to the organization

The importance the organization places on your project directly influences the chances for your project's success. When conflicting demands for scarce resources arise, resources are usually given to the project that the organization feels will provide the greatest benefit. Therefore, determine the following:

✔ **How your project relates to the organization's top priorities.**

Consult the following sources to learn about your organization's top priorities:

- **Long-range plan:** Formal report that identifies your organization's overall direction, specific performance targets, and individual initiatives for the next one to five years

- **Annual budget:** Detailed list of the categories and individual initiatives on which all organization funds will be spent during the year

- **Capital appropriations plan:** Itemized list of all expenditures over an established minimum amount planned for facilities and equipment purchases, renovations, and repairs during the year

- **Managers' annual performance objectives:** Specific tasks and desired accomplishments that'll be considered when conducting each manager's annual performance appraisal

In addition, determine whether specific commitments related to your project's completion have been made to external customers or upper management.

✔ **How you could make it relate more closely to the organization's top priorities.** If your project isn't specifically identified in any of these documents, can you help others understand how your project will support other initiatives that are included in the long-range plan, your manager's performance objectives, and so on?

Ask people to consider what would happen if you didn't perform your project. If they honestly feel it would make no difference, explore ways to modify your project so that it will make a difference. If you can't figure out how to modify your project so that it will make a difference to the organization, consider suggesting that the project be cancelled before any more work is done. Organizations are consistently overworked and understaffed — spending precious time and resources on a project that people agree will "make no difference" is the last thing you want to do.

More likely, people realize that your project will make a difference. Your job is to stop them from losing sight of this.

### Being exhaustive in your search for information

You're seeking information that's sensitive, sometimes contradictory, and often discussed verbally (not in writing). Getting it won't always be easy. Here are some tips that can help:

✔ **Get information from all possible sources.**

✔ **Whenever possible, get information from primary sources.** A *primary source of information* is the place where the original information you're seeking is contained. A *secondary source of information* is someone else's report of the information contained in the primary source.

Suppose your project was discussed in a report of alternative projects to be considered for the coming year. The report itself is a primary source of information; someone who reads the report is a secondary source.

The further removed from the original your source is, the more likely that the information contained in it differs from the real information.

✔ **Written sources are the best.** Check relevant minutes from meetings, correspondence, e-mail, reports from other projects, long-range plans, budgets, capital improvement plans, market requirement documents, and cost-benefit analyses.

✔ **Speak to two or more people from the same area to confirm information shared.** Different people have different styles of communication as well as different perceptions of the same situation. Speak with more than one person and compare their messages to determine any contradictions.

✔ **When speaking with people, arrange to have at least one person in addition to yourself present.** This allows two different people to interpret what they heard from the same individual.

✔ **Put down in writing all information obtained from personal meetings.** Share your written notes and summaries with others who were present at the meeting. This helps ensure that your interpretation of the messages shared was correct, and it serves as a reminder of agreements made.

✔ **Plan to meet at least two times with key audiences.** Your first meeting starts them thinking about issues. Allow some time for them to think over your initial discussions, as well as to think of new ideas related to the issues you raised. A second meeting also gives you a chance to clarify any ambiguities or inconsistencies from the first session.

✔ **Wherever possible, confirm the information you learn in personal meetings with information from written sources.** It's important to determine people's perceptions. It's equally important to compare perceptions and opinions with factual data. Discuss any discrepancies you identify with the people with whom you speak.

Be sure to ask people to let you know when they learn of any information that may relate to project audiences, needs, and priorities. Often, people ignore these issues after the project plan is prepared and approved. The longer the project, though, the greater the chances that people and priorities will change. The sooner you know about any changes, the better able you will be to deal with them.

## Defining where your project starts and where it stops

Sometimes your project stands alone, but more often, it's part of one or more related efforts, all of which are designed to achieve a common result. You want to avoid duplicating the work of these other projects and, where appropriate, you want to ensure that you coordinate your work with them.

The statement of your project's scope should describe clearly when your project starts and when it ends. Suppose that you've been assigned a project to develop a new product for your organization. You may describe your project scope as follows.

> This project will entail designing, developing, and testing a new product.

If you feel your statement is in any way ambiguous, you may clarify your scope further by stating what you will not do, as follows:

> This project won't include finalizing the market requirements or launching the new product.

Here are some tips for making sure your scope description is clear.

- ✔ **Check for hidden inferences.** Suppose you determine that your boss has asked you to design and develop a new product. You may check to be sure that she's not assuming that you'll also perform market research to determine what the characteristics of the new product should be.

- ✔ **Use words that clearly describe intended activities.** Suppose your project includes the implementation of a new information system. Are you sure that everyone defines "implementation" in the same way? For instance, do people expect that "implementation" will include:

  - Installing the new software

  - Training people to use the new software

  - Evaluating the new software's performance

- Fixing problems identified in the new software

- All of the above

- Something else

✔ **Confirm your understanding of your project's scope with your project's drivers and supporters.** A colleague told me of an assignment she received from her boss to prepare for the competitive acquisition of certain equipment. She developed a plan for her project to include selection of the vendor, award of the contract, and production and delivery of the equipment. Her boss was stunned when she estimated the project would require six months and $500,000; he thought it should take no more than two months and cost less than $25,000.

After a brief discussion with her boss, my colleague realized she was just supposed to select the potential vendor and not actually to place the order for the equipment and have it delivered. Although she had clarified her misunderstanding, she still wondered aloud, "But why would we select a vendor if we didn't want to actually buy the equipment?"

Of course, she missed the point. The question wasn't whether the company ever planned to buy the equipment. Certainly, unless company plans changed dramatically, the desire and intention to buy the equipment was the whole reason for her project. Instead, the question was whether her project was to include the purchase of the equipment or whether that would be handled by a different effort in the future.

## Defining your approach to the work on the project

Your *project strategy* is the general approach you plan to take to perform the work highlighted in your project scope. Examples of a project strategy include the following:

✔ We'll buy the needed supplies from an outside vendor.

✔ We'll conduct our training in instructor-led sessions.

Your project strategy will help determine whether you're able to meet the demands and expectations of your audiences. At the earliest point in your thinking about the project, find out whether any of your audiences has preconceived ideas about how the project should be approached or how it should *not* be approached.

When selecting a strategy

✔ Consider your organization's usual approaches for handling similar projects.

## Facing challenging expectations

When faced with challenging expectations, try the following:

✔ **Be careful not to assume a particular approach just because you've always used it in the past.** A client of mine was criticized recently for buying a piece of equipment from the vendor the organization had used for several years. It turned out this vendor was charging 20 percent more than other vendors for the same item. When asked why he hadn't checked out the other vendors, he replied that the organization had been using this vendor for years and no one had complained before.

✔ **Be careful not to prejudge others' willingness to use different approaches.** Years ago, I was working to get a proposal out the door by the end of the week. I needed a full day of secretarial support to finish all of the administrative details so that the proposal could be mailed by the close of business on Friday. However, the company's secretaries were all tied up with other assignments. When I went to my boss to tell him we wouldn't be able to get the proposal out on time, he asked me why. I told him that all the secretaries were busy on other assignments and that the company had always turned down any requests I had made in the past to hire temporary secretarial help. He stunned me by saying that if the choice was between hiring a temp and missing the due date, I should hire a temp!

✔ Where possible, choose a strategy with the least risks, uncertainties, and uncontrollables. You don't just want a strategy that *may* work, you want one with the greatest chance that it *will* work.

✔ For riskier projects, consider developing one or more backup strategies, in case your primary strategy runs into problems. A different strategy may be the answer for meeting an apparently unachievable performance expectation.

## Innovating your approach

A colleague of mine had been assigned the task to train all sales representatives in his company in a new order entry process. The company had several hundred sales representatives located throughout the country, and he was to have the training completed within one month. In the past, he had delivered all company training in instructor-led, on-site programs. After some preliminary consideration, though, he was convinced that it would take at least three months to design and present to all the sales representatives around the country an instructor-led program. He was ready to tell his boss that the task was impossible, when a colleague suggested he consider presenting the training through his company's intranet. Using this new strategy, he completed the project ahead of schedule!

A strategy isn't a detailed list of activities to be performed. That list is derived from your project Work Breakdown Structure, which is described in detail in Chapter 3.

If you haven't yet chosen a strategy as you prepare your Statement of Work, rather than not addressing it at all, make a note in that document that it is *to be determined* (TBD), which means that a strategy hasn't yet been chosen. This note will also remind you that, at some point in the future, you have to develop a strategy.

## What exactly are you trying to achieve?

*Objectives* are results to be achieved through the performance of your project. Objectives may include the creation of products and services or the impact realized through the application of these products and services. The more clearly you can define your project's objectives, the greater your chances for achieving project success.

Include the following elements to make your objective clear and specific:

- ✔ **Statement:** A brief narrative description of what you want to achieve

- ✔ **Measures:** One or more indicators you will use to assess your achievement

- ✔ **Performance targets:** The value of each measure that defines success

Suppose you're assigned or take on a project to revise the format of an existing report that summarizes monthly sales activity. You may frame your project's objective as shown in Table 2-1.

| Table 2-1 | An Illustration of a Project Objective | |
|---|---|---|
| *Statement* | *Measures* | *Performance Targets* |
| Create a revised report that summarizes monthly sales activity | | |
| | Content | Report must include the following data for each product line:<br>• Total number of items sold<br>• Total sales revenue<br>• Total returns |

| Statement | Measures | Performance Targets |
|---|---|---|
| | Schedule | Report must be operational by August 31 |
| | Budget | Development expenditures are not to exceed $40,000 |
| | Approvals | New report format must be approved by<br>• Vice president of sales<br>• Regional sales manager<br>• District sales manager<br>• Sales representatives |

Sometimes, people try to avoid setting a specific performance target for a measure by establishing a range within which performance will be deemed successful. This is just avoiding the issue.

Suppose you're a sales representative and your boss said that you would be successful if you achieved between $20 million and $25 million in sales for the year. As far as you're concerned, you will be 100 percent successful as soon as you reach $20 million. Most likely, however, your boss will only consider you to be 100 percent successful when you reach $25 million. While it appeared that you and your boss had reached agreement, in fact you had not.

## Clarifying objectives

At the start of my training sessions, I ask people what they hope to gain from attending. Every once in a while, someone tells me his boss had directed him to attend and that he didn't want to learn anything in particular. I used to think there was no way I could fail to satisfy this person's desire, as long as I kept him in the room for the entire session. Through experience, though, I realized that this person presented the greatest challenge for me. Because the person hadn't clarified exactly what it was that he wanted to learn, he wouldn't participate as actively during the session and he would miss many opportunities to see how topics we were exploring may help him deal with situations that he typically faced at his job. Further, I had no way of knowing whether I was addressing the right issues at the right level for this person, and whether he was learning what he needed and wanted. In truth, the chances that this person would leave the session having worked on those skills and techniques that can help him most at his job were small, at best.

### Making your objectives clear and specific

The more clear and specific your project objectives are, the greater the chance you'll be able to achieve them. Here are some tips for developing clear objectives.

- **Less is more.** Be brief when describing an objective. If you take an entire page to describe a single objective, most people won't even read it. And, even if they do, the chances are that your objective isn't clear and is subject to multiple interpretations.

- **Don't use technical jargon or acronyms.** There's no end to the array of technical terms and acronyms you find in the workplace today. Each industry (such as telecommunications, finance, pharmaceuticals, and insurance) has its own vocabulary, as does each company within an industry. Within companies, different departments (such as accounting, legal, and information services) have *their* own jargon. It's not unusual today that the same TLA *(three letter acronym)* can mean two or more different things in the same organization!

  To make matters worse, people often don't ask if they aren't familiar with a term, because they fear it will make them appear to be ignorant or less qualified for their jobs. Your best bet is not to use acronyms at all; just use the words themselves. If you feel that you have to use an acronym, define it the first time it's used on a page.

- **Make your objectives SMART, as follows:**

  - **S**pecific: Define your objective clearly, in detail, with no room for misinterpretation.

  - **M**easurable: Specify the measures or indicators you will use to determine whether you met your objective.

  - **A**ggressive: Set objectives that are challenging and that encourage people to stretch beyond their comfort zones.

  - **R**ealistic: Set objectives that the project team believes it can achieve.

  - **T**ime-sensitive: Include the date by which you will achieve the objective.

- **Make your objectives controllable.** Make sure that you and your team believe you have the ability to influence whether you achieve each objective. If you don't believe you can influence whether or not you achieve an objective, you won't commit to achieve it, and most likely you won't even try to achieve it. In that case, it becomes not an objective but a wish.

- **Identify all objectives.** Time and resources are always scarce, so if you don't specify an objective, you won't (and shouldn't) work to achieve it.

✔ **Be sure both drivers and supporters agree on your project's objectives.** When drivers buy in to your objectives, you feel confident that achieving them will constitute true project success. When supporters buy in to your objectives, you have the greatest chance that people will work their hardest to achieve those objectives.

## Anticipating resistance to clearly defined objectives

Not everyone is excited about committing to specific objectives. Here are some reasons people give for not being too specific, along with some suggestions for how you can address them.

✔ **Too much specificity stifles creativity.** Creativity is to be encouraged; the question is where and when. You want people to be creative when figuring ways to meet objectives, not when trying to determine the objectives. You want to determine with certainty what others expect from your project, not what they may expect. The more clearly you can describe their actual wants, the easier it is to determine whether and how you can meet them.

✔ **Your project entails research and new development, and you can't tell today what you will be able to accomplish.** Objectives are targets, not guarantees. Certain projects have more risk associated with them than others. When you haven't done something before, you can't be sure that it's possible or, if it is possible, how long it'll take and how much it'll cost. It's still essential, though, to state at the outset what you'd like to achieve and what you think is possible, even though you may have to change your objectives as the project progresses.

✔ **What if interests or needs change.** Objectives are targets, based on what you know and expect today. If things change in the future, you may have to revisit one or more objectives to see if they're still relevant and feasible or if they, too, should be changed.

✔ **While specific objectives help you determine when you have succeeded, they also make it easier to determine when you haven't.** Yep. That's true.

Sometimes you find out unexpected things when you ask others to be specific, such as the following:

✔ A requestor, after being asked, can't tell you specifically what he wants his project to achieve. If you begin his project now, there's a greater chance you'll waste time and resources working to produce results he later decides he doesn't want.

✔ A requestor, after being asked, refuses to tell you specifically what he wants his project to achieve. You later realize that the requestor was resisting your effort to take away his power to control you by making arbitrary changes that you're not able to anticipate. In this situation, the requestor isn't only interested in your project's outcomes, but he also wants a vehicle to satisfy his needs for power and control.

# Defining the Boundaries

You'd like to operate in a world where all things are possible — that is, where you can do anything you want to achieve your desired results. Your clients and your organization, on the other hand, want to believe that you can achieve everything they ask with minimal or no cost to them. Of course, neither situation is true.

Defining the restrictions on how you approach your project helps to introduce reality in your plans and helps clarify expectations. Think in terms of the following:

- **Limitations:** Restrictions that others place on the results you have to achieve, the time frames you have to meet, the resources you can use, and the way you can approach your tasks
- **Needs:** Requirements you determine must be met in order to achieve project success

## Identifying limitations

When defining limitations, your job is to determine what's in the minds of others who will influence or be affected by your project. At this point, you're not concerned with whether or not you can satisfy their limitations — you just want to identify them.

### Understanding the types of limitations

Others often have preset expectations or requirements with regard to

- **Results:** The products and impact of your project.
- **Time frames:** By when certain results must be produced. Your project must be done by June 30. You don't know yet whether it's possible to finish by June 30, you just know that someone else expects it then.
- **Resources**: The type, amount, and when they will or will not be available. Resources are everything necessary for you to perform your project work, including people, funds, equipment, raw materials, facilities, information, and so on.
- **Activity performance:** The strategies and approaches for performing different tasks. You've been told that you must use your organization's printing department to reproduce the user's manuals for the new system you're developing. You don't yet know what the manual will look like, how long it will be, the number of copies you'll need, or when you'll need them. Therefore, you can't know whether your organization's printing department is capable of satisfactorily reproducing the manuals. But

you do know that, at this point, someone in the organization expects that the printing department can handle the order and that you'll have them do the work.

Be careful of a vague limitation. Not only does a vague limitation provide poor guidance for how you should proceed to satisfy that limitation, it can be demoralizing for people who have to deal with it. Here are some examples:

✔ **Schedule limitation:**

- Vague: "Finish this project as soon as possible." All work has to be done as soon as possible, so this statement really tells you nothing you didn't already know. With this limitation, you're afraid that, with no advance warning, your audience will suddenly demand your project's final results.

- Specific: "Finish this project by close of business, June 30."

✔ **Resource limitation:**

- Vague: "You can have an analyst part time in May." How heavily can you count on this analyst? From the analyst's point of view, how can she juggle all of the assignments given to her in the same time period if she has no idea how long each one will take?

- Specific: "You can have an analyst four hours per day for the first two weeks in May." If people can't be specific when they tell you about a constraint, you can't be sure that you will be able to honor their request. The longer they wait to be specific, the more likely that you won't be able to adhere to the constraint while successfully completing your project.

## Determining your project's limitations

Determining limitations is a fact-finding mission, so your job is to identify and examine all possible sources of information. You don't want to miss anything and you want to clarify any conflicting information. After you know what people expect, you can set about determining how (or if) you can meet those expectations. Try the following approaches:

✔ **Consult your audiences.** Check with drivers about limitations regarding desired outcomes; check with supporters about limitations concerning work approach and resources.

✔ **Review relevant written materials.** Such materials may include long-range plans, annual budgets and capital-appropriations plans, cost-benefit analyses, feasibility studies, reports of related projects, minutes of meetings, and individuals' performance objectives.

✔ **When you identify a limitation, be sure to note its source.** Confirming a limitation from different sources increases your confidence in its accuracy. Resolve conflicting opinions about a limitation as soon as possible.

### Including limitations in your plan

You can reflect limitations in your project in two ways. You can choose to incorporate them directly into your plan. If a key driver says you have to finish your project by September 30, you may choose to set September 30 as your project's completion date. Of course, because September 30 is the outside limit, you may also choose to set a completion date of August 31. In this case, the limitation influences your target but isn't equivalent to it.

You can also identify any project risks that exist because of a particular limitation. If you feel the target completion date is unusually aggressive, the risk of missing that date may be significant. You'll want to develop plans to minimize and manage the risk throughout your project. See Chapter 14 for more information on how to assess and plan for risks and uncertainties.

## Determining needs

Start thinking as soon as possible about what situations or conditions must come to pass for you to be able to complete your project successfully. Most needs will relate to resources required to support project performance. The following are examples:

- **Personnel:** "I need a technical editor for a total of 40 hours in August."

- **Budget:** "I need a budget of $10,000 for computer peripherals."

- **Other resources:** "I need access to the test laboratory during the month of June."

Be as specific as you can. The more specific you are, the easier it is for others to understand your needs and the more likely they are to meet them.

Sometimes you can identify needs very early in your thinking about your project. More often, however, particular needs surface as you try to create a plan that addresses the expectations of the drivers. Your list of needs will grow as you continue to plan out your project.

# Dealing with Unknowns in the Planning Process

As you proceed through your planning process, you can identify issues or questions that may affect your project's performance. Unfortunately, just identifying these issues or questions doesn't help you address them.

For every issue you identify, decide what assumption you will make regarding the issue that you'll then build into your planning process. Plan actions you can take to make your assumption become a reality. Consider the following examples:

✔ **Issue:** How much money will you get to perform your project?

**Approach:** Assume you'll get $50,000 for your project. Plan out your project to spend up to but no more than $50,000. Develop detailed information to demonstrate why it's important that you receive a project budget of $50,000 and share that information with key decision makers.

✔ **Issue:** When will you get authorization to start work on your project?

**Approach:** Assume you'll receive authorization to start work on August 1. Plan your project work so that no activities start before August 1. Explain to key people why it's important that your project start on August 1 and work with them to facilitate your project's approval by that date.

Consider all project assumptions when you develop your project's risk management plan. See Chapter 14 for a discussion on how to assess and manage project risks and uncertainties.

# Developing a Statement of Work

Figure 2-1 illustrates a systematic approach to help you prepare your Statement of Work. As the figure suggests, take the following steps to determine your project's purpose, objectives, constraints, and assumptions and to write your Statement of Work.

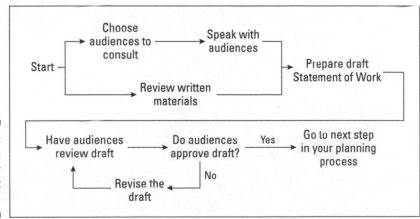

**Figure 2-1:** Developing your Statement of Work.

1. **Identify audiences, people who are looking for the results of your project or will be needed to support it.**

2. **Meet with some or all of those people and find out what they think is desirable and feasible to achieve.**

3. **At the same time that you're doing Steps 1 and 2, review all written materials related to your project.**

4. **Combine the information from your personal meetings and your materials review to prepare a draft of a Statement of Work.**

5. **Have the people with whom you met in Step 2 review your draft Statement of Work and ask them to formally approve it (that is, to approve it in writing).**

6. **If the people agree with the information in the draft Statement of Work and formally commit to support it, move on to the next step in your planning process.**

7. **If some or all of the people give you comments and suggestions about the draft, incorporate those suggestions into a revised draft Statement of Work and ask the people to review and approve the revised document.**

8. **Continue until you obtain all necessary approvals.**

On occasion, you may find that one or more reviewers won't approve your draft Statement of Work, even after several revisions. If this happens and you believe that you've done all you can to respond to their suggestions and concerns, ask yourself:

Are you willing to proceed without their support?

If your answer is "yes," do the following:

1. **Make a written record of your attempts to get their approval and the reasons why they didn't give it.**

2. **Record their lack of approval in your risk management plan (see Chapter 14 for how to identify, assess, and manage project risks).**

3. **Move on to the next step in your planning process.**

If your answer is "no," find someone at a higher level in the organization who can help you resolve the issue (this is the perfect time to ask for help from your project champion).

# Chapter 3

# Getting from Here to There

*In This Chapter*
▶ Using a hierarchical breakout to develop a project Work Breakdown Structure
▶ Knowing how much detail is enough
▶ Planning for uncertain activities
▶ Incorporating past experience in your Work Breakdown Structure
▶ Dealing with unknown activities

The keys to successful project planning and performance are completeness and continuity. You want to identify and consider all important information in your project plan, and you want to remember and address all aspects of your plan during project performance. This chapter shows you how.

Your organized approach for describing project work provides the basis for scheduling and resource planning, defining roles and responsibilities, assigning work to team members, capturing key project performance data, and reporting on project work done.

## Dividing and Conquering

My biggest concern when I start a new project is remembering to plan for all important pieces of work. My second biggest concern is accurately estimating required time and resources for all work. To address both issues, I develop a logical framework to define all work that will have to be performed for the project to be completed.

I have a friend who loves to assemble jigsaw puzzles. My friend readily attacks 5,000 piece puzzles — he even tackles those where 80 percent of the puzzle is sky (so all of the pieces are basically the same color)! But a while back, my friend confided that he thought he'd met his match. My friend's acquaintance gave him a box containing a 5,000-piece puzzle of the United States to assemble. His acquaintance suggested that, before my friend started on the puzzle, he may first want to examine the pieces in the box to determine whether any were missing and, if so, which ones. My friend just laughed. He knew how he would identify any missing puzzle pieces: He would attempt to assemble the puzzle, and if any holes in the picture remained when all the pieces had been used, well, I guess the conclusion would be obvious. How else could he do it?

You've probably had the same experience with your project assignments. Suppose you're asked to design and present a training program. You and a few colleagues work intensely for a couple of months choosing the content, designing the materials, selecting the instructors, arranging for the facilities, and inviting the participants. A week before the session, you ask your colleagues if they had made arrangements for the training manuals to be printed. Your colleagues say they hadn't thought about having the manuals printed; you declare that you hadn't either because you thought they would deal with all of the final details. It turns out that printing the manuals had been overlooked because everyone thought someone else would handle it. Now you have a training session to be presented in a week and neither time nor money to print the needed materials. It's crisis time.

How could this situation have been avoided? By using an organized approach to identify all necessary project work in the planning stage, you could've planned for this essential activity.

## Thinking in detail

The most important guideline to remember when identifying and describing project work is to think in detail! I find that people consistently underestimate the time and resources needed for work because they just don't realize everything they have to do to complete their tasks.

Suppose you're asked to write a report of the proceedings of your team's most recent meeting. Your first task is to estimate the time and resources you'll need to prepare this report. Because you've written many reports before, you figure it should take you a few days. But, how confident are you in this estimate? Are you sure you've considered all of the activities that writing the report will entail?

The key to describing your work is decomposition, breaking down a piece of work into its component parts. Preparing the report will actually entail three separate activities: writing a draft report, reviewing the draft, and preparing the final report. Preparing the final report, in turn, will involve two separate activities: writing the final report and printing the final report.

Follow two guidelines to decompose activities correctly:

✔ **No gaps:** All work in the activity must be identified in the subactivities you define. *No gaps* means that all of the work that goes into writing the report is encompassed in its three subactivities. If you feel that there's more work that has to be done, define another subactivity to include it.

✔ **No overlaps:** The same work can't be included in more than one of your subactivities. As an example, you can't say that writing the draft report will involve having people review preliminary versions of the draft if all reviews are included under reviewing the draft.

Detailing your work in this way forces you to think about all the work that must be performed to complete each activity. It increases your confidence that you haven't overlooked anything important, and it lets you develop more accurate and realistic estimates of the time and resources needed for you to complete your project.

## Thinking of hierarchy

Thinking in detail is critical; however, you also need to identify all of the work required for your project to be complete. If you fail to identify a major part of your project work, you won't have the chance to be detailed! Your task is to be both comprehensive and specific.

My friend's jigsaw puzzle dilemma (discussed in the previous section) suggests an approach that'll help you achieve your goal. My friend could count the pieces before starting to assemble the puzzle to determine whether any piece was missing. However, knowing that he only had 4,999 pieces wouldn't help him determine which particular piece was missing. He needs a structure to divide up the 5,000 pieces into smaller groups that he can examine and understand. Suppose my friend divides the entire puzzle of the United States into 50 separate puzzles, one for each state, each of which consists of 100 pieces. Because he knows the United States is comprised of 50 states, he's confident that each piece of the puzzle will be in one and only one of the boxes. Suppose he takes it a step further and divides each state into northeast, northwest, southeast and southwest sections, which should each contain 25 pieces. My friend could then count the number of pieces in each box to see if any were missing. If would be a lot easier to determine which piece of 25 pieces was missing from the box representing the northeast sector of New Jersey than to figure out which piece was missing from the 5,000 piece puzzle of the entire United States.

Figure 3-1 shows how you use the same approach of classifying an item into its component parts to describe the details of the work for your project. A *Work Breakdown Structure* is an organized, hierarchical representation of all work to be performed in your project, broken out in sufficient detail to support planning, assignment of roles and responsibilities, and ongoing monitoring and control.

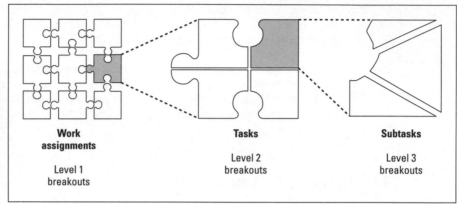

**Figure 3-1:** Developing a structure to detail all project work.

**Work assignments**

Level 1 breakouts

**Tasks**

Level 2 breakouts

**Subtasks**

Level 3 breakouts

The different levels of detail include

- **Level 1:** Work assignment
- **Level 2:** Task
- **Level 3:** Subtask
- **Level 4:** Subsubtasks

Consider that you're planning to develop and present a new training program for your organization. Your first question is, "What major pieces of work have to be done for this project to be completed?" You may identify the following:

- Determine the needs
- Design the program
- Develop the materials
- Test the program
- Present the program

Next, you consider "Determine the needs." You ask, " What major pieces of work have to be done for this portion of the project to be completed?" You may determine that you have to

    ✔ Identify people who have an interest in the program

    ✔ Interview some of these people

    ✔ Review written materials that discuss needs for the program

    ✔ Prepare a report of the needs the program will address

Don't stop now, you're on a roll! Consider "Interview some of these people." Again, you ask, "What major pieces of work have to be done for this portion of the project to be completed?" You decide that you have to

    ✔ Select the people to be interviewed

    ✔ Prepare the questions you will ask during the interviews

    ✔ Schedule the interviews

    ✔ Conduct the interviews

    ✔ Write up the results of the interviews.

But why stop here? You can break each of these five pieces of work into finer detail. And then you can break those pieces into finer detail. How far should you go? The following sections can help.

### Asking three key questions

Determining how much detail you need isn't a trivial task. Experienced project managers often have difficulty deciding when to say when. A client told me of a situation she had recently experienced. Her boss had asked her to plan out her work for the next 12 months, by breaking down her proposed activities into 20-minute intervals! She was a strong supporter of project management, but she wondered, "Wasn't this going a bit too far?"

You want to describe your work in sufficient detail to support accurate planning and meaningful tracking, but not in so much detail that the additional time spent in developing and maintaining your plans and reporting your progress isn't justified. Asking the following three questions is one approach to determine if an activity is sufficiently detailed.

    ✔ Can you accurately estimate the resources you will need to perform the activity? Resources include personnel, equipment, raw materials, money, facilities, information, and so on.

    ✔ Can you accurately estimate how long the activity will take to perform?

    ✔ If you had to assign the activity to someone else, are you confident that he or she would understand exactly what to do?

If your answer to any one of these questions is "no," break down the work into finer detail.

Your answers to these questions depend on how familiar you are with the work to be done, how critical the activity is to the success of your project, what would happen if something went wrong with the activity, who you may assign to perform the activity, how well you know that person, and so on. In other words, it depends on your judgment.

If you're a little uneasy about answering these three questions, here's an even easier test: Break your activity into more detail, if you feel that

- ✔ It'll take significantly longer than two calendar weeks to complete
- ✔ It'll require significantly more than 80 hours of full-time work to complete

Remember, these are just guidelines. Suppose you estimate that you need one week and three days on the calendar to prepare a report, that's sufficient detail. How about two weeks and two days? That's also sufficient detail. But what if you figure that it'll take about two to three months to finalize the requirements for your new product? You need to break it down into more detail because there's too much uncertainty surrounding what you think you'll do in those two to three months for you to have any confidence in your time or resource estimates or your ability to clearly assign the task to someone else to perform.

### Making assumptions to clarify planned work

Sometimes you feel that work isn't defined in sufficient detail, but that certain unknowns stop you from defining it further. How do you resolve this dilemma? Make assumptions!

As an example, suppose "Conduct the interviews" needs to be sufficiently detailed to allow you to estimate the required time and resources to perform it, but you can't detail it further because you don't know how many people you will be interviewing and how many separate sets of interviews you will conduct. If you assume you will interview five groups of seven people each, you can then develop specific plans for arranging and conducting each of these sessions.

Be sure to write your assumptions down, so that you remember to change your plan appropriately, if it turns out you'll actually conduct more or less than five sessions. See the discussion in Chapter 2 for more information about detailing assumptions.

### Using action verbs at the lowest levels of detail

Use action verbs at the lowest levels of detail, to clarify the nature of the work you intend to be performed. This clarity will improve your time and resource estimates, your work assignments to team members, and your tracking and reporting.

Consider the assignment to prepare a report. Suppose you choose to break this project into three work assignments: draft, reviews, and final. If that's all the description you provide, you haven't stated clearly whether you mean to include, under draft, any or all of the following activities:

- ✔ Collect information for the draft
- ✔ Determine length and format expectations and restrictions
- ✔ Handwrite the draft
- ✔ Review the draft

If you worded the activity as "Design and handwrite the draft," your intended scope of work is clearer.

### Using a Work Breakdown Structure for large and small projects

You develop Work Breakdown Structures for very large projects, very small projects, and everything in between. Building a skyscraper, designing a new airplane, researching and developing a new drug, and revamping your organization's information systems are all described with Work Breakdown Structures. So, too, are writing a report, scheduling and conducting a meeting, coordinating your organization's annual blood drive, and moving into your new office. The size of the Work Breakdown Structures for these different projects will vary immensely, but the hierarchical scheme used to develop them is the same.

On occasion, you may look at a detailed Work Breakdown Structure and decide that it makes your project more complex than it really is. Let's face it, looking at 100 tasks all written out on paper can be a little unnerving, not to mention 10,000 tasks! The truth is, though, the project's complexity was there all the time; the Work Breakdown Structure just displays it. In fact, by clearly portraying all aspects of the work to be done, it actually simplifies your project.

### Looking at an example

Consider an example to see how developing a Work Breakdown Structure helps you develop a more accurate and achievable estimate of the time you need to complete your work. Figure 3-2 illustrates a portion of a Work Breakdown Structure for a project to collect certain information from several identified populations.

Suppose your boss asked you to estimate how long it will take to survey people to determine the characteristics that a new product being considered for development should have. Based on some quick, initial thinking, you figure you'll need to contact people in your headquarters office, in two regional activity centers, and from a sampling of your current clients. You tell your boss, "Between one and six months."

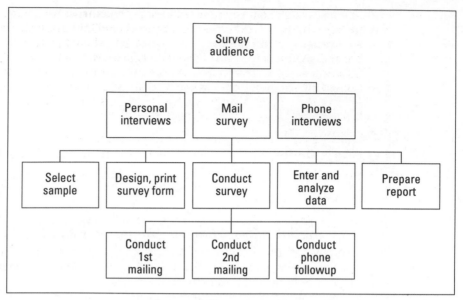

**Figure 3-2:**
Developing
a Work
Breakdown
Structure
for
conducting
surveys.

Have you ever noticed that people aren't happy when you respond to their question of how long something will take with an answer of "Between one and six months"? You figure that finishing anytime before six months will meet your promise; your boss is expecting that, with some hard work, you'll be done in one month. The truth is, though, that you don't have a clue how long it will take, because you don't yet know the work you have to do.

Developing a Work Breakdown Structure encourages you to define a clear picture of exactly what you'll do and, correspondingly, how long it'll take. First, you decide to do three different types of surveys: personal interviews with people in the headquarters office, phone conference calls with people at the two regional activity centers, and a mail survey of a sample of the client population. All three need to be detailed further, but suppose you focus on just the mail survey. People who've done mail surveys before tell you you'll have to perform five activities:

✔ **Selecting a sample of clients to survey:** You figure it should take one week to select your sample of clients if the sales department has a current listing of all company clients. You check with them and they do.

✔ **Designing and printing a survey questionnaire:** You get lucky. A colleague tells you she thinks a similar survey was conducted of a different target population a year ago and that there may be some extra questionnaires around. You find that a local warehouse has 1,000 of these questionnaires and, when you check, you determine that they'll be perfect for your survey. How much time do you allow for designing and printing the questionnaires? Zero!

✔ **Sending out the survey and receiving the returns:** You consult with people who've done these surveys before and find out, if you can accept a response rate of 70 percent or greater, you should plan on a three phased approach for conducting the survey. Mail out your first set of questionnaires and collect responses for four weeks. Then mail out a second set of questionnaires to the nonrespondents and wait another four weeks. Finally, conduct phone follow-ups for two more weeks with the people who have still not responded.

✔ **Entering and analyzing the data:** You figure it'll take about two weeks to enter and analyze the amount of data you anticipate receiving.

✔ **Preparing the final report:** You estimate two weeks to prepare the final report.

Your estimate of the time to complete your mail survey is 15 weeks. Because you have clarified the work to be done and how you'll do it, not only are you more specific, but you also have a higher confidence in your number!

## Special situations

With a little bit of thought, you can break most work into detailed components. However, several special situations require some creativity.

### Representing an iterative activity

Suppose you plan to perform an activity that could require an unknown number of repetitive cycles, such as obtaining approval of a report you've written. In reality, you'll write a draft and submit it for review and approval. If the reviewers approve the draft, you'll proceed to the next activity (such as having the final version typed). If the reviewers don't approve the draft, you'll revise it to incorporate their comments and then resubmit it for a second review and approval. If it's now approved, you'll proceed to the next activity; if not, you'll revise it again, and so on.

A *conditional activity* is an activity that'll be performed if certain conditions come to pass. Unfortunately, there are no conditional activities in a Work Breakdown Structure. You plan to perform every activity that you include. Therefore, you can represent this situation in two ways.

✔ You can define a single activity as "Review/revise report" and assign one duration to that activity. You would be saying, in effect, that you can perform as many iterations as possible within the established time period.

✔ You can assume the number of revisions you think will be needed in order to receive approval and include each of these reviews and revisions as separate activities in your Work Breakdown Structure. This approach defines a separate milestone at the end of each review and revision, which allows more meaningful tracking of progress.

Assuming that three reviews and two revisions will be required doesn't guarantee that your draft will be approved after the third review. If your draft is approved after the first review, you move on to the next activity immediately (that is, you don't perform two revisions just because the plan assumed you would!). However, if you still haven't received approval after the third review, you continue to revise the document and submit it for further review until you do obtain approval. Of course, you have to go back and reassess your plan after you finally receive approval to determine the impact of the additional iterations and to see if you need to change future activities to keep on schedule and/or within your budget.

Remember, a plan isn't a guarantee of the future; it's your statement of what you'll try to achieve. If you're unable to achieve your plan, you must revise your plan accordingly (and promptly).

### Handling an activity with no obvious break points

Sometimes there is no apparent way to break down an activity into two-week intervals. And sometimes it just doesn't seem necessary. Even in these situations, divide the activity into smaller chunks just to remind you to check periodically to ensure that the initial schedule and resource projections for the overall activity are still valid.

A number of years back, I met a young engineer at one of my training sessions. Soon after he joined his organization, he'd been given an assignment to design and build a piece of equipment for a client. When he asked his procurement office to order the raw materials he needed to make the equipment, he was told that the material would be delivered in six months. He was told to notify the procurement office if he hadn't received the raw materials by the promised date. Being young, inexperienced, and new to the organization, he wasn't comfortable trying to fight this "established procedure." So he waited for six months.

When he hadn't received his raw materials after the six months were up, he notified the procurement office. The procurement specialist learned that there had been a fire in the vendor's facilities five months earlier that had caused all production to stop. Production had just been resumed the previous week, and the vendor estimated his materials would be shipped in about five months!

In essence, his Work Breakdown Structure had identified one activity, "Buy raw materials," with a single duration of six months. He argued that, after placing the order, nothing else was to happen until five and one half months passed, at which time work on his order would be started and the final materials would be delivered to him in two weeks. How was he to break this activity down further?

I suggested he could have divided the waiting time into one month intervals, and he could have called at the end of each month to see if anything had occurred which changed the projected delivery date. While checking wouldn't have prevented the fire, he would have learned about it five months sooner and could've made other plans immediately.

### Planning a long-term project

A long-term project presents a different challenge. Often, the activities you perform a year or more in the future depend on the results of the work you do between now and then. Even if you could accurately predict today the activities you will perform then, the further into the future you plan, the more likely that something will change and require you to modify your plans.

When developing a Work Breakdown Structure for a long-term project, do it in phases.

✔ Plan in detail (that is, down to activities that take two weeks or less to complete) for the first three months.

✔ Plan the remainder of the project in less detail, perhaps detailing the planned work in packages that you estimate will take between one and two months.

✔ At the end of the first three months, revise your initial plan to detail your activities for the next three months in components that will take two weeks or less to complete.

✔ Modify any future activities as necessary, based on the results of your first three months' work.

✔ Continue revising your plan in this way throughout the project.

# Creating and Displaying Your Work Breakdown Structure

You can use several different approaches to develop and display your project's Work Breakdown Structure. Each is effective under different circumstances.

## Considering different approaches to detailing an activity

You can break an activity into detail by the following:

✔ **Product components:** Floor plan, training manuals, screen design, or promotional literature

✔ **Functions:** Design, launch, review, or test

> ✔ **Geographical areas:** Region 1 or the northwest
>
> ✔ **Organizational units:** Marketing, operations, or facilities

Product component and function are the most commonly used schemes.

When you choose the scheme you want to use to break out an activity, stick with that scheme to prevent possible overlap in categories.

Consider that you wanted to develop finer detail for the activity called "Prepare report." You may choose to break out the detail according to function, as follows:

> ✔ Write draft report
>
> ✔ Have draft report reviewed
>
> ✔ Write final report

Or, you may choose to break it out by product component, as follows:

> ✔ Chapter 1
>
> ✔ Chapter 2
>
> ✔ Chapter 3

However, don't try to break it out by using some elements from both, as follows:

> ✔ Chapter 1
>
> ✔ Chapter 2
>
> ✔ Chapter 3
>
> ✔ Have draft report reviewed
>
> ✔ Write final report

This breakout creates confusion, because the activity "Prepare the final version of Chapter 3" could be included in either of two categories — "Chapter 3" or "Write final report."

Consider the following factors when deciding which scheme to use to detail an activity:

> ✔ **What higher-level milestones will be most meaningful when reporting progress?** Will it be more helpful to report that all work on Chapter 1 is completed or that all work on the entire draft of the report is done?
>
> ✔ **How will responsibility be assigned?** Will one person be responsible for drafting, reviewing, and finalizing Chapter 1 or will one person be responsible for all work on the drafts of Chapters 1, 2, and 3?

> ✔ **How will the work actually be done?** Will the drafting, reviewing, and finalizing of Chapter 1 be handled separately from the same activities for Chapter 2, or will all chapters be drafted together, reviewed together, and finalized together?

## Identifying your Work Breakdown Structure entries

Figure 3-3 illustrates a useful scheme for numbering your Work Breakdown Structure entries.

> ✔ The first number refers to the work assignment under which the activity is classified

> ✔ The number after the first period refers to the task under which the activity is classified

> ✔ The number after the second period refers to the subtask under which the activity is classified

**Figure 3-3:**
A useful scheme for identifying your Work Breakdown Structure activities.

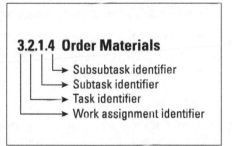

**3.2.1.4  Order Materials**
→ Subsubtask identifier
→ Subtask identifier
→ Task identifier
→ Work assignment identifier

As an example, consider the following activity illustrated in Figure 3-3:

3.2.1.4. Order Materials

This activity is subsubtask 4 under subtask 1 under task 2 under work assignment 3. This scheme lets you easily see where any individual activity fits in your Work Breakdown Structure.

## Developing your Work Breakdown Structure

How you develop your Work Breakdown Structure depends upon how familiar you and your team are with your project, whether similar projects have been successfully performed in the past, and how many new methods and approaches will be used. Choose one of the following two approaches, depending upon your project's characteristics:

- ✔ **Top down:** Start at the top level and systematically develop increasing levels of detail for all activities

- ✔ **Brainstorming:** Generate all activities you can think of that will have to be done and then group them into categories

In either case, consider using stick-on notes to support your work. Write activities on stick-on notes as you identify them and put them on the wall. Add to, remove, and regroup them as you continue to think through your work. This approach encourages open sharing of ideas and helps all people appreciate in detail the nature of the work that'll be done.

### Top-down approach

Use the following top-down approach for projects with which you or others are familiar. Proceed as follows:

1. **Specify all work assignments required for the entire project to be finished.**

2. **Determine all tasks required to complete each work assignment.**

3. **As necessary, specify the subtasks required to complete each task.**

4. **Continue in this way until you have adequately detailed your entire project.**

### Brainstorming approach

Use the following brainstorming approach for projects involving untested methods and approaches or for ones you and your team members have not done before.

1. **On a single list, write any and all activities you think will have to be performed for your project.**

   - Don't worry about overlap or level of detail.

   - Don't discuss activity wording or other details.

   - Don't make any judgments about the appropriateness of the activity.

   - Write everything down!

2. **Study the list and group the activities into a few major categories with common characteristics.**

   These will be your work assignments.

3. If appropriate, group activities under a particular work assignment into a small number of tasks.

4. Consider each category you have created and use the top-down approach to determine any additional activities that may have been overlooked.

## Displaying your Work Breakdown Structure in different formats

You can use several different formats to display your Work Breakdown Structure.

### The organization-chart format

Figure 3-4 shows how you can draw your Work Breakdown Structure in an organization-chart format. This format effectively portrays an overview of your project and the hierarchical relationships of different work assignments (and perhaps tasks) at the highest levels. However, because this format requires a lot of space to draw, it's less effective for displaying large numbers of activities.

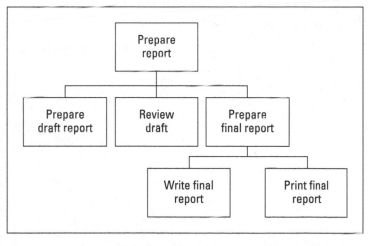

**Figure 3-4:**
Drawing your Work Breakdown Structure in an organization-chart format.

### The indented-outline format

The indented-outline format illustrated in Figure 3-5 is another way to display your Work Breakdown Structure. It's easier to read and understand a complex Work Breakdown Structure with many activities if it's displayed in this format.

**Figure 3-5:**
Drawing
your Work
Breakdown
Structure in
an indented-
outline
format.

**Prepare report**

1.0 Prepare draft report

2.0 Review draft report

3.0 Prepare final report

    3.1 Write final report

    3.2 Print final report

Consider using a combination of the organization chart and indented-outline formats to explain your Work Breakdown Structure for a large project. Display the work assignments and possibly the tasks in the organization chart format and then portray the detailed breakout for every task in the indented-outline format.

### The bubble-chart format

The bubble-chart format illustrated in Figure 3-6 is particularly effective for supporting the brainstorming process. You interpret the bubble chart as follows:

- The bubble in the center represents your entire project.

- Lines from the center bubble lead to work assignments.

- Lines from each work assignment lead to tasks related to that work assignment.

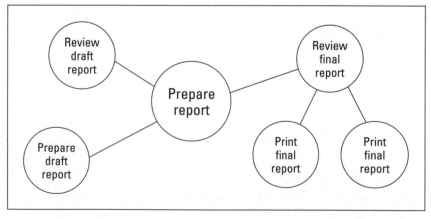

**Figure 3-6:**
Drawing
your Work
Breakdown
Structure in
a bubble-
chart
format.

The freeform nature of the bubble chart makes it effective for easily record-ing thoughts generated in a brainstorming process. You can also easily rearrange activities as you proceed with your analysis.

The bubble chart isn't effective for displaying your Work Breakdown Structure to audiences who aren't familiar with your project. Use the bubble chart to develop your Work Breakdown Structure but transpose the chart into an organization chart or indented outline format to present it to others.

## Some tips and hints

Follow these guidelines to improve the quality and utility of your Work Breakdown Structure:

- **Involve the people who'll be doing the work in the development of your Work Breakdown Structure.** If possible, involve them when the plan is developed initially. If they join the project after the plan is devel-oped, have them review and critique the Work Breakdown Structure before they begin work.

- **Review and include information from Work Breakdown Structures that were developed for similar projects.** Review plans and consult people who've worked on previous projects similar to yours. Incorporate the information you learn in your Work Breakdown Structure.

- **Keep your Work Breakdown Structure current.** If you add, delete, or change activities during your project, be sure to reflect this in your Work Breakdown Structure.

- **Make assumptions regarding uncertain activities.** If you aren't certain whether you'll do a particular activity, make an assumption and prepare your Work Breakdown Structure based on that assumption. Be sure to document that assumption. If your assumption proves to be wrong during the project, change your plan to reflect the true situation.

- **Remember that your Work Breakdown Structure only identifies the subelements of an activity; it doesn't depict the order in which activi-ties are performed.** There is nothing wrong with including activities from left to right or top to bottom in the approximate order in which you will perform them. However, you may have difficulty showing detailed interrelationships among activities in complex projects in the Work Breakdown Structure format. The purpose of the Work Breakdown Structure is to ensure you identify all activities. Developing your project's schedule by considering the order in which activities will be performed is explored in Chapter 4.

# Using templates

A *Work Breakdown Structure template* is a predesigned Work Breakdown Structure that contains typical activities for projects similar to yours.

### Drawing upon previous experience

A Work Breakdown Structure template reflects the cumulative experience gained from doing numerous projects of a particular type. As you perform more projects, you add activities to the template that you overlooked in earlier projects and you remove ones that proved not to be needed. Using templates can save you time and improve your accuracy.

Suppose you prepare the budget for your department each quarter. After doing a number of these budgets, you know most of the activities required to obtain the necessary inputs, draft the budget, solicit approvals, and print it in final format. Each time you finish another budget, you revise your Work Breakdown Structure template to include any new information you gleaned from your recently completed project.

The next time you start to plan out a quarterly budget preparation project, you begin your Work Breakdown Structure with the Work Breakdown Structure template that you've been developing from your past projects. You then add and subtract activities as appropriate for this particular budget preparation.

Templates can save time and improve accuracy. However, don't inhibit people's active involvement in the development of the Work Breakdown Structure by using a template that's too polished. Lack of people's involvement can lead to missed activities and lack of commitment to project success.

### Improving your Work Breakdown Structure templates

When using templates, keep the following in mind:

- ✔ **Develop templates for frequently performed tasks, as well as for entire projects.** Templates for the annual organization blood drive or the submission to the Food and Drug Administration of a newly developed drug are valuable. However, so are templates for individual tasks that are part of these projects, such as awarding a competitive contract and having a document printed. Templates for tasks can be incorporated into a larger Work Breakdown Structure for an entire project where these tasks will be performed.

- ✔ **Develop and modify your Work Breakdown Structure template from previous projects that worked, not from plans that looked good.** Often you develop a detailed Work Breakdown Structure at the start of your project, but you don't revise it during the project to add activities that you overlooked in your initial planning. If you update your Work Breakdown Structure template from the Work Breakdown Structure you prepared at the start of your project, it won't reflect what you learned during the actual performance of the project.

✔ **Use templates as starting points, not ending points.** Make it clear to your team members and others with whom you consult that the Work Breakdown Structure template is the start of your Work Breakdown Structure for your project, not the final version. Every project differs in some ways from similar ones in the past. If the template isn't critically examined, you'll miss activities that weren't performed in previous projects but that need to be included in this one.

✔ **Continually update your templates to reflect the experience gained from performing different projects.** The post-project evaluation is an excellent opportunity to review and critique your original Work Breakdown Structure. See Chapter 15 for information on how to plan and conduct one. At the end of your project, take a moment to revise your Work Breakdown Structure template to reflect the lessons learned.

# Identifying Risks While Detailing Your Activities

In addition to helping you to identify activities that you know you'll have to perform, developing a Work Breakdown Structure also helps you identify unknowns that may cause problems on your project. As you think through the work required to complete your project, you'll often identify some considerations that'll affect how or whether you can perform one or more activities in the project. Sometimes you know this information with certainty, and sometimes it's unknown. Identifying and dealing effectively with unknowns can dramatically increase your chances for success with your project.

Unknown information you feel you need can fall into either of two categories:

✔ **A known unknown:** Information that you don't have but someone else does.

✔ **An unknown unknown:** Information that you don't have because it doesn't yet exist.

You deal with known unknowns by finding out who has the information and determining what the information is. You deal with unknown unknowns either by developing contingency plans to be followed when you find out the information or by trying to influence the value of the information.

Refer to the part of the Work Breakdown Structure in Figure 3-2, which details the work to conduct a mail survey of a sample of your organization's client population. The first task is "Select a sample to survey." Early in your project planning, you don't know whether a file with all of your customers' names exists. If it does, selecting a sample to survey will take about one week. If it doesn't, you'll have to create one, and selecting the sample will take about four weeks.

Whether or not the file exists is a known unknown; you don't know but someone else does. You deal with this unknown by calling people in sales to see if they know whether such a file exists.

Developing the Work Breakdown Structure helps you identify a situation where something could compromise your chances for project success. You then must decide how you want to deal with it. See Chapter 14 for further discussion on how to identify and manage project risks and uncertainties.

# Defining What You Need to Know about Your Activities

After breaking your project work down in sufficient detail, describe all of the important information about your lowest level activities. This information is collected and maintained in a *Work Breakdown Structure dictionary* for larger projects.

The Work Breakdown Structure dictionary contains the following information for each lowest level activity:

- **Work detail:** Narrative description of work processes and procedures that'll be performed to accomplish the activity

- **Inputs:** Work products from other activities that'll be used in the work of this activity

- **Outputs:** Products or results produced upon completion of this activity

- **Roles and responsibilities:** How team members will work with each other on each of the projects' activities

- **Duration:** Time on the calendar that you estimate this activity will take

- **Required resources:** People, funds, equipment, facilities, raw materials, information, and so on that you'll require to do the work associated with this activity

Sometimes the following information is also included:

✔ **Immediate predecessors:** Activities that must be completed right before the activity you're considering can be started

✔ **Immediate successors:** Activities that can be started as soon as the activity you're considering is finished

# Taking Different Paths to the Same End

Early in the development of your Work Breakdown Structure, it's often helpful to consider two or more different hierarchical schemes to describe your project. Considering your project from two or more perspectives helps you identify activities you may overlook.

Suppose a local community wants to open a halfway house for substance abusers. Figures 3-7 and 3-8 depict two different schemes, both of which you can use to detail the work to open this Community Based Treatment Facility.

Figure 3-7 defines the following project components as work assignments:

✔ Staff

✔ Facility

✔ Residents (people who will be living at the facility and receiving services)

✔ Community training

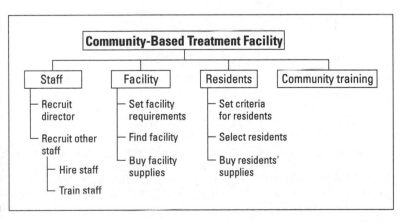

**Figure 3-7:**
One Work Breakdown Structure for preparing to open a community-based treatment facility.

**Community-Based Treatment Facility**

| Staff | Facility | Residents | Community training |
|---|---|---|---|
| — Recruit director | — Set facility requirements | — Set criteria for residents | |
| — Recruit other staff | — Find facility | — Select residents | |
| — Hire staff | — Buy facility supplies | — Buy residents' supplies | |
| — Train staff | | | |

Figure 3-8 defines the functions as work assignments:

✔ Planning

✔ Recruiting

✔ Buying

✔ Training

The same lowest-level activities are included in both Work Breakdown Structures.

**Figure 3-8:**
Another
Work
Breakdown
Structure
for
preparing to
open a
community-
based
treatment
facility.

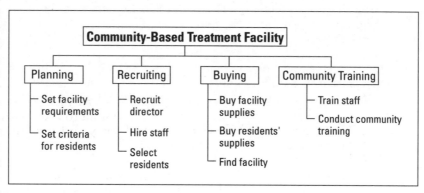

When you think about your project in terms of major functions to be performed (instead of project components to complete), you realize that you forgot the following activities:

✔ You have no planning activity for your hiring of staff.

✔ You have no activity to buy staff supplies.

✔ You forgot to include an activity to plan your community training.

After you identify the activities you overlooked, you can represent them in either of the two Work Breakdown Structures.

Be sure you choose one Work Breakdown Structure to use for your project before you leave your planning phase. Nothing will confuse people faster than trying to use two or more different Work Breakdown Structures to describe the same project during its performance.

# Chapter 4

# You Want This Done When?

*In This Chapter*

▶ Developing and analyzing a network diagram

▶ Estimating activity durations

▶ Meeting schedule constraints

▶ Displaying your schedule

*P*roject assignments always have deadlines. You may not be sure exactly what your project is to accomplish, but you want to know when it has to be finished. Unfortunately, often when you find out, your immediate reaction may be that you don't have enough time!

The truth is, when you first receive your project assignment, you usually don't know how long it'll take to complete. Your first reactions are often based more on fear and anxiety than on facts, especially if you're trying to juggle multiple responsibilities and the project is at all complex.

You need an organized approach to clarify how you propose to perform your project's activities, what schedules are possible at the outset, and what you may consider doing to meet deadlines that initially appear to be unrealistic. This chapter helps you prepare plans that are achievable and to respond to changes that occur throughout the life of your project.

## Analyzing Schedule Possibilities

The total time required to perform a group of activities depends on the following:

✔ **Duration:** How long each individual activity will take

✔ **Sequence:** The order in which you perform the activities

Suppose you were assigned a project consisting of ten activities that each required one week to complete. How long would it take you to complete your project? Truth is, you can't tell. Your project could be finished in one week, if you could perform all the activities at the same time and you had sufficient resources to do this. Your project may take ten weeks if you had to do the activities one at a time in sequential order. Or, your project could take between one and ten weeks if you had to do some of the activities in sequence.

You consider the activity durations and interdependencies in your head when you develop a schedule for a small project. For projects with more than 15 to 20 activities, many of which you can perform at the same time, you need a method to guide you through your analysis.

## Drawing network diagrams

A *network diagram* is a flow chart that illustrates the order in which you'll perform the activities in your project. Think of the network diagram as your project's test laboratory: It gives you a chance to try out different project strategies before actually performing the work.

Network diagrams include three elements:

- ✔ **Event:** A significant occurrence in the life of your project; sometimes called a *milestone* or a *deliverable*. Events take no time and consume no resources; they occur instantaneously. Think of them as signposts that signify you've reached a certain point in your trip to project completion. Events mark the start or finish of an activity or a group of activities. Examples of events are "draft report approved" and "design begun."

    You may see the word "event" used differently in other contexts from the way I define it in this book. Suppose you read that the premier social event of a post-election year was the presidential inaugural ball. In project management terms, the inaugural ball is an activity rather than an event, because it takes time and *lots* of resources!

- ✔ **Activity:** Work required to move from one event to the next in your project. Activities take time and consume resources; they're described by action verbs. Examples of activities are "design report format" and "identify needs for new product."

- ✔ **Span time:** The actual calendar time required to complete an activity; also called *duration* or *elapsed time.* The amount of work effort required, people's availability, and whether two or more people can work on an activity at the same time all affect the activity's span time. *Capacity* (for example, a computer's processing speed and the pages per minute that a copier can print) and availability of nonpersonnel resources also affect span time.

Understanding the basis of span time helps you to figure out ways to reduce it, if necessary. As an example, suppose you have to test a software package you just purchased. You estimate that you have to run the package for 24 hours on a computer to do a complete test. If you're allowed to use the computer for only six hours in any one day, the span time for your software test is four days.

Suppose you wanted to cut the span time for your software test in half. Doubling the number of people assigned to the activity won't do it; but getting approval to use the computer for 12 hours a day will.

The units of time are used to describe two related but different activity characteristics. Span time describes duration; *work effort* is the number of hours a person would have to work on the activity to complete it.

Suppose four people had to work full-time at the same time for five days to complete an activity. The activity's span time is five days. The work effort required is 20 person-days (four people multiplied by five days). See Chapter 5 for further discussion of work effort.

Pure *delay* can also add to an activity's span time. Suppose your boss has to approve a report you wrote. You put the report in your boss's in box and it sits there for four days and seven hours. Your boss then removes it, reads it for one hour, and signs it. The activity's span time is five days; the work effort invested is one hour.

No matter how complex your project, its network diagram is comprised of these same three elements.

## Using one of two formats for network diagrams

You can draw network diagrams in either of two formats:

- **Activity-on-the-arrow:** Also referred to as the *classical* or *traditional* approach
- **Activity-in-the-box:** Also referred to as *activity-in-the-node* or *precedence diagramming*

These two formats are interchangeable; there's nothing you can represent in one that you can't also represent in the other. The only difference between the two formats is in the symbols used to represent the three elements.

## The advantages of clearly defining activities and events

The more clearly you define activities and events:

✔ The more accurately you can estimate needed time and resources

✔ The easier it is to assign the task to someone else to perform

✔ The more meaningful your tracking becomes

You may also hear the following terms used to refer to the flow chart of your project's activities:

✔ **Precedence diagram:** Another term for a network diagram in the activity-in-the-box format

✔ **Dependency diagram:** Another term for a network diagram in either format

✔ **PERT chart:** Refers to a network diagram in the activity-on-the-arrow format

PERT is an acronym that stands for Program Evaluation and Review Technique. PERT was created in the 1950s to plan the Polaris weapon system's design and development. PERT is an analytical technique that allows you to assign optimistic, pessimistic, and most likely estimates for an activity's span time, when you don't expect that repeated performances of the activity will take the same time. You use probabilities to determine the likelihood that individual activity span times and overall project duration will fall within specified limits.

### Using the activity-on-the-arrow diagramming approach

The activity-on-the-arrow approach uses distinct symbols to describe each of the three elements of the diagram:

✔ A circle represents an event

✔ A line with an arrowhead represents an activity

✔ The letter "t" represents span time

Every activity starts from and ends in an event. Figure 4-1 presents a simple example. When you reach Event A (represented by the circle on the left), you're allowed to perform Activity 1 (represented by the arrow). You estimate that Activity 1 will take two weeks to complete (described in the caption beneath the arrow). Upon completing Activity 1, you reach Event B (represented by the circle on the right).

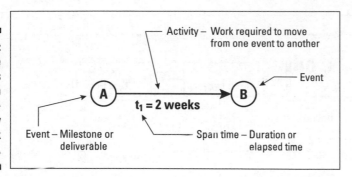

Figure 4-1:
The three
symbols
used in an
activity-on-
the-arrow
network
diagram.

In case you were wondering, the length of the arrow representing an activity is not proportional to the activity's span time.

Occasionally, a fourth symbol is used in this diagramming scheme: A *dummy activity* is an activity with 0 span time that's used to represent a required dependency between events. Suppose Bill and Susan both have to approve your system's design before you can consider your overall design complete and proceed to implement it. You would represent this in a network diagram by defining two separate events, "Bill's approval received" and "Susan's approval received," and having a dummy activity start from each one and end in the "Overall system design completed" event.

### Using the activity-in-the-box diagramming approach

The activity-in-the-box approach uses only two symbols to describe the three elements of the diagram:

- ✔ A box represents both an event and an activity. You can tell whether a box represents an event or an activity by looking at its span time. If the span time is 0, it's an event. In addition, the boxes representing events are sometimes highlighted by making their lines bold, double, and so forth.

- ✔ The letter "t" represents span time.

Figure 4-2 presents a simple illustration. When you reach Event A (represented by the box on the left), you're allowed to perform Activity 1 (represented by the box in the middle). Upon completing Activity 1, you reach Event B (represented by the box on the right). The arrows only indicate the direction of workflow.

**Figure 4-2:**
The two
symbols
used in an
activity-in-
the-box
network
diagram.

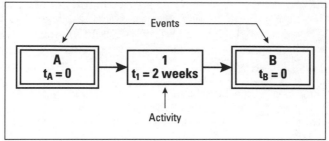

Figure 4-2 illustrates how you can use the activity-in-the-box approach to represent both events and activities. In this approach, however, the use of events is optional; you can have one activity lead directly to another, with no event in between.

### Choosing a format for drawing your network diagram

The two diagramming formats are interchangeable — there isn't anything that you can represent in one that you can't represent in the other. However, consider the following when you choose which approach to use:

- ✔ **The activity-on-the-arrow approach represents each element with a unique symbol.** This is especially helpful if you're just learning network diagrams, because you'll tend not to confuse activities and events.

- ✔ **The activity-in-the-box approach allows you to draw out your entire project without defining any events.** This approach often takes less time and space to draw, because you aren't required to define events if you see no need for them.

- ✔ **The more commonly used integrated project management software packages use the activity-in-the-box approach.**

I use the activity-in-the-box approach for the rest of this chapter, because you'll find it simpler to understand and easier to enter your plans into an integrated project management software package, should you decide to use one to support your project planning and control.

## Analyzing your network diagram

Think of your project as if it were a trip that you and several friends will take. Each of you has his or her own car and will travel a different route to arrive at your final destination. During your trip, two or more of your routes will cross at certain places. Your agreement is that all people who are scheduled to pass through a common point must arrive at that point before anyone can proceed on to the next leg of his or her journey. The trip is over when all of you reach your final destination.

You would certainly not want to undertake a trip this complex without first planning it out on a roadmap. Planning your trip on a roadmap allows you to determine how long the entire trip will take, identify potential difficulties you may encounter along the way, and consider alternate routes to get to your final destination quickly.

Your network diagram is the roadmap for your project. The legs of each person's journey are the activities that project team members will perform, and milestones signify the start or end of the legs. A *path* is any sequence of activities that you perform during your project.

Use the following two rules to draw and interpret your network diagram. After you understand these rules, analyzing the diagram is a snap:

✔ **Rule 1:** After you finish an activity or reach an event, you can proceed to the next activity or event, as indicated by the arrow(s) leaving from that activity or event.

✔ **Rule 2:** To be able to start an activity or reach an event, you must complete all activities and reach all events from which arrows entering that activity or event emanate.

Figure 4-3 illustrates a network diagram drawn in the activity-in-the-box format. Rule 1 says that after you start your project (that is, when your reach the event called "Start"), you can work on Activities 1 or 3. That means you can do Activity 1, Activity 3, or both Activities 1 and 3. In other words, they're independent of one another.

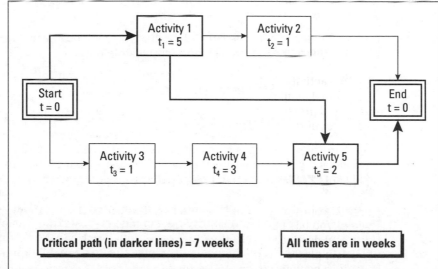

**Figure 4-3:** Example of a network diagram.

Critical path (in darker lines) = 7 weeks

All times are in weeks

It also means you can choose to do neither of the activities. Rule 1 is an "allowing" relationship, not a "forcing" relationship. It says that you *can,* if you choose, work on the activities to which the arrows from the event called "Start" lead; it doesn't say that you must work on any of them. Of course, if you don't work on any of them, your project will be in a state of delay. That, however, is your choice.

Rule 2 says that you can start working on Activity 2 as soon as you complete Activity 1, because the arrow from Activity 1 is the only one leading into Activity 2. Rule 2 is a "forcing" relationship. If arrows from three activities entered Activity 2, the diagram doesn't indicate that you can start working on Activity 2 by completing any one of the three activities that you choose. The activities from which all three arrows emanate *must* be completed before you can start to work on Activity 2.

Determine the following information from the network diagram to figure out what schedules are possible to achieve and how you'd do it.

- ✔ **Critical path:** A sequence of activities in your project that takes the longest time to complete

- ✔ **Noncritical path:** A sequence of activities that you can delay by some amount and still finish your overall project in the shortest possible time

- ✔ **Slack time:** The maximum amount of time that you can delay an activity and still finish your project in the shortest possible time

- ✔ **Earliest start date:** The earliest date that you can possibly start an activity

- ✔ **Earliest finish date:** The earliest date that you can possibly finish an activity

- ✔ **Latest start date:** The latest date that you can start an activity and still finish your project in the shortest possible time

- ✔ **Latest finish date:** The latest date you can finish an activity and still finish your project in the shortest possible time

The length of your project's critical path(s) defines how long your project will take to complete. If you want to get your project done in less time, consider ways to shorten the time to complete the critical path. Monitor critical-path activities closely during project performance, because any delays in critical-path activities will delay your final project completion.

Remember that your project can have two or more critical paths at the same time. In fact, every path in your project can be critical if they all take the same amount of time to complete. This is a high-risk situation, because a delay in any activity will immediately cause the final completion of the project to be delayed.

Critical paths can change as your project unfolds. Sometimes activities on the critical path are finished so early that the total time to complete the path becomes less than that required to complete one or more other paths. It's also possible that activities on a path that's initially noncritical are sufficiently delayed that the time to complete the path exceeds that of the current critical path.

### The forward pass — determining critical paths, noncritical paths, and earliest start and finish dates

Your first step in analyzing your project's network diagram is to start at the beginning of your project and see how fast you can complete the activities along each path of your project until you reach your project's finish. This start-to-finish analysis is called the *forward pass*.

You can perform a forward pass through the diagram illustrated in Figure 4-3 as follows:

Rule 1 says you can consider working on Activities 1 or 3 as soon as the project starts (that is, as soon as you reach the event called "Start"). First consider the upper path comprised of Activities 1 and 2:

- ✔ The earliest you can start Activity 1 is the moment the project starts.

- ✔ The earliest you can finish Activity 1 is the end of week 5 (add Activity 1's estimated span time of five weeks to its earliest start time, which is the start of the project).

- ✔ Rule 2 says the earliest you can start Activity 2 is the beginning of week 6, since the arrow from Activity 1 is the only one entering Activity 2.

- ✔ The earliest you can finish Activity 2 is the end of week 6.

So far, so good. Now consider the path at the bottom of the diagram, comprised of Activities 3, 4, and 5.

- ✔ The earliest you can start Activity 3 is the moment the project starts.

- ✔ The earliest you can finish Activity 3 is the end of week 1.

- ✔ The earliest you can start Activity 4 is the beginning of week 2.

- ✔ The earliest you can finish Activity 4 is the end of week 4.

Now you see something a little different. According to Rule 2, the two arrows entering Activity 5 indicate you can't start Activity 5 until you finish both Activity 1 and Activity 4. Even though you can finish Activity 4 by the end of week 4, you can't finish Activity 1 until the end of week 5. Therefore, the earliest you can start Activity 5 is the beginning of week 6.

This situation illustrates the following guideline:

> If two or more activities lead to the same activity, the earliest date you can start the activity is equal to the latest of the earliest finish dates for these activities.

In the example, the earliest finish dates for Activity 4 and Activity 1 are the ends of weeks 4 and 5, respectively. Therefore, the earliest date you can start Activity 5 is the beginning of week 6.

Is your head spinning yet? Take heart, the end is in sight.

- ✔ The earliest you can start Activity 5 is the beginning of week 6.
- ✔ The earliest you can finish Activity 5 is the end of week 7.
- ✔ The earliest you can finish Activity 2 is the end of week 6. Therefore, the earliest you can finish the entire project (and reach event called "End") is the end of week 7.

So far, you've found out the following information about your project:

- ✔ The length of the critical path is seven weeks, the shortest time in which the project can be completed. There is one critical path that takes seven weeks; it includes the event called "Start," Activity 1, Activity 5, and the event called "End.'
- ✔ Activity 2, Activity 3, and Activity 4 are not on critical paths.
- ✔ The earliest dates you can start and finish each activity in your project are summarized in Table 4-1.

| Table 4-1 | Earliest Start and Finish Dates for Figure 4-3 | |
|-----------|------------------------------------------------|---|
| *Activity* | *Earliest Start Date* | *Earliest Finish Date* |
| 1 | Beginning of week 1 | End of week 5 |
| 2 | Beginning of week 6 | End of week 6 |
| 3 | Beginning of week 1 | End of week 1 |
| 4 | Beginning of week 2 | End of week 4 |
| 5 | Beginning of week 6 | End of week 7 |

### *The backward pass — determining slack times and earliest start and finish dates*

You're half way home. Now you need to determine how much you can delay the activities along each path of your project and still finish the project at the earliest possible date. This finish-to-start analysis is called the *backward pass*.

You found out from the forward pass that the earliest date you can reach the event called "End" is the end of week 7. However, Rule 2 says you can't reach the event called "End" until Activities 2 and 5 are both completed. Therefore, if you want to finish your project by the end of week 7, the latest you can finish Activities 2 and 5 is the end of week 7. Again, consider the lower path comprised of Activities 3, 4, and 5.

✔ You must start Activity 5 by the beginning of week 6, at the latest, if you want to finish it by the end of week 7.

✔ Rule 2 says you can't start Activity 5 until you finish Activity 1 and Activity 4. Therefore, you must finish Activity 1 and Activity 4 by the end of week 5, at the latest.

✔ Hence, you must start Activity 4 by the beginning of week 3, at the latest.

✔ You must finish Activity 3 before you can work on Activity 4. Therefore, you must finish Activity 3 by the end of week 2, at the latest.

✔ You must start Activity 3 by the beginning of week 2, at the latest.

Finally, consider the upper path.

✔ You must start Activity 2 by the beginning of week 7, at the latest.

✔ You can't work on Activity 2 until you finish Activity 1. Therefore, you must finish Activity 1 by the end of week 6, at the latest.

Now again, you see something a little different. You must finish Activity 1 by the end of week 5 to allow work on Activity 5 to start at the beginning of week 6 and by the end of week 6 to allow work on Activity 2 to start at the beginning of week 7. Finishing Activity 1 by the end of week 5 will satisfy both requirements. This situation illustrates the following guideline:

> If two or more arrows leave from the same activity or event, the latest date by which you must finish the activity or reach the event is the earliest of the latest dates by which you must start the activities or reach the events to which these arrows lead.

In this example, the latest start dates for Activity 2 and Activity 5 are the beginning of week 7 and the beginning of week 6, respectively. Therefore, the latest date by which you must finish Activity 1 is the end of week 5. The rest is straightforward: You must start Activity 1 by the beginning of week 1, at the latest.

The latest dates by which you must start and finish each activity in your project are summarized in Table 4-2.

| Table 4-2 | Latest Start and Finish Dates for Figure 4-3 | |
|---|---|---|
| *Activity* | *Latest Start Date* | *Latest Finish Date* |
| 1 | Beginning of week 1 | End of week 5 |
| 2 | Beginning of week 7 | End of week 7 |
| 3 | Beginning of week 2 | End of week 2 |
| 4 | Beginning of week 3 | End of week 5 |
| 5 | Beginning of week 6 | End of week 7 |

Sometimes, you may feel that you get bogged down in all these calculations. Consider writing the earliest and latest start dates and the earliest and latest finish dates at the top of each box. It makes the whole process seem much simpler. See how this looks in Figure 4-4.

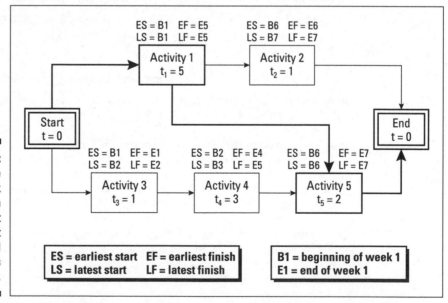

**Figure 4-4:**
Example network diagram with earliest and latest start and finish dates written in.

Finally, determine the slack time associated with each activity in one of two ways, as follows:

✔ Subtract the earliest possible start date from the latest allowable start date

✔ Subtract the earliest possible finish date from the latest allowable finish date

Table 4-3 presents the slack times for each activity in the example. If an activity's slack time is 0, the activity is on a critical path.

| Table 4-3 | Slack times for Figure 4-3 |
|---|---|
| *Activity* | *Slack Time (Weeks)* |
| 1 | 0 |
| 2 | 1 |
| 3 | 1 |
| 4 | 1 |
| 5 | 0 |

Slack time is actually associated with a sequence of activities rather than with an individual activity. Table 4-3 indicates that both Activities 3 and 4, which are on the same path, have slack times of 1 week. However, if Activity 3 is delayed by a week, Activity 4 will have 0 slack time.

## Fleshing out your diagram

To draw your project's network diagram, you must decide the order in which you will perform your project's activities.

A *predecessor* to Activity 4 is an activity you must complete before you can work on Activity 4. An activity is an *immediate predecessor* to Activity 4 if you don't have to perform any other activities between finishing it and starting on Activity 4.

Determine the immediate predecessors for every activity in your project and you have all the information you need to draw your project's network diagram. Relationships between activities can be based on several considerations:

✔ **Required relationships:** Relationships that must be observed if project work is to be successfully completed

  • **Legal requirements:** Federal, state, and local laws or regulations that require certain activities to be done before others. As an example, consider a pharmaceutical company that has developed a new drug in the laboratory and has demonstrated its safety and effectiveness in clinical trials. They'd like to start producing and selling the drug immediately, but they can't. Federal law requires that the company first obtain Food and Drug Administration (FDA) approval of the drug before they can start to sell it.

- **Procedural requirements:** Company policies and procedures that require certain activities to be done before others. Suppose you're developing a new piece of software for your organization. You've finished your design and you want to start programming the software. However, your organization follows a systems development methodology that requires that an established management oversight committee formally approve your design before you can start your development.

✔ **Discretionary relationships:** Relationships you choose to establish between activities

- **Logical relationships:** Logical relationships involve choosing to do certain activities before others because it seems to make the most sense. Suppose you're writing a report. Because much of Chapter 3 will depend upon what you write in Chapter 2, you decide to write Chapter 2 first. You could write Chapter 3 first or work on both at the same time, but that would increase the chance that you would have to rewrite some of Chapter 3 after you had finished Chapter 2.

- **Managerial choices:** These are arbitrary decisions to work on certain activities before others, perhaps because they are harder, more apt to have problems, and so on.

Decide upon the immediate predecessors for your project's activities in one of two ways:

✔ **Front-to-back:**

- Select the first activity or activities you'll perform as soon as your project starts.

- Consider one of these activities and decide which activity or activities you'll perform as soon as you finish your chosen activity.

- Continue in this way until you've considered all activities in the project.

✔ **Back-to-front:**

- Identify the last activity or activities you'll perform before your project is over.

- Choose one of these activities and decide which activities you'll perform immediately before you start on the chosen activity.

- Continue on in this manner until you've considered all activities in your project.

In either case, record your project's immediate predecessors in the simple table illustrated in Table 4-4.

| Table 4-4 | Immediate Predecessors | |
|---|---|---|
| Work Breakdown Structure Code | Activity Description | Immediate Predecessors |
| 1 | (Include activity name) | None |
| 2 | (Include activity name) | 1 |
| 3 | (Include activity name) | None |
| 4 | (Include activity name) | 3 |
| 5 | (Include activity name) | 1, 4 |

Determine precedence based on the nature and requirements of the activities, not on the resources you think will be available. Suppose Activities A and B could be performed at the same time; however, you figure you'll be assigning the same person to do them both. Don't make A the immediate predecessor for B, because the person can work on only one activity at a time. If you show that they can be done at the same time, you'll be able to evaluate the impact on your project if you're unexpectedly told that you have another resource who can help out with this work.

See Chapter 5 for a discussion on how to determine when people are over-committed and how to resolve these situations.

For simple projects, consider creating your network diagram by using stick-on notes to represent your activities and events and attaching them to chart paper or a wall. For more complex projects, consider using an integrated project management software package. See Chapter 16 for a discussion of how to use software to support your project planning and control, and check out *Microsoft Project For Dummies* by Martin Doucette (IDG Books Worldwide, Inc.) for the lowdown on the most popular project-management software package.

## Using a network diagram to analyze a simple example

Consider the following example of preparing for a picnic to illustrate how you can use the network diagram to determine schedule possibilities and ways to meet people's expectations. (I'm not suggesting that you plan all your picnics this way, but it does illustrate the technique!)

It's Friday evening after a very tense week. You and your friend are considering what you can do on the weekend to unwind and relax. The forecast for Saturday is for sunny and mild weather, and you both decide that you'll visit a local lake for a picnic tomorrow. You're concerned that you get the most enjoyment possible from your picnic. So, you both decide to plan this outing carefully by drawing and analyzing a network diagram.

Table 4-5 illustrates the seven activities you decide you must perform to prepare for your picnic and get to the lake.

| Table 4-5 | Activities Required for Your Picnic at the Lake | | |
|---|---|---|---|
| **Activity** | | **Who Will Do the Work** | **Duration (Minutes)** |
| **Identifier** | **Description** | | |
| 1 | Load car | You and your friend | 5 |
| 2 | Get money from bank | You | 5 |
| 3 | Make egg sandwiches | Your friend | 10 |
| 4 | Drive to lake | You and your friend | 30 |
| 5 | Decide which lake | You and your friend | 2 |
| 6 | Buy gasoline | You | 10 |
| 7 | Boil eggs (for egg sandwiches) | Your friend | 10 |

In addition, you both agree to observe the following constraints:

✔ You and your friend will start all activities at your house on Saturday morning at 8:00 a.m. — you can't do anything before that time.

✔ You must complete all activities before your project is done.

✔ You can't change who must do the different activities.

✔ The two lakes you're considering are in opposite directions from your house, so you have to decide which lake you'll visit before you begin your drive.

First, you decide the order in which you'll perform these various activities. In other words, you determine the immediate predecessors for each activity. The following dependencies are required:

↳ Your friend must boil the eggs before he or she can make the egg sandwiches.

↳ You both must decide which lake you'll visit before you can start your drive.

How you do the rest of the activities is up to you. You may consider the following approach:

↳ Decide which lake you'll visit before you do anything else.

↳ As soon as you both decide on the lake, you drive to the bank to get money.

↳ After you get money from the bank, you get gasoline.

↳ As soon as you both decide on the lake, your friend starts to boil the eggs.

↳ As soon as the eggs are boiled, your friend makes the sandwiches.

↳ As soon as you get back with the gas and your friend is finished making the egg sandwiches, you load the car.

↳ You start your drive to the lake, right after you both load the car.

Table 4-6 illustrates these predecessor relationships that you've defined.

| Table 4-6 | Predecessor Relationships for Your Picnic | |
|---|---|---|
| *Activity* | | *Immediate Predecessors* |
| *Identifier* | *Description* | |
| 1 | Load car | 3, 6 |
| 2 | Get money from bank | 5 |
| 3 | Make egg sandwiches | 7 |
| 4 | Drive to lake | 1 |
| 5 | Decide which lake | None |
| 6 | Buy gasoline | 2 |
| 7 | Boil eggs (for egg sandwiches) | 5 |

Draw the network diagram for your project from the information in this table, as follows.

1. **Start your project with a single event, "Start."**

2. **Next, find all activities that have no immediate predecessors — they can all be started as soon as you begin your project.**

In this case, Activity 5 is the only such activity.

3. **Start your diagram by representing these relationships, as illustrated in Figure 4-5.**

   Represent this activity in a box, and draw an arrow from the event called "Start" to this box.

**Figure 4-5:**
Starting
your picnic-
at-the-lake
network
diagram.

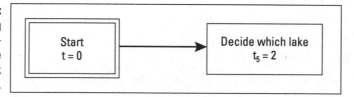

4. **Find all activities that have Activity 5 as an immediate predecessor.**

   Your table says there are two, Activities 2 and 7. Represent them in boxes, and draw arrows from Activity 5 to these boxes.

5. **Continue on in the same way.**

   Recognize from the table that Activity 6 is the only activity that has Activity 2 as an immediate predecessor. Draw a box representing Activity 6 and draw an arrow from Activity 2 to Activity 6.

   The table shows further that Activity 3 is the only activity that has Activity 7 as an immediate predecessor. Draw a box representing Activity 3 and draw an arrow from Activity 7 to Activity 3. Your diagram-in-progress is depicted in Figure 4-6.

**Figure 4-6:**
Continuing
your picnic-
at-the-lake
network
diagram.

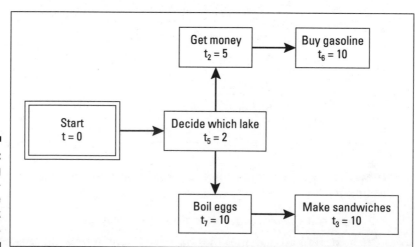

Now you realize that Activity 1 has both Activities 3 and 6 as immediate predecessors. Draw a box representing Activity 1 and draw arrows from Activity 3 to Activity 1 and from Activity 6 to Activity 1.

The rest is pretty straightforward. Activity 4 is the only activity that has Activity 1 as its immediate predecessor. Therefore, draw a box representing Activity 4 and draw an arrow from Activity 1 to Activity 4. Finally, draw a box representing the event called "End" and draw an arrow from Activity 4 to the event called "End."

Figure 4-7 depicts your project's complete network diagram.

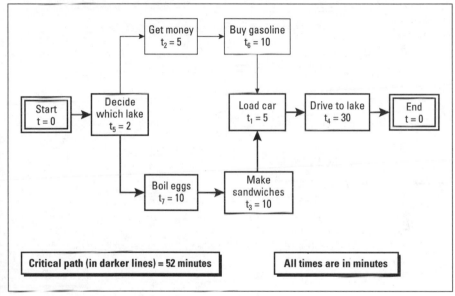

**Figure 4-7:** Completed picnic-at-the-lake network diagram the activity-in-the-box format.

Now for the important questions. First, how long will it take you to get to the lake for your picnic?

✔ The upper path, consisting of Activities 2 and 6, takes 15 minutes to complete.

✔ The lower path, consisting of Activities 7 and 3, takes 20 minutes to complete.

✔ Because the critical path is the longest path through your project, the path consisting of Activities 5, 7, 3, 1, and 4, is the critical path. It'll take you 57 minutes to get to the lake if you follow the plan outlined in your network diagram.

Can you delay any activities and still get to the lake in 57 minutes? If so, which ones?

✔ The upper path, consisting of Activities 2 and 6, is a noncritical path.

✔ The network diagram reveals that Activities 5, 7, 3, 1, and 4 are on the critical path and, therefore, can't be delayed at all if you want to get to the lake in 57 minutes.

✔ However, Activities 2 and 6 can be performed at the same time as Activities 7 and 3. Activities 7 and 3 will take 20 minutes to perform, while Activities 2 and 6 will take 15 minutes. Therefore, Activities 2 and 6 have a total slack time of 5 minutes.

Figure 4-8 illustrates the network diagram for this project drawn in the activity-on-the-arrow format. Event A is equivalent to "Start" and Event I is equivalent to "End" in Figure 4-7.

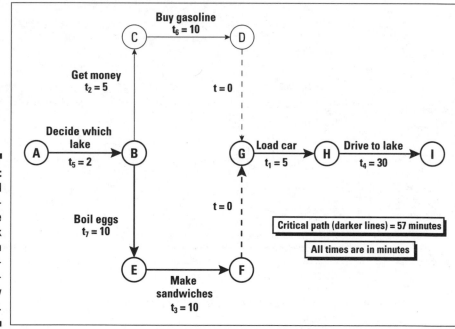

**Figure 4-8:** Completed picnic-at-the-lake network diagram in the activity-on-the-arrow format.

By the way, you've drawn events at the start and end of each activity in Figure 4-8, but you haven't named them yet. Choose names that describe the point reached in your project. Where possible, a useful approach is to consider the activity that you've just completed. As examples:

✔ Event B, the end of Activity 5, "Decide which lake," may be named "Decision reached."

✔ Event C, the end of Activity 2, "Get money," may be named "Money obtained," and so on.

A *simple* event is one that represents the completion of a single activity. Defining simple events at the end of all activities in the activity-on-the-arrow format makes it easier to monitor and report on activity performance status. If Activity 1 has multiple predecessors, instead of having arrows representing each of the predecessors coming directly into the event from which Activity 1 leaves, do the following:

- ✔ Have each of the predecessors end in a simple event.
- ✔ Tie them all together into a single event using dummy activities.
- ✔ Have Activity 1 leave from that single event.

This technique is illustrated in Figure 4-8. You must finish Activity 6, "Buy gasoline," and your friend must finish Activity 3, "Make sandwiches," before you both can load the car. Rather than have both activities lead directly into Event G, Activity 6 ends in Event D, "Gasoline purchased," and Activity 3 ends in Event F, "Sandwiches made." You then draw dummy activities from Events D and F into Event G, which may be defined as "Ready to load car."

# Developing Your Project's Schedule

Developing your actual schedule requires finding a combination of activities, resources, and activity performance sequences that gives you the greatest chance of meeting your audiences' expectations with the least risk.

## Developing your initial schedule

Develop your first attempt at your project schedule as follows.

1. **Describe your project's objectives, constraints, and assumptions (see the discussion of Statement of Work in Chapter 2).**

2. **Detail your project's activities (see the discussion of Work Breakdown Structures in Chapter 3).**

3. **Identify immediate predecessors for all activities in your project.**

4. **Estimate span times for all activities in your project.**

5. **Identify any intermediate and final dates that must be met.**

6. **Identify all activities or events outside your project that affect the performance of your project's activities.**

7. **Draw your network diagram.**

8. **Analyze your project's network diagram to determine the identity and length of all critical paths and the slack times of noncritical paths.**

If the completion date you develop this way is acceptable to your audiences, you're done with your scheduling. However, if your audiences want you to finish faster than your initial schedule allows, your analyses are just beginning.

# Avoiding the pitfall of "backing in" to your schedule

Beware of developing a schedule by "backing in." *Backing in* is the process of starting at the end of a project and working your way back toward the beginning, identifying activities as you go and estimating durations that eventually will add up to the amount of time that you've been given. Using this approach substantially decreases the chances that you'll meet the schedule you develop, for the following reasons:

- You may miss activities, because your focus is more on meeting a time constraint than ensuring you identify all required work

- Your span time estimates are based on what you can allow activities to take, rather than what they'll actually require.

- The order in which you propose to perform activities may not be the most effective one.

I was reviewing a colleague's project plan a while back, and I noticed she'd allowed one week for her final report to be reviewed and approved. When I asked her if she thought this estimate was realistic, she replied that it certainly was not, but that she had to put it in for the entire project plan to work out. In other words, she was using time estimates that totaled up to the number she wanted to reach, rather than ones that she felt could actually be achieved.

# Meeting an established time constraint

Suppose you have to find a way to complete your project in less time than your initial schedule allows. Consider the following options for all critical path activities:

- **Recheck the original span time estimates.**

    • Be sure the activity's work is clearly described.

    • If past performance was used as a guide for developing the span times, recheck to be sure all aspects of your current situation are the same as the situation on which your time estimates are based.

    • Ask other experts to review and validate your estimates.

- Ask the people who'll actually be doing the work on these activities to review and validate your estimates.

✔ **Consider using more experienced personnel.** Sometimes more experienced personnel can get work done in less time. Of course, using more experienced people may cost you more money. Further, you're not the only one in your organization who'll want those more experienced personnel, so they may not always be available!

✔ **Consider different strategies for performing them.** As an example, if you were going to do work internally, consider contracting it out. Or, if you were planning on contracting work out, consider doing it internally.

✔ **Consider removing them from the critical path by doing them in parallel with one or more other critical path activities.**

*Fast tracking* entails performing two or more activities at the same time to reduce the overall time to complete a project. While it's possible to get done faster if you use this approach, there's also more risk that portions of your work may have to be redone.

As you find ways to reduce the lengths of critical paths, monitor paths that aren't initially critical to ensure that they haven't become critical. If one or more has become critical, use these same approaches to reduce their length.

## Reducing the required time

How would you apply some of these approaches to your picnic at the lake? If arriving at the lake in 57 minutes is okay, your analysis is done. But suppose you and your friend agree that you must get to the lake no later than 45 minutes after you start on Saturday morning. What changes can you make in your initial plan to save you 12 minutes?

You may be tempted to change the estimated time for the drive from 30 minutes to 18 minutes, figuring that you'll just drive faster. Unfortunately, this won't work if you really feel that the drive will take 30 minutes! Remember, your plan represents an approach that you believe has a chance to work (though not necessarily one that's guaranteed). If you'd have to drive at speeds in excess of 100 miles per hour over dirt roads to drive to the lake in 18 minutes, reducing the time for the drive to 18 minutes has no chance of working.

### Performing activities at the same time

You'll have to be creative if you want to be able to develop a plan that will both save time and have a chance of working. Here's a first thought:

✔ Assume there's an Automatic Teller Machine (ATM) next to your gas station. If you pull into a full service gas island, you can get money from the ATM while the attendant fills up your car's gas tank.

✔ If you followed this strategy, you'd be able to perform Activities 2 and 6 at the same time in a total of 10 minutes, instead of the 15 minutes you indicated in Figure 4-7.

At first glance, it seems that you can cut the total time down to 52 minutes by making this change. Look again. These two activities aren't on the critical path, so reducing the time it takes to complete them has no impact on the overall project schedule at all! (In case you thought you could spend the extra five minutes you'll be home helping your friend to make the egg sandwiches, remember you agreed, for this example, that you and your friend could not swap jobs.)

Okay, back to the drawing board. Start with your 57-minute solution and remember you must reduce the length of the critical path if you want to save any time. Here's another idea: Both you and your friend are in the car for the drive to the lake, but only one of you is driving while the other is just sitting in the car. You could volunteer to do the driving and your friend could load the fixings for the sandwiches into the car and make the sandwiches during the drive to the lake. This would take a 10-minute activity off the critical path.

The question is, though, how much time will this change actually save? Examine the diagram in Figure 4-7 to figure out the answer as follows:

✔ The upper path comprised of Activities 2 and 6 takes 15 minutes, and the lower path comprised of Activities 7 and 3 takes 20 minutes. Because the lower path is the critical path, removing five minutes from the lower path will save five minutes in the overall time to complete the project. At this point, there are two critical paths, each taking 15 minutes.

✔ Taking an additional five minutes off the lower path doesn't save any more time for the overall project because the upper path still takes 15 minutes. It does, however, add five minutes of slack to the lower path.

Figure 4-9 reflects this change in your network diagram.

Consider again using your first idea and getting money at the ATM while an attendant fills up your car with gas. This now saves you five minutes, because the upper path is now critical.

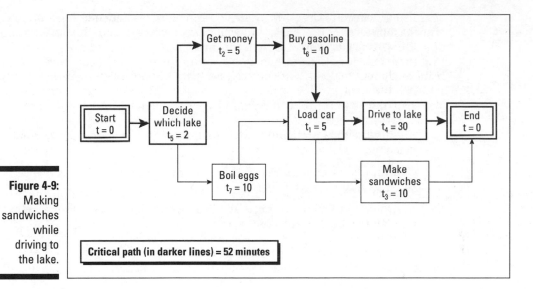

**Figure 4-9:**
Making
sandwiches
while
driving to
the lake.

Finally, you can decide which lake to visit and load the car at the same time, which will save you an additional two minutes. The final 45-minute solution is illustrated in Figure 4-10.

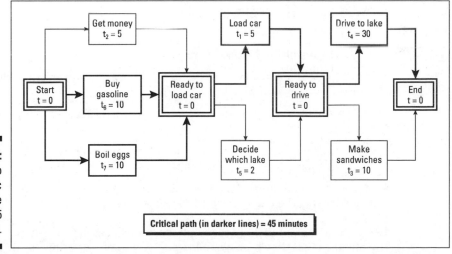

**Figure 4-10:**
Getting to
your picnic
at the lake
in 45
minutes.

Consider a situation where you have to complete two or more activities before you can work on two or more new ones. Represent this in your diagram by defining an event that represents the completion of the two or more activities and drawing arrows from these activities to this event. Then draw arrows from that event to the other activities that can then be started.

This is illustrated in Figure 4-10. Once you complete the activities "Get money," "Buy gasoline," and "Boil eggs," you can perform the activities "Load car" and "Decide which lake." You represent this by drawing arrows from each of the first three activities to a newly-defined event, "Ready to load car," and arrows from that event to the activities "Load car" and "Decide which lake."

To recap, if you want to shorten your project's schedule:

1. **Find the critical path and reduce its time until a second path becomes critical.**

2. **Continue to shorten both critical paths by the same amount until a third path becomes critical.**

3. **Continue to shorten all three by the same amount until a fourth path becomes critical, and so on.**

If you feel that this analysis is becoming complicated, you're right. You do pay the following prices to perform a group of activities faster:

✔ **Increased planning time:** You have to detail precisely all the activities and their interrelationships; you can't afford to make mistakes.

✔ **Increased risks:** The list of assumptions grows, and it becomes more likely that one or more of the assumptions will not come to pass.

In the picnic-at-the-lake example, you've made the following assumptions to arrive at a possible 45-minute solution:

✔ You can get right into a full service island at the gas station when you pull in at a little after 8:00 a.m.

✔ Attendants are available to fill up your tank as soon as you pull into the full-service island.

✔ The ATM is available and working when you pull into the full-service island.

✔ You and your friend can load the car and make a decision together without getting into an argument that takes an hour to resolve.

✔ Your friend can make sandwiches while driving in the car without totally destroying the car's interior in the process.

However, when you identify assumptions, you can either take steps to increase the chances that they'll prove to be true or you can develop contingency plans, in case they don't come to pass.

Consider your assumption that you can get right into a full service island as soon as you pull into the gas station at a little after 8:00 a.m. on Saturday morning. First, you can ask the gas station owner whether your assumption is reasonable. Unfortunately, when you ask, the gas station owner tells you Saturday morning is the busiest time of the week and he can't give you any idea of how long you'll have to wait. When you tell him how important it is that you get into the full-service island at that time so you can get to your picnic by 8:45 a.m., he apologizes but says there's nothing he can do.

As another thought: You ask if it would make a difference if you paid him $100 in cash. He immediately guarantees he will cordon off the full service island from 7:55 a.m. until 8:20 a.m. and assign two attendants to stand there, one with a nozzle and the other with a charge receipt ready to be filled out. He guarantees you, if you get in by about 8:00 a.m., you'll be out in 10 minutes with gas in the tank and a smile on your face! You've just learned that most uncertainty can be reduced for a price! Your job is to determine how much you can reduce the uncertainty and what it will cost.

### Devising an entirely new strategy

So you have a plan for getting to the lake in 45 minutes. It's not guaranteed to work, but at least it gives you a chance. However, suppose your friend now tells you he or she really needs to get to the lake in 10 minutes, instead of 45! Chances are your immediate reaction is, "Impossible!" You figure creative planning is one thing, but how can you get to the lake in 10 minutes when the drive to the lake takes 30 minutes by itself?

Without realizing it, you just changed your criterion for project success from achieving a desired result, where it belongs, to performing a series of activities, where it doesn't. Your project's success is arriving at the lake for your picnic, not performing a predetermined set of activities. The seven activities you formulated were fine, as long as they allowed you to get to the lake within your established constraints. But if the activities won't allow you to achieve success as you now define it, consider changing the activities.

You do some checking, and you find out that you can rent a helicopter for $500 per day that'll fly you and your friend to the lake in 10 minutes. However, you figure that you both were thinking about spending a total of $10 on your picnic, for admission to the park at the lake. Clearly it's absurd to spend $500 to get to a $10 picnic. So you don't even tell your friend about the possibility of renting the helicopter; you just reaffirm that it's impossible. Unfortunately, you didn't know the reason why your friend wanted to get to the lake in 10 minutes. It turns out that if he or she can get to the lake in 10 minutes, he or she can make a $10,000 profit on a business deal. Is it worth it to spend $500 to make $10,000? Sure. But you didn't know about the $10,000.

When developing schedule options, it's not your job to take away someone else's authority to make the schedule decision. Instead, you want to identify all possible options and their associated costs so that the decision maker can make an informed decision by considering all possibilities.

### Subdividing activities

Often, another way you can reduce the time to complete a sequence of activities is by subdividing one or more of the activities and performing some parts of them at the same time.

Figure 4-11 illustrates how your friend can save seven minutes when boiling your eggs and making your egg sandwiches as he or she prepares for your picnic.

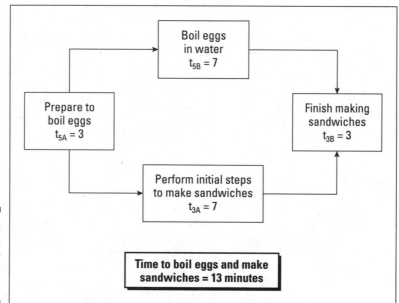

**Figure 4-11:**
Reducing span time by subdividing an activity.

✔ **Divide the activity of boiling into two parts.**

- Prepare to boil eggs: Remove the pot from the cupboard, take the eggs out of the refrigerator, put the water and the eggs in the pot, put the pot on the stove, and turn on the heat — estimated span time of three minutes.

- Boil eggs in water: Allow the eggs to boil in a pot until they're hard — estimated span time of seven minutes.

✔ **Divide the activity of making the egg sandwiches into two parts.**

- Perform initial steps to make sandwiches: Take the bread, mayonnaise, lettuce, and tomatoes out of the refrigerator; take the wax paper in which you will wrap the sandwiches out of the drawer; put the bread on the wax paper; put the mayonnaise, lettuce, and tomatoes on the bread — estimated span time of seven minutes.

• Finish making sandwiches: Take the eggs out of the pot, shell them, slice them, put them on the bread, slice the sandwiches, finish wrapping the sandwiches — estimated span time of three minutes.

Note that the total time for the original activity to boil the eggs is still ten minutes (three minutes to prepare and seven minutes in the water) and the total time for the original activity to make the sandwiches is still ten minutes (seven minutes for the initial steps and three minutes to finish up).

✔ **Perform the activities as illustrated in Figure 4-11.**

• Prepare to boil eggs.

• When your preparations are done, simultaneously boil the eggs in water and perform the initial steps to make the sandwiches.

• When these two activities are both done, finish making the sandwiches.

By describing in more detail exactly how you would perform these activities, you're able to complete the two activities in 13 minutes instead of 20.

# Estimating Activity Duration

A *span time estimate* is your best sense of how long it'll actually take to perform an activity. It's not how long you'd like it to take or how long someone tells you it must take, but how long you think it really will take.

Unrealistically short span time estimates can actually cause an activity to take longer than necessary because:

✔ Not identifying the reasons why an activity will take a certain amount of time makes it difficult for you to come up with strategies that may reduce the time.

✔ If people believe estimates are totally unrealistic, they won't even try to meet them.

Estimation is not negotiating or bartering.

Suppose your boss asks you to complete a project in six months. You explore all possible alternative strategies and determine you can't complete the project in less than 12 months. After some back and forth negotiating, you and your boss agree that you'll complete the project in nine months.

If you were both being honest initially, you've just guaranteed the project's failure. You agreed to complete the project three months before it's possible. Your boss agreed to accept the final product three months after he or she needs it.

If you weren't both being honest initially, you each learned something about the other. You learned that, whenever your boss gives you an end date, you should add 50 percent to it (nine months is 50 percent more than six months). Your boss learned that when you state the earliest date you can finish an assignment, he or she should subtract 25 percent from it (nine months is 25 percent less than 12 months).

Unfortunately, at the worst, you've reached an agreement that defines a performance target that isn't acceptable to either of you. At the best, you've learned not to trust the information either one of you shares with the other!

## Describing what happens

When estimating an activity's span time, first describe the following components of the activity:

- **Work performed by people:** Physical and mental activities people perform. Examples include writing a report, assembling a piece of equipment, and thinking of ideas for an ad campaign.
- **Work performed by nonhuman resources:** Testing software on a computer and printing a report on a high-speed copy machine are examples.
- **Processes:** Physical or chemical reactions. Concrete curing, paint drying, and chemical reactions in a laboratory are examples.
- **Time delays:** Passage of time where no resource is performing any work. Time delays are typically due to the availability of resources. The need to reserve a conference room two weeks prior to holding a meeting is an example.

## Considering resource characteristics

The following types of resources may be needed to support project work:

- **Personnel**
- **Equipment**
- **Facilities**
- **Raw materials**
- **Information**
- **Funds**

For each resource needed to support or perform the activity's work, determine its:

- **Capacity**: Productivity per unit time period
- **Availability:** When on the calendar a resource will be available

## Finding sources of supporting information

When you've clearly described all aspects of your activity, consult the following information sources to develop your span time estimate:

- Historical records of how long it took to perform similar activities in the past
- People who've performed similar activities in the past
- People who'll be working on the activities
- Experts familiar with the type of activity, even if they haven't performed work exactly like it before

## Improving activity span time estimates

Practice the following to improve the accuracy of your span time estimates:

- Define your activities clearly: Minimize the use of technical jargon and describe associated work processes fully (see Chapter 3 for further discussion).
- Subdivide your activities until you estimate that your lowest level activities will take two weeks or less.
- Define activity start and end points clearly.
- Minimize the use of fudge factors.

A *fudge factor* is an amount of time you add to your best estimate of span time, "just to be safe." An example would be adding an additional 50 percent to all your initial time estimates. Fudge factors compromise your planning for several reasons:

- Work tends to expand to fill the time allotted for it: If you may be able to finish an activity in two weeks but you use a 50 percent fudge factor and indicate a span time of three weeks, the likelihood you'll finish in less than three weeks is almost zero.
- People use fudge factors as an excuse to avoid studying activities in sufficient depth to enable developing viable performance strategies.

✔ Others lose faith in the accuracy and feasibility of your plan because they know you're playing with numbers instead of thinking things through in detail.

No matter how hard you try, it's sometimes difficult to estimate how long an activity will take. Activities you haven't done before, activities you'll perform far in the future, and activities with a history of unpredictability are examples. In these cases:

✔ Make the best estimate you can by following the above approaches and guidelines.

✔ Monitor closely as your project unfolds to identify anything that may cause you to change your initial estimate.

✔ Reflect any changes in your project schedule as soon as you become aware of them.

# Displaying Your Project's Schedule

Your network diagram doesn't contain your schedule; it presents information you will consider to develop your schedule. Consider the following formats to present your schedule, after you've selected your actual dates:

✔ **Key-events report:** A table that lists events and the dates on which you plan to reach them

✔ **Activities report:** A table that lists activities and the dates on which you plan to start and end them

✔ **Gantt chart:** A graph illustrating on a timeline when each activity will start, be performed, and end

✔ **Combined milestone chart and Gantt chart:** A graph illustrating on a timeline when activities will start, be performed, and end, as well as when selected events will be achieved

Your 45-minute schedule for your picnic at the lake is presented in a key-events report, an activities report, and a Gantt chart in Figures 4-12, 4-13, and 4-14, respectively.

Consider the following when choosing the format to display your schedule:

✔ A key-events report and an activities report are more effective for indicating specific dates.

✔ The Gantt chart provides a clearer picture of the relative lengths of activities and their overlap.

| Key Event | Person Responsible | Date Due (minutes after start) | Comments |
|---|---|---|---|
| Ready to load car | You and your friend | 10 | Critical path |
| Ready to drive | You and your friend | 15 | Critical path |
| End: arrived at lake | You and your friend | 45 | Critical path |

**Figure 4-12:** Representing your picnic-at-the-lake schedule in a key-events report.

> **Note: This list includes several key events you have defined for your project. If you want to, you can choose to define and represent an event at the end of each activity.**

**Figure 4-13:** Representing your picnic-at-the-lake schedule in an activities report.

| Activity | Person Responsible | Start Date (minutes after start) | End Date (minutes after start) | Comments |
|---|---|---|---|---|
| 1. Load car | You and your friend | 10 | 15 | Critical path |
| 2. Get money | You | 0 | 5 | |
| 3. Make egg sandwiches | Your friend | 15 | 25 | |
| 4. Drive to lake | You and your friend | 15 | 45 | Critical path |
| 5. Decide which lake | You and your friend | 10 | 12 | |
| 6. Buy gasoline | You | 0 | 10 | Critical path |
| 7. Boil eggs | Your friend | 0 | 10 | Critical path |

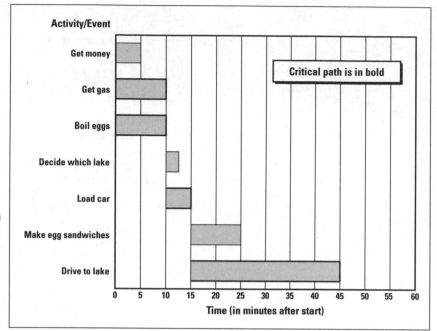

**Figure 4-14:**
Representing
your picnic-
at-the-lake
schedule in
a Gantt chart.

# Chapter 5

# Estimating Resource Requirements

*In This Chapter*

▶ Describing people's skills and capabilities

▶ Assessing your project's personnel needs

▶ Managing multiple commitments

▶ Planning for other resources

▶ Developing your project budget

*I* remember reading the following exasperated declaration written by a stressed out project manager: "We've done so much with so little for so long [that] they now expect us to do everything with nothing!"

The truth is, of course, you can't accomplish anything for nothing; everything has a price. We live in a world of limited resources and not enough time. There will always be more work to do than time and resources will allow. Your job is to decide which tasks to pursue and to do everything possible to succeed on those activities you choose to undertake. Identifying and planning for the resources you'll need to perform your project allows you to:

✔ Explain to those who'll have to support your project what they'll have to contribute.

✔ Ensure that the resources are available when they're needed.

✔ Develop more accurate and realistic schedules.

✔ Monitor your resource expenditures to identify and address possible overruns.

Some organizations have systems and procedures that detail and track every resource used on every project performed, while others don't formally plan or track project resources at all. However, this information will be invaluable to help you ensure project success, whether or not your organization requires that you consider it.

# Establishing Whom You Need, How Much, and When

Your project's success rests on your ability to enlist the help of the right people to perform necessary work. Successful personnel planning requires the following:

- Identifying the skills and knowledge needed to perform your project's activities
- Specifying the people who'll work on each activity
- Determining how much effort they'll have to invest to complete their assignments
- Determining when over the life of a task they'll invest their time, if they work on the task less than full time

If you have the opportunity to influence which people will support your project, the personnel planning described in the following sections will help you get the most qualified people. If you're arbitrarily assigned people or if your team already exists, the planning in the next sections can help you make the best use of their individual skills and knowledge.

## Describing people's skills and knowledge

A Skills Roster, illustrated in Figure 5-1, is a convenient format to display the skills and knowledge of people who may work on your project.

Figure 5-1: Displaying people's skills, knowledge, and interests in a Skills Roster.

|  | Bill | Mary | Sue | Ed |
|---|---|---|---|---|
| Technical writing |  |  | ◉▲ | △ |
| Legal research | △ | △ |  | ● |
| Graphic design | ◉▲ |  | ○ | ◉▲ |
| Questionnaire design | ○ |  |  | △ |

● – Primary skill or knowledge    ○ – Secondary skill or knowledge    △ – Interest

The left-hand column in the Skills Roster identifies skill and knowledge areas, and the top row lists the people's names. At the intersection of the rows and columns, you describe each person's particular skills, knowledge, and interests.

The following scheme is used to describe skill and knowledge level:

- ✔ **Primary capability:** Person is able to assume a lead role in an assignment requiring this skill or knowledge

- ✔ **Secondary capability:** Person has some training or experience in the skill or knowledge area but should work under another person's guidance

- ✔ **Interest:** Person would like to work on assignments involving this skill or knowledge

The Skills Roster in Figure 5-1 tells you that Sue is qualified to lead technical writing assignments and that she'd like to work on this type of assignment. Ed is qualified to lead legal research tasks, but he would prefer not to work on them. He would like to work on questionnaire design activities, but he has no skills or knowledge in this area.

By the way, you may figure that you'd never assign Ed to work on a questionnaire design activity because he has no relevant skills or knowledge. However, if you were trying to find more people who can develop questionnaires, Ed would be a prime candidate. Because he wants to work on these types of assignments, he most likely would be willing to put in extra effort to learn the necessary capabilities.

You can use a variety of numerical or alphanumeric codes to describe a person's skill, knowledge, or interest level. As an example, relative levels of skill, knowledge, or interest can be represented with the following numerical scale:

- **5:** Outstanding

- **4:** Above Average

- **3:** Average

- **2:** Limited

- **1:** Minimal

You may also choose to include some indicator of the experience people have had working on activities requiring the indicated skills and knowledge.

In addition to serving as a guideline to help you request the appropriate people to work on your project activities, a Skills Roster can reveal gaps and weaknesses in staff skills and knowledge that can guide the following:

- ✔ **Training:** The organization can develop or make available training to address the deficiencies.

- ✔ **Career development:** Individuals develop skills and knowledge that are in short supply to increase their opportunities to assume greater responsibilities in the organization.

✔ **Recruiting:** Recruiters can look for candidates who have skills and knowledge in short supply in the organization, in addition to the primary skills and knowledge they will need for their primary jobs.

Because of their potential use in different areas of the organization, group managers and supervisors, training departments, and employee recruiting departments may already have Skills Rosters prepared for some or all of the staff. If you decide to create one yourself or to help someone else in your organization create one, proceed as follows:

1. **Develop a complete list of the skill and knowledge areas that may be required for anticipated project assignments.**

2. **Develop a list of all people who will be included in the Skills Roster.**

3. **Have people on your list rate their proficiency in each skill and knowledge area, as well as their interest in working on assignments in each area.**

4. **Have each person's direct supervisor rate the person's skill, knowledge, and interest.**

5. **Compare the ratings made by the person and his or her supervisor and reconcile any differences.**

6. **Prepare a final version of the Skills Roster.**

Comparing your own ratings of your skills, knowledge, and interests with those made by your supervisor can help you identify situations that may lead to future performance problems. The following are typical situations, associated problems, and possible solutions after you and your supervisor become aware of the discrepancy:

✔ **You rate your skills and knowledge in an area higher than your supervisor rates them.**

• Potential situation: You may feel that your supervisor is unfairly choosing not to give you more challenging assignments with greater responsibility.

• Possible solution: Your supervisor can give you a more challenging assignment and monitor your performance closely. If all goes well, your supervisor's opinion of your capabilities will improve. If you have problems with the assignment, you can work out a plan with your supervisor to develop any skills or knowledge that you may be lacking.

✔ **You rate your skills and knowledge in an area lower than your supervisor rates them.**

• Potential situation: You check with your supervisor about the smallest issues and decisions because you feel you're not qualified to deal with them yourself.

- • Possible solution: Your supervisor can explain to you initially why he or she feels you are qualified to handle your assignment, and your supervisor can point out to you when you handle issues correctly and why.

✓ **You have interests in areas that your boss doesn't know about.**

- • Potential situation: You miss out on opportunities to work on assignments.

- • Possible solution: Frequently talk with your supervisor about your interests and why you think you'd perform well on assignments in these areas.

✓ **Your boss thinks you have interests in areas where you don't.**

- • Potential situation: You're repeatedly given assignments in which you have little or no interest, you become bored and disinterested in work, and your productivity suffers.

- • Possible solution: Discuss your interests with your boss; ask your boss if you can do some work in your special-interest areas, in addition to handling the normal assignments where your special skills may be needed.

In a project environment, you often work with people you don't know well or haven't spent much time with before. Making a special effort to learn about their skills, knowledge, and interests helps you to make more appropriate use of their special talents, and also improves their morale and productivity.

## *Estimating needed commitment*

Planning out your personnel needs begins with identifying whom you need and how much effort he or she will have to invest. You can display this information in a Human Resources Matrix, as illustrated in Figure 5-2.

**Figure 5-2:**
Displaying personnel needs in a Human Resources Matrix.

| Activity | | Personnel (Person-hours) | | |
|---|---|---|---|---|
| **Work Breakdown Structure Code** | **Description** | **J. Jones** | **F. Smith** | **Analyst** |
| 2.1.1 | Design questionnaire | 32 | 0 | 24 |
| 2.1.2 | Pilot questionnaire | 0 | 40 | 60 |
| 2.2.1 | Prepare instructions | 40 | 24 | 10 |

The Human Resources Matrix displays individual resources that will work on an activity and the work effort that each resource will invest in the activity.

*Work effort* or *person effort* is the actual time a person spends working on an activity. Work effort is expressed in units of person-hours, person-days, person-weeks, and so forth. On occasion, you may still hear people express work effort in units of man-hours or man-days. This is just a less politically acceptable way of expressing the same concept!

Work effort is related to, but different from span time or duration. Work effort is a measure of resource use; span time is a measure of time passage. Consider the work effort required to complete "design questionnaire" in the Human Resources Matrix illustrated in Figure 5-2. According to the Matrix, this activity requires J. Jones for 32 person-hours and an unnamed analyst for 24 person-hours.

This information alone, however, doesn't tell you the span time of the activity. If both people can work on the activity at the same time, if they're both assigned 100 percent to the project to do their respective work and if there are no other aspects of the task that will take additional time, the activity may be finished in four days. However, if either person is available for less than 100 percent time, if one or both worked overtime, or if one person had to finish his or her work before the other could start, the span time would be different.

See Chapter 4 for more discussion of span time.

### Describing needed personnel

A *lowest-level activity* is an activity in your Work Breakdown Structure that's not divided into further detail. See Chapter 3 for further discussion.

Identify all personnel that will have to work on each lowest-level activity in your project. You can identify personnel by listing the following:

- **Name:** The name of the person who'll do the work
- **Position description:** The position description or title of the person who'll eventually do the work
- **Skills and knowledge:** The specific skills and knowledge that anyone assigned to the task will have to possess

Early in your planning, specify needed skills and knowledge, if possible, such as "a person who can develop work process flow charts" or "a person who can use Microsoft PowerPoint." If you can identify the exact skills and knowledge that a person must have to do a particular task, you increase the chances that the proper person will be assigned. On occasion, a position description or title such as "operations specialist" is used to identify needed resources. Doing this assumes that the position description or title accurately describes the skills and knowledge that anyone with the position description or title would have. Unfortunately, titles are often vague and position descriptions are frequently out of date. Therefore, this is a risky way for you to try to get the right person for the job.

Very often, you identify people you want on your project by name. The reason is simple: If you've worked with someone before and he or she has done a good job, you want to work with that person again. Unfortunately, while this is great for the ego of the person whom everyone requests, it often reduces the chances that you'll get the best person for your project. People who develop reputations for excellence are often requested for more time than they have available. If you don't specify the particular skills and knowledge needed, the manager who has to find a substitute for the person you requested by name won't know what skills and knowledge the substitute should have.

### Estimating required work effort

For all lowest-level activities in your project, estimate the work effort that each person will have to invest to complete his or her assigned portion of the work. Develop your work effort estimates as follows:

- ✔ **Describe in detail all work to be done when performing the activity.** Include work directly and indirectly related to the activity. Examples of work directly related to an activity include writing a report, meeting with clients, performing a laboratory test, and designing a new logo.

  Examples of work indirectly related to an activity include receiving skills or knowledge training required to perform activity-related work and preparing periodic activity progress reports.

- ✔ **Consider history.** Past history doesn't guarantee future performance. It does, however, provide a guideline for what's possible. Determine whether the activity or parts of the activity have been performed before. If they have, review written records to determine the work effort spent on the activity in the past. If written records weren't kept, consult with people who've done the activity before to determine their estimate of the work effort they spent.

  When using prior history to support the estimates of required work effort, be sure the work was performed as follows:

  - By people with qualifications and experience similar to those of the people anticipated for your project

  - Using facilities, equipment, and technology that's similar to that planned for your project

  - In a time frame similar to the one you anticipate for your project activity

✔ **Have the person who'll do the work participate in estimating the required work effort.** Having people participate in developing work effort estimates for activities they'll perform provides two benefits: Their understanding of everything that goes into performing the activity is improved and their commitment to do the work for the estimated level of work effort is increased.

If you know who'll be working on the activity at the time you're developing your initial plan, have those people participate then. If people join the project team at the start of the project or during the project, have them review and comment on the plans that have been developed.

✔ **Consult with experts familiar with this type of activity, even if they haven't performed work exactly like it before.** Experience and knowledge from all sources will improve the accuracy of your estimate.

### Factoring in productivity, efficiency, and availability

Being assigned to a project full time doesn't mean that you'll be able to perform project work at peak productivity 40 hours per week for 52 weeks per year. Other personal and organizational activities will reduce the actual number of hours you'll be available to do your project work. Therefore, consider each of the following factors when determining the number of hours that people will have to be assigned to your project to complete their work:

✔ **Productivity:** The results you produce per unit of time that you and your project team spend working on the activity. Your productivity is affected by the following:

- Knowledge and skills: The raw talent and capability you have to perform a particular task.

- Prior experience with similar tasks: Familiarity with the work required and the typical problems encountered for a particular task.

- Sense of urgency: The drive you have to generate the desired results within established time frames. Urgency will influence your focus and concentration on an activity.

- Ability to switch back and forth among several tasks: Your comfort moving to a second task as soon as you hit a roadblock in your first one, so that you won't sit around stewing about your frustrations and wasting time.

- The quality and setup of your physical environment: Proximity and arrangement of furniture and support equipment, as well as the availability and condition of equipment and resources that you use to perform your work.

✔ **Efficiency:** The proportion of time on the job that you and your project team spend on project work, as opposed to organizational tasks that aren't related to specific projects. Your efficiency is affected by the following:

- The time you spend on non-project-specific professional activities, including attending general organization meetings, handling incidental requests about issues with which you are familiar, and reading technical journals and periodicals about your field of specialty.

- The time you spend on personal activities, such as getting a drink of water, going to the restroom, organizing your work area, conducting personal business on the job, and talking about nonwork related topics with coworkers.

The more time you spend each day on these non-project-specific activities, the less time you'll have available to work on your project assignments.

A number of years ago, I read of a study that determined that, on the average, a typical employee spends about four hours of an eight-hour work day working on preplanned project activities and work assignments. The interviewers in this study spoke with people in more than 100 organizations, with a wide range of job responsibilities. This means that the typical employee in this study was working at an efficiency of about 50 percent!

I have since found several organizations that have done similar studies of their own operations. These organizations all found workers' efficiency to be about 75 percent. But remember, of course, that these organization studies were biased. The people surveyed wanted their organization to think they were spending most of their time working on planned project assignments, and the organization wanted to believe this was the case. Still, the organization studies found that people spent about 25 percent of each day doing something other than preplanned, project related activities!

✔ **Availability:** The portion of time you and your project team are at the job, as opposed to on leave. Your availability is determined by organization policy. Determine your potential availability by specifying the number of days each year staff can use for annual leave, sick leave, holiday leave, administrative leave, personal leave, mental health leave, and so on.

### *Supporting your estimates with historical data and experience*

How you reflect efficiency in your personnel planning depends on whether and how you track your work effort. You don't have to factor in a separate measure for efficiency if you base your estimate on historical data from a time-recording system and either of the following situations is true:

✔ **Your time sheet has one or more categories to record time spent on non-project-specific work *and* you report accurately by activity your actual time expenditures**

If this is the case, the historical information represents the actual number of hours people recorded to do the activity in the past. These numbers reflect the actual time spent working on the activity in the past, and you can comfortably use these numbers to predict the number of hours you can expect to record to do this activity this time.

✔ **Your time sheet has no category for recording your time on non-project-specific work, but you report accurately (by activity) the time you spend on work-related activities, and you apportion in a consistent manner your non-project-specific work among the available project activities.**

The historical information again reflects the actual number of hours that people recorded to do the activity in the past. In this instance, the recorded hours will include some portion of time spent on non-project-specific work, as well as on the activity itself. However, if your time-recording practices haven't changed, these data will suggest the number of hours you will record (for both project and nonspecific work) to do the activity this time.

# Be careful to distinguish between efficiency and availability

A while back, I met a person in one of my training sessions who was convinced that he took efficiency into account when he estimated needed levels of resources for his projects. He explained to me that his organization had performed an internal study and determined that each year, a typical employee spent about 25 percent of his or her time on sick leave, holiday leave, vacation leave, personal leave, and administrative leave. Therefore, he defined "full-time availability" to be 120 person hours each month, which was 75 percent of the approximately 160 person hours an employee was potentially available to work during a month. (He derived his estimate of 160 person hours potentially available by multiplying 8 hours per day by five days a week by four weeks per month — admittedly, this is an approximation.)

I explained to him that the 120 person-hours he derived was the total time an employee was available each month, and, unfortunately, that people didn't work at 100 percent efficiency for all the hours they were available. I told him that, to be accurate, he should consider that a person had about 90 productive hours each month that could be spent on project work, if you consider that the person worked at 75 percent efficiency. (I determined 90 person-hours by multiplying the 160 hours potentially available by the 75 percent availability factor and that number by the 75 percent efficiency factor.)

His reaction to my suggestion was interesting: He completely rejected my analysis! He said that he refused to tell the people on his project that they only had to do six hours of work for every eight hours they charged to his project. He didn't realize that they were doing this already. He could recognize it and reflect it in his plans or he could ignore it; but ignoring it didn't change the reality.

On the other hand, you do have to consider factoring in a separate measure of efficiency if you base your estimate on the personal opinions of people with experience performing similar activities or who will be doing this activity.

If you'll be doing the activity yourself, estimate the required work effort assuming you could work at 100 percent efficiency. (In other words, don't worry about normal interruptions during the day, consider you are working on one task at a time, and so forth.) Then take your estimate and modify it to reflect efficiency as follows:

- ✔ If you'll be recording your time accurately on a time sheet that has one or more categories to record time spent on non-project-specific work, don't include an efficiency factor.

- ✔ If you'll be recording your time accurately on a time sheet that has no categories to record time spent on non-project-specific work, include an efficiency factor.

As an example, suppose you estimate you need 30 person-hours to perform a task (if you could be 100 percent efficient), and your time sheets have no categories for recording non-project-specific work. If you consider you'll actually be closer to 75 percent efficient, you'd plan to charge 40 person-hours to your project to complete the task, because 75 percent of 40 person-hours is 30 person-hours, the amount you said you really needed.

The following time sheet practices will cause the data collected to be inaccurate:

- ✔ You aren't allowed to record overtime spent.

- ✔ You fill out your time sheet for the entire period several days before the period is over.

- ✔ You copy the work effort estimates from the project plan onto your time sheet each period.

If any of these situations exist in your organization, don't use data from time sheets to support your work effort estimates for your current project.

Failing to consider efficiency when estimating and reviewing work effort invested can lead to incorrect conclusions about people's performance. Suppose your boss assigns you a project on Monday morning. He tells you he thinks it'll take about 40 person-hours to finish, but he really needs it completed by Friday, close of business. Suppose further that you work intensely all week and you finish the task by Friday close of business. In the process, you record on your time sheet that you spent 55 person-hours on it.

If your boss doesn't realize that his initial estimate of 40 person-hours was based upon your working at 100 percent efficiency, he'll think you took 15 hours longer to do the assignment than you should have. On the other hand, if your boss recognizes that 55 person-hours on the job translates into about 40 person-hours of work on specific project tasks, your boss will appreciate that you invested extra effort to meet his aggressive deadline.

Although your performance is the same, overlooking the impact of efficiency makes you appear less capable, while correctly considering it makes you appear intensely dedicated.

The longer your involvement in an assignment, the more important it will be to consider efficiency and availability. Suppose you decide you have to spend one hour on an assignment. You can figure your availability is 100 percent and your efficiency is 100 percent, so you'll need to allow yourself to charge one hour to your project. If you need to spend six hours on an assignment, you probably can figure that your availability will be 100 percent, but you must consider that your efficiency will be 75 percent (or whatever planning figure you decide to use). Therefore, you should allow yourself to charge one workday (eight work hours) to the project to ensure you'll be able to spend the six hours working on your task.

If you plan to devote one month or more to your assignment, recognize that you most likely will take some leave days during that time. Even though your project budget won't have to pay for your annual or sick leave, recognize that being available for one person-month means that you'll have about 97 hours available for productive work on your project task, assuming 75 percent efficiency and 75 percent availability (2,080 hours total in a year ÷ 12 months in a year × .75 × .75).

Consider the following numbers when estimating personnel requirements:

| Table 5-1 | Person-Hours Available for Project Work | | |
|---|---|---|---|
| | **Productive Person-Hours Available** | | |
| | *100 percent efficiency, 100 percent availability* | *75 percent efficiency, 100 percent availability* | *75 percent efficiency, 75 percent availability* |
| **1 person-day** | 8 | 6 | 4.5 |
| **1 person-week** | 40 | 30 | 22.5 |

|  | 100 percent efficiency, 100 percent availability | 75 percent efficiency, 100 percent availability | 75 percent efficiency, 75 percent availability |
|---|---|---|---|
| **1 person-month** | 173 | 130 | 98 |
| **1 person-year** | 2080 | 1560 | 1170 |

Develop your own planning figures if your organization has different numbers for efficiency or availability.

Beware of the hierarchical work-effort estimate. Suppose you plan to assign a particular task to Harry's group. However, Harry will pass the assignment to Mary, who will pass it to Beth, who will pass it to Joe, who'll actually do the required work.

You ask Harry to estimate the work effort required to complete the task. Harry in turn asks Mary who asks Beth who asks Joe. Joe estimates it'll take two person-weeks of actual work to complete the task. However, Joe, Beth, Mary and Harry all know the organization has determined that people work at 75 percent efficiency, so each individually reflects this factor in his or her estimate, to be realistic. Joe tells Beth it will take 2.7 person-weeks; Beth tells Mary it will take 3.6 person-weeks; Mary tells Harry it will take 4.8 person-weeks; and Harry tells you it will take 6.4 person-weeks!

The problem, of course, was communication. Each person separately included a factor in his or her estimate to represent efficiency, without telling the others. Including this factor one time is appropriate; including it four times is wasteful and misleading.

### Tips to improve work effort estimates

Practice the following to improve the accuracy of your work effort estimates:

- ✔ Define your activities clearly: Minimize the use of technical jargon and describe associated work processes (see Chapter 3 for further discussion).
- ✔ Subdivide your activities until you estimate that your lowest level activities will take two person-weeks or less.
- ✔ Minimize the use of fudge factors (see Chapter 4).
- ✔ Update work effort estimates when project personnel or task assignments change.

## *Juggling multiple commitments*

Determining whether you're overcommitted is straightforward, if you work on only one activity at a time. Suppose you plan to work on several activities that are partially overlapping during a particular time period. Then you must decide when during each activity you will put in your hours to see if your multitasking has left you overcommitted.

### *Preparing your initial analysis*

Start your analysis by developing:

- ✔ A Human Resources Matrix
- ✔ A Person Loading Graph or Person Loading Chart for each individual in the Human Resource Matrix

Suppose that you plan to work on Tasks 1, 2, and 3 of a project. Table 5-2 depicts the person-hours you plan to spend on each task (consider that efficiency has already been reflected in these estimates).

| Table 5-2 | Proposed Work Effort on Three Activities |
|-----------|------------------------------------------|
| *Activity* | *Level of Effort (Person-Hours)* |
| Task 1 | 60 |
| Task 2 | 40 |
| Task 3 | 30 |

Figure 5-3 illustrates when you propose to perform Tasks 1, 2, and 3. According to the Gantt Chart, you'll perform Task 1 in weeks 1, 2, and 3, Task 2 in weeks 2 and 3, and Task 3 in weeks 3, 4, and 5.

The Gantt chart at the top of Figure 5-3 indicates Task 1 will take three weeks, Task 2 will take two weeks, and Task 3 will take three weeks. Table 5-2 suggests you'll spend 60 person-hours (50 percent of the available time), 40 person-hours (50 percent of the available time) and 30 person-hours (25 percent of the available time) on Tasks 1, 2, and 3, respectively. Therefore, you'd have no problem completing your work on each one if you didn't have to work on them at the same time.

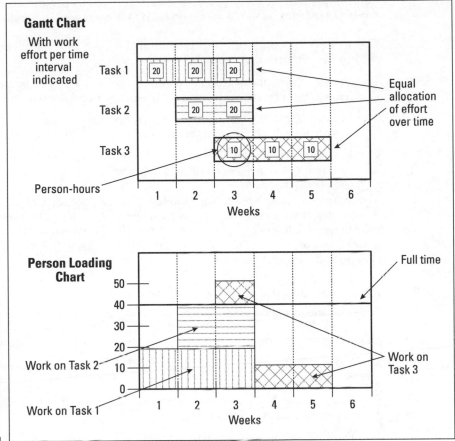

**Figure 5-3:**
Planning to work on several activities over the same time period.

But your initial plan has you working on both Tasks 1 and 2 in week 2 and on all three tasks in week 3. You'll have to make the following decision, to see whether you'll be able to do your work on all three activities as they are currently scheduled:

> When over the life of each activity will you put in your required time?

As a starting point, assume you'll spend your time evenly over the life of each task. That means you'll work 20 hours a week on Task 1 during weeks 1, 2, and 3, 20 hours a week on Task 2 during weeks 2 and 3, and 10 hours a week on Task 3 during weeks 3, 4, and 5. This initial allocation of your work effort by task is illustrated on the Gantt chart at the top of Figure 5-3.

Determine the total effort you'll have to devote to the project each week by adding up the hours you'll spend on each task each week, as follows:

- ✔ In week 1, you'll work 20 person-hours on Task 1 for a total commitment to the project of 20 person-hours.

- ✔ In week 2, you'll work 20 person-hours on Task 1 and 20 person-hours on Task 2, for a total commitment to the project of 40 person-hours.

- ✔ In week 3, you'll work 20 person-hours on Task 1, 20 on Task 2 and 10 on Task 3, for a total commitment to the project of 50 person-hours.

- ✔ In weeks 4 and 5, you'll work 10 person-hours on Task 3, for a total commitment to the project of 10 person-hours.

These commitments are displayed in the "Person Loading Graph" of Figure 5-3. A quick review reveals that this plan has you working 10 hours of overtime in week 3. If you're comfortable putting in this overtime, this plan will work. If you aren't, you have to come up with an alternative strategy to reduce your week 3 commitments.

### Resolving potential resource overloads

Consider the following strategies to avoid overcommitting yourself:

- ✔ Allocate your time unevenly over the duration of one or more activities.

- ✔ Take advantage of any slack time that may exist in your assigned activities.

- ✔ Assign some of the work you were planning to do in the third week to someone else on your project.

- ✔ Have new people assigned to your project.

- ✔ Hire an external vendor or contractor to perform some of the work you had originally planned to do yourself.

Suppose you choose to spend your hours unevenly over the duration of Task 1, as depicted in Table 5-3. Figure 5-4 illustrates how this will remove the need for overtime in the third week.

| Table 5-3 | Proposed Work Effort Each Week on Task 1 |
|---|---|
| *Time Period* | *Level of Effort (Person-Hours)* |
| Week 1 | 30 |
| Week 2 | 20 |
| Week 3 | 10 |

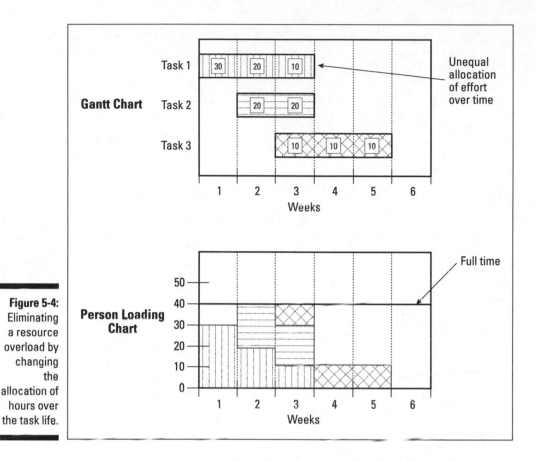

**Figure 5-4:**
Eliminating
a resource
overload by
changing
the
allocation of
hours over
the task life.

Figure 5-5 illustrates how you can remove the need for overtime in the third week by taking advantage of slack time that may be associated with Task 3. If Task 3 had at least one week of slack time associated with it, you could reduce your total work on the project in the third week to 40 person-hours by delaying both the start and end of Task 3 by one week. See Chapter 4 for a detailed definition and discussion of slack time.

You can display detailed allocations of work effort by time period in a tabular format, as well as in a graphical format. Figure 5-6 presents the information from the Person Loading Graph of Figure 5-3 in an individual Person Loading Chart. Prepare a separate individual Person Loading Chart for each person on your project team.

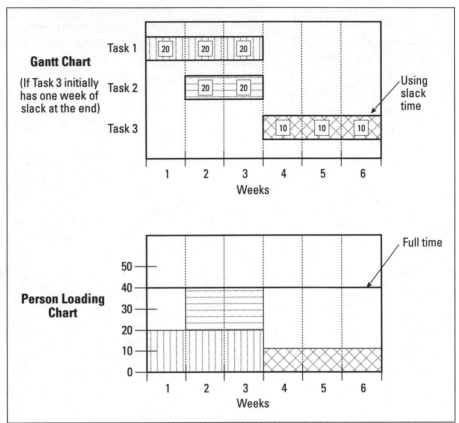

**Figure 5-5:**
Eliminating
a resource
overload by
changing
the start and
end dates of
a task with
slack time.

| | Person-hours | | | | | |
|---|---|---|---|---|---|---|
| | Week 1 | Week 2 | Week 3 | Week 4 | Week 5 | Total |
| Task 1 | 20 | 20 | 20 | | | 60 |
| Task 2 | | 20 | 20 | | | 40 |
| Task 3 | | | 10 | 10 | 10 | 30 |
| Total | 20 | 40 | 50 | 10 | 10 | 130 |

**Figure 5-6:**
Example of
an individual
Person
Loading
Chart.

Detail the total hours that each person will spend on your project in a summary Person Loading Chart, as illustrated in Figure 5-7. The entries in your row for weeks 1 through 5 are the same as those in the "Total" row of the individual Person Loading Chart in Figure 5-6.

This chart helps you to

✔ Identify who may be available to share some of the load for people who are overcommitted.

✔ Determine the personnel budget for your project by multiplying the number of hours people will work on the project by their weighted labor rates. (See "Two approaches for estimating indirect costs" section at the end of this chapter.)

| | Person-hours | | | | | |
|---|---|---|---|---|---|---|
| | Week 1 | Week 2 | Week 3 | Week 4 | Week 5 | Total |
| **You** | 20 | 40 | 50 | 10 | 10 | 130 |
| **Bill** | 10 | 20 | 10 | 30 | 10 | 80 |
| **Mary** | 15 | 10 | 20 | 10 | 30 | 85 |
| **Total** | 45 | 70 | 80 | 50 | 50 | 295 |

**Figure 5-7:** Illustration of a summary Person Loading Chart.

### Coordinating assignments across multiple projects

You can use this planning approach to manage resource assignments across projects, if you prepare Person Loading Graphs or Charts for each project.

Figure 5-8 illustrates a Person Loading Chart that presents the total hours committed for each person in your group for those months. This chart is derived from the summary Person Loading Charts for the projects on which they'll be working.

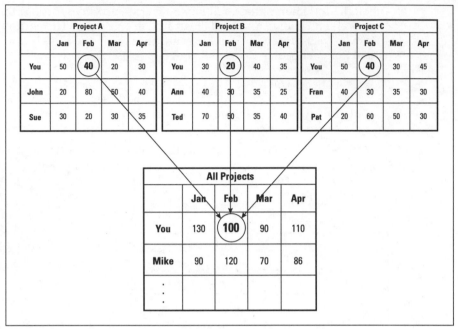

**Figure 5-8:**
Using
Person
Loading
Charts to
plan your
time on
several
projects.

Suppose you'll be working on three projects in January, February, and March. Consider your current plans for February. You're already committed to work on Projects A, B, and C for 40, 20, and 40 person-hours, respectively. If someone wants you to devote 80 person-hours to Project D in February, you have several options. If you assume that you have a total of 160 person-hours available in the month, then you can devote 60 person-hours to Project D with no problem. However, you don't have the other 20 available. You may consider the following:

✔ Finding someone to assume 20 person-hours of your work on Projects A, B, and C in February

✔ Shifting your work on one or more of these projects to January or March

✔ Working overtime

# *Working in Everything Else*

Plan for all other resources, such as equipment and facilities, the same way you plan for personnel. Develop the following:

✔ A resources matrix (for all nonpersonnel resources)

✔ Individual usage charts (for each nonpersonnel resource)

✔ A summary usage chart (for all nonpersonnel resources)

Figure 5-9 illustrates a resources matrix for nonpersonnel resources. The following information is displayed for every lowest-level activity in your project:

✔ The nonpersonnel resources you'll need to perform the activity: Examples include computers, copiers, and use of a test laboratory.

✔ The total amount of each resource you'll need.

**Figure 5-9:**
An
illustration
of a
resources
matrix.

| Activity | | Amount of Resource Required (Hours) | | |
|---|---|---|---|---|
| Work Breakdown Structure Code | Description | Computer | Copier | Test Lab |
| 1.2.1 | Design layout | 32 | 0 | 0 |
| 2.1.4 | Prepare report | 0 | 40 | 0 |
| 3.3.1 | Design device | 40 | 0 | 32 |

Figure 5-9 suggests you'll need 40 hours of computer time and 32 hours of the test laboratory to design a device.

Estimate the amount of each resource you'll need by examining the nature of the task and the capacity of the resource. As an illustration, determine the amount of copier time you'll need to reproduce a report as follows:

✔ Estimate the number of report copies you'll need.

✔ Estimate the number of pages per copy.

✔ Specify the copier capacity in pages per minute.

✔ Multiply the first two numbers together to determine the amount of copier time you'll need to reproduce your reports.

Figure 5-10 illustrates a computer usage chart that displays when over the life of a task you plan to use the computer required to support it. The chart suggests you'll need 10 hours of computer time for Task 1 in weeks 1, 2, and 3, respectively.

|  | Computer Time Required (Hours) | | | | | |
|---|---|---|---|---|---|---|
|  | Week 1 | Week 2 | Week 3 | Week 4 | Week 5 | Total |
| Task 1 | 10 | 10 | 10 |  |  | 30 |
| Task 2 |  | 20 | 20 |  |  | 40 |
| Task 3 |  |  | 10 | 20 | 30 | 60 |
| Total | 10 | 30 | 40 | 20 | 30 | 130 |

**Figure 5-10:**
Illustration of a computer usage chart.

# Estimating the Dollars

All project resources cost money. In a world of limited resources, you're constantly deciding how to get the most return for your investment. Therefore, estimating a project's costs is important for several reasons:

✔ It enables you to assess anticipated benefits, with respect to anticipated costs, to see whether the project makes sense.

✔ It allows you to see if you can get the funds necessary to support the project.

✔ It provides a criterion as you monitor your ongoing performance to help you ensure you'll have sufficient funds to complete the project.

I recognize that you may not have to develop detailed budgets for your projects. You may never receive reports of your expenditures and financial status during your project. In fact, your organization may not even associate expenses incurred with the projects to which they relate! However, understanding how project costs are defined and can be used will make you a better project manager and increase your chances of project success.

## Different types of project costs

A *project budget* is a detailed, time-phased estimate of the costs of all resources required to perform your project. Your budget is typically developed in stages, from an initial rough estimate to a detailed budget estimate through a completed, approved project budget. On occasion, you may even revise your approved budget while your project is in progress to reflect changes in planned work and results.

*Direct costs* are expenditures for resources that are used solely to perform project activities. Direct costs include salaries paid to the people who work on your project; materials, supplies, and equipment bought for your project; travel to perform work on your project; and subcontracts for services performed for your project.

*Indirect costs* are expenditures that are incurred to support project activities but that aren't tracked individually. Indirect costs fall into two categories:

- **Overhead costs:** Expenditures for resources used to perform project activities, but which are difficult to subdivide and allocate directly. Examples include employee benefits, office space rent, supplies, and the rental or purchase of furniture, fixtures, or equipment used to support work on your project.

- **General and administrative costs:** Expenditures that keep your organization operational (if your organization didn't exist, you couldn't perform your project). Examples include salaries of your contracts department, finance department, and top management, as well as fees for accounting and legal services.

You realize that you need an office to work on your project activities and you know that office space costs money. However, your organization has an annual lease for office space that requires 12 monthly installments be paid to your landlord. The office space is broken into many individual offices and work areas, and people are performing numerous projects in these offices at any one time. Unfortunately, you have no clear record of the portion of each month's rent check that goes to pay for the office space you use to work on your project. Your office space is an indirect project cost.

Suppose you're planning to design, develop, and produce a company brochure. Direct costs for this project may include the following:

- Labor: Salaries paid to you and others for the hours you spend working on the brochure

- Materials: The special paper stock on which you will copy the brochure

- Travel: The costs for the miles you drive to investigate different firms that could design your brochure cover

- Subcontract: The services of an outside company that will design the cover art for your brochure

Indirect costs for this project may include the following:

- Employee benefits: Employee benefits earned by you and others in addition to your salary while you're working on the brochure

- Rent: The cost of the office space you use when you're developing the copy for the brochure

✔ Equipment: The computer you use to compose the copy for the brochure

✔ Management and administrative salaries: A portion of the salaries of upper managers and staff who perform the administrative duties necessary to keep your organization functioning

## Developing your project budget

Develop your project budget in stages, as follows:

✔ **Rough order-of-magnitude estimate:** An initial estimate of costs that's based on a general sense of the type of work the project will likely entail. Sometimes this estimate is more a statement of what someone is willing to spend than of what the project will really cost. You typically don't detail this estimate by lowest level project activity because you usually prepare it in a short amount of time before you've identified the needed project activities.

Whether or not people choose to accept it, initial budget estimates included in annual plans and long-range plans are typically rough order-of-magnitude estimates.

✔ **Detailed budget estimate:** An itemization of the estimated costs for each project activity. You prepare this estimate by developing a detailed Work Breakdown Structure (see Chapter 3) and estimating the costs associated with all lowest-level activities.

✔ **Completed, approved project budget:** A detailed project budget that essential people approve and agree to support.

### Refining your budget as you move through your project

A project moves through five phases as it evolves from an idea to a reality:

✔ **Conceive**

✔ **Define**

✔ **Start**

✔ **Perform**

✔ **Close**

See Chapter 1 for more discussion of these phases. The budget-development activities that you perform in each phase are summarized in Table 5-4.

| Table 5-4 | Budget-Development Activity in the Project Phases |
|---|---|
| *Project Phase* | *Budget Activity* |
| Conceive | Develop rough order-of-magnitude estimate |
| Define | Develop detailed budget estimate |
| | Obtain completed, approved project budget |
| Start | Review budget, after personnel and resources are assigned to the project |
| | Obtain approved, revised budget, if necessary |
| Perform | Identify situations that may require changes to the approved project budget |
| | Obtain approved, revised budget, as needed |
| Close | Identify situations that may require changes to the approved project budget |
| | Obtain approved, revised budget, as needed |

A rough order-of-magnitude estimate is prepared in the conceive phase. Rather than an actual estimate of costs, this estimate often represents an amount that can't be exceeded, if your project is to have an acceptable return for the investment. Your confidence in this estimate is low, because it isn't based on detailed analyses of the activities you will perform.

Develop your detailed budget estimate in the definition phase, after you specify your required project activities. Get your detailed budget approved before you leave this phase.

Review your approved budget in the start phase, when you identify the people who will be working on your project and start to develop formal agreements for the use of equipment, facilities, vendors, and other resources. Get any required budget changes approved before you move to the perform phase.

Monitor project activities and related occurrences throughout the perform and close phases to determine when budget revisions are necessary. Develop them and get them approved as soon as possible.

You may not personally be involved with all steps in the development of your project budget. If you join your project after some initial planning has been done, be sure to review the plans and resolve any questions and issues you may identify.

### Estimating project costs

Develop your detailed project budget estimate by using a combination of the following approaches:

✔ **Bottom-up:** Develop detailed cost estimates for each lowest-level activity in the project Work Breakdown Structure and add these estimates together to obtain the total project budget estimate.

✔ **Top-down:** Examine the estimated cost of each major work assignment in the Work Breakdown Structure to confirm its reasonableness.

Develop your bottom-up budget estimate as follows:

1. **Consider each lowest-level activity in turn.**

2. **Determine direct labor costs for each activity by multiplying the number of hours each person will work on the activity by the person's hourly salary.**

   Direct labor costs can be estimated by:

   • Using the salary of each person on the project

   • Using the average salary for people with a particular job title, in a certain department, and so on

   Suppose you need the services of a graphic artist to design overheads for your presentation. The head of the graphics department estimates the person will have to spend 100 hours on your project. If you knew Harry (with a salary rate of $30/hour) would be assigned to the activity, you could estimate your direct labor costs to be $3,000. However, if the director doesn't know whom she will assign to your project, you may consider using the average salary for a graphic artist in your organization to estimate the direct labor costs.

3. **Estimate the direct costs for materials, equipment, travel, contractual services, and other resources for each activity.**

4. **Determine the indirect costs that will be allocated to each activity.**

   You typically estimate indirect costs as a fraction of the planned direct labor costs for the activity. In general, your organization's finance department determines this fraction annually by

   • Estimating organization direct labor costs for the coming year

   • Estimating organization indirect costs for the coming year

   • Dividing the estimated indirect costs by the estimated direct labor costs

   Some organizations express this indirect cost rate as a percentage that's determined by multiplying the fraction by 100.

Choosing the detailed method you'll use to estimate indirect costs requires you to weigh the potential accuracy of the estimate against the effort needed to develop it. See the "Two approaches for estimating indirect costs" sidebar.

Table 5-5 illustrates how you would present a typical budget estimate. Suppose you're planning a project to design and produce a company brochure. You've developed the following information:

✔ You estimate you'll spend 200 person-hours on the project and Mary will spend 100 person-hours.

✔ Your salary rate is $30/hour and Mary's is $25/hour.

✔ You'll have to buy stationery on which to copy the brochures; you estimate the cost to be $1,000.

✔ You estimate you'll incur $300 in travel costs to visit vendors and suppliers.

✔ You expect to pay an external company $5,000 do the artwork for the brochure.

✔ Your organization has developed a combined indirect cost rate of 60 percent.

| Table 5-5 | Project Budget for Designing and Producing a Company Brochure | |
|---|---|---|
| **Cost Category** | **Cost** | **Total** |
| Direct Labor | | |
| You: 200 hours @ $30/hour | $6,000 | |
| Mary: 100 hours @ $25/hour | $2,500 | |
| Total Direct Labor | | $8,500 |
| Indirect Costs @ 60 percent | | $5,100 |
| Other Direct Costs | | |
| Materials | $1,000 | |
| Travel | $300 | |
| Subcontract | $5,000 | |
| Total Other Direct Costs | | $6,300 |
| TOTAL PROJECT COSTS | | $19,900 |

# Two approaches for estimating indirect costs

Following are two approaches typically used for estimating indirect costs associated with an activity:

**Option 1: Use one rate for overhead costs and another rate for general and administrative costs.**

✔ Your finance department determines the overhead rate by calculating the ratio of all projected overhead costs to all projected direct salaries.

✔ Your finance department determines the general and administrative rate by calculating the ratio of all projected general and administrative costs to the sum of all projected direct salaries, overhead costs, and other direct costs.

✔ You determine the overhead costs associated with an activity by multiplying the direct salaries for that activity by the overhead rate.

✔ You determine the general and administrative costs associated with an activity by multiplying the sum of direct salaries, calculated overhead costs, and other direct costs for the activity by the general and administrative rate.

**Option 2: Use one indirect cost rate for all overhead and general and administrative costs.**

✔ Your finance department determines the combined indirect cost rate by calculating the ratio of all projected overhead costs to all projected direct salaries.

✔ You determine the indirect costs associated with an activity by multiplying the direct salaries for that activity by the indirect cost rate.

Some organizations develop *weighted labor rates*, which combine hourly salary and associated indirect costs. As an example, suppose your salary is $30/hour, and your organization's indirect cost rate is 0.5. Your weighted labor rate would be $45/hour (equal to $30 + (0.5 × $30)).

The top-down cost encourages you to consider the relative emphases you contemplate placing on the different aspects of your project. As an example, suppose you plan to develop a new piece of equipment. You develop a bottom-up cost estimate that suggests the project will cost $100,000, broken out as follows for each of the major work assignments:

✔ Design ($60,000)

✔ Development ($15,000)

✔ Testing ($5,000)

✔ Production ($20,000)

However, experience with similar projects suggests that approximately 40 percent of the total budget for this type of project should be spent on design, rather than the 60 percent that your estimate indicates. It appears that you've planned a design phase for a $150,000 project rather than for a $100,000 project.

You have two choices: You can either reexamine the activities under design to see whether you can devise an alternative strategy or you can request an additional $50,000 for your project. Whatever you do, don't just arbitrarily change the numbers without a strategy for how you will perform the necessary work for the new figures!

Identify all issues and uncertainties as you develop your project budget estimate. Develop plans for managing their potential impact on your project in a risk-management plan. See Chapter 14 for a more detailed discussion.

# Part II
# Organizing the Troops

The 5th Wave          By Rich Tennant

"...and what makes you think you're a leader of men all of a sudden?"

# In this part . . .

The key to successful projects is people — using their capabilities to the fullest, encouraging their mutually supportive work efforts, and sustaining their ongoing commitment to your project's success.

In this part, I identify the various people who affect the work environment in a project-oriented organization. I suggest how you can define the roles that team members will play on your project and approaches for encouraging people to work together supportively.

# Chapter 6

# The Who and the How of Project Management

*In This Chapter*

▶ Distinguishing the project organization from the traditional organization

▶ Clarifying the roles of different people in the matrix organization

▶ Recognizing key tips for increasing the chances for success

*I*n the traditional work environment, your supervisor gives you work assignments, completes your performance appraisals, approves your salary increases, and authorizes your promotions. However, increasing numbers of organizations are moving away from this traditional structure toward one in which people other than your functional manager also direct your work assignments. This new set of working relationships supports faster and more effective response to the diverse array of projects your organization typically performs.

Working successfully in this new project-oriented organization requires that you recognize the different people who define and influence your work environment, understand their unique roles, and know how to work with them to create the greatest chances for successfully completing your projects.

# Defining the Organizational Environment

Over the years, projects have evolved from organizational afterthoughts to major vehicles for conducting current business and developing future capabilities. The approaches for organizing and managing projects have evolved, as well.

## Centralized structure

The traditional or centralized approach for handling projects within an organization is illustrated in Figure 6-1. In this structure, individual units are established to handle all work in particular specialty areas, such as human resources, training, or information systems.

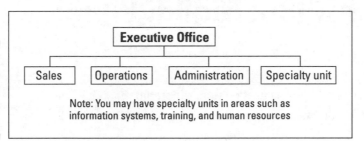

Figure 6-1:
A centralized
structure for
administering
projects.

Note: You may have specialty units in areas such as information systems, training, and human resources

Each unit reports to a manager at the corporate level, and any needs that arise in the organization for projects in a particular specialty area are submitted to the appropriate organizational unit. As an example, if the manufacturing group needs a new production-control system, the information systems unit would be asked to develop it.

This is also referred to as a *fixed-group structure,* because the specialty areas are established parts of the organization. People proficient in the technical skills and knowledge required to perform typical projects are permanently assigned to the group.

Working on projects within this structure offers certain benefits:

- ✔ **Centralized control over project selection:** All project requests are submitted to the manager of a group. The manager then chooses which projects to perform, based upon the relative benefits to the organization, other priority factors that may be identified, and the amount of time staff has available to do the required work.

- ✔ **One set of management procedures and reporting systems for all projects:** A consistent set of management procedures can be established to guide essential group processes, such as change management, conflict resolution, decision making, and project-progress reviews. Information systems needed to support these processes can be developed to support consistent planning and management of all projects performed by the group.

- ✔ **Established working relationships among people who are on your project team:** Projects assigned to your group are performed by combinations of the people employed in your unit. Therefore, over time you become familiar with each person's skills, knowledge, and operating style. You also come to know which people you can count on to honor their promises and commitments.

✓ **Clearly established lines of authority to more easily set priorities and resolve conflicts:** All project assignments are made or approved by the director of your specialty area. Therefore, choices for how to resolve conflicting demands on your time can be made by one person.

✓ **Clear authority that increases pressure for people to honor their commitments:** The specialty area's manager completes the performance appraisals for the unit's staff. Therefore, how you complete your project assignments can be directly reflected in your performance appraisals.

✓ **Clearly defined career path for people in the unit:** Promotions and increased job responsibilities depend upon your successful performance on your project assignments. This further reinforces the chances that people will successfully complete their project tasks.

However, working in a centralized structure also presents the following challenges:

✓ **Slow response time to project requests:** Groups throughout the organization are competing against each other for the services of a specialty area with a fixed number of staff. The size of the staff may cause certain projects to be delayed. In fact, the very process of having to justify performing one project rather than others submitted from all over the organization may take a significant amount of time.

✓ **Difficult to manage the peaks and valleys in staff workloads:** Because people are assigned full time to be in a specialty group, you're looking for project work to keep them busy for close to 100 percent of their time. Unfortunately, project requests don't always come in a smooth stream, and the requests you do receive may not require the services of people who are available at that time.

✓ **People's lack of familiarity with areas that request their area's services:** People in specialty units are hired for their technical proficiency with the types of projects the unit normally performs. However, they often have limited experience with the business areas requesting their services. As an example, a person from an information services group assigned to develop a repair parts inventory-control system may have extensive experience with inventory control systems but little or no experience with the repair parts operation in your organization.

## Functional structure

The functional structure was developed to be more responsive to needs of different organizational areas. In the *functional* structure, separate units addressing the same specialty are established in the organization's different functional groups, as illustrated in Figure 6-2. As an example, you may have three separate information services units assigned to sales, operations, and administration, respectively. Each specialty unit would respond only to the requests of the functional group in which it's located.

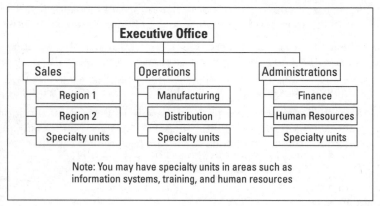

**Figure 6-2:**
A functional structure for administering projects.

The functional structure is a fixed-group structure, because the specialty units are permanent parts of the organization. As such, it offers many of the advantages of the centralized structure that are listed in the "Centralized structure" section. In addition,

- ✔ **People in the specialty unit have a better understanding of the functional area that they'll support.** Because each specialty unit only addresses the needs of one functional group, you can staff the unit with people who are both technically proficient in the unit's area of expertise and experienced in the functional group's operations.

- ✔ **Organizational units don't have to compete with one another to get the support of their specialty groups.** A specialty unit addresses only the needs of the functional group in which it's located. This reduces the competitiveness and tension that arise when groups compete for scarce resources from the same pool.

However, the functional structure also raises the following concerns:

- ✔ **Possibility that different work procedures and reporting systems will be used to guide projects in the same specialty area.** Because each functional group has its own specialty units, each of those specialty units can set up and use its own systems and procedures.

- ✔ **More difficult to make major investments in equipment and facilities needed to support a unit's technical work.** Suppose your organization's sales and marketing group and operations group both had their own publications units. Suppose further that both units wanted to buy a new document printer and sorter that cost $100,000. Both groups had $75,000 in their budgets that they could spend on such a machine, and each estimated it had work to keep the machine busy about 60 percent of the time. Neither group by itself had sufficient workload to justify the purchase or sufficient funds to make it. However, the two units working together would have both sufficient need and sufficient funds to buy one machine.

✔ **Chance for overlap or duplication among projects in the same specialty area performed for different organizational groups.** Because groups in the same specialty area are located in different parts of the organization, there's no requirement for the groups to tell each other what they're working on or when they get similar or overlapping project requests. In fact, sometimes one group undertakes a project similar to one being handled by another unit, because it wants to retain technical and administrative control. Unfortunately, this often results in duplicate or wasted effort.

## *Matrix structure*

With increasing frequency, projects in today's organizations involve and affect many functional areas. Successful performance requires that these different areas work in concert to produce results that address people's individual and collective needs.

*Matrix management* was devised to enable a quick and efficient response to projects that must be performed under these conditions. Figure 6.3 illustrates that, in a matrix management environment, people from different parts of the organization are assigned to work on projects as they are created. The project manager and team members may be assigned to the project for less than or equal to 100 percent of their time.

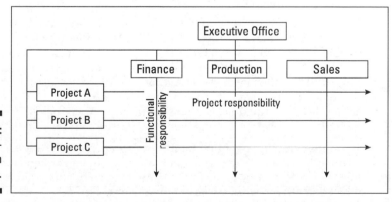

**Figure 6-3:**
Matrix-
organization
structure.

Matrix management offers numerous benefits, including the following:

- **Teams can be assembled rapidly.** You have a larger resource pool from which to choose your project team so you don't have to wait for a select few people to finish their current assignments before they can start on your project. Additionally, this approach reduces the need to have to go through the time-consuming process of hiring someone new from the outside.

- **Scarce expertise can be applied to different projects, as needed.** Often, your project may require a small amount of effort from a person with highly specialized knowledge or skills. Your project alone couldn't provide full-time support for this person, but he or she could be supported by working part time on several projects.

- **It's easier to get buy-in from team member's functional units.** Units that have to work on a project or will be affected by its outcome are more likely to support the project if they're confident that the project team hears their concerns and issues.

- **Consistent systems and procedures can be used for projects of the same type.** In a matrix environment, a single functional group sets procedures for how work in its specialty area will be done. Because this group lends its staff to work on different projects throughout the organization, members of the group perform their work in accordance with the technical standards and approaches that their functional group has established.

For all its potential benefits, the matrix environment also introduces some new challenges that must be successfully addressed:

- **Team members respond to two different managers.** The team member's functional manager coordinates his or her assignments to different projects, completes the person's performance appraisal, and approves requests for leave. The project manager coordinates project work assignments and project team support.

- **Team members working on multiple projects may have to address competing demands for their time.** Each team member has at least two people giving him or her direction — a project manager and a functional manager. In addition, if the team member is working on more than one project, he or she may have more than one project manager. Some of these people who have some claim to the team member's time may be at similar levels in the organization's hierarchy, which makes it even more difficult to resolve conflicting demands for the person's time.

- **Team members' may not be familiar with each other's styles and knowledge.** Because team members may not have worked extensively together before, they may require some time to become comfortable with each other's work styles and behaviors.

- **Potential lack of focus on your project team and its goals, as opposed to each person's individual assignment.** Team members often represent their functional areas on different project teams and perform tasks associated with those areas. A procurement specialist from the purchasing department may, for example, be responsible for buying equipment and supplies for all projects on which he or she is a team member. In such a case, the specialist may become less concerned that a project's overall goals are met and more concerned that goods and services are bought on time and in accordance with the organization's procurement policies.

✔ **Multiple work processes and reporting systems used by different team members.** Team members will be familiar with the systems and processes used in their functional units. They'll have to be encouraged to develop common procedures and systems that all team members can use for their specific projects.

# Recognizing the Key Players in a Matrix Environment

In a matrix environment, the following people play critical roles in every project's success:

✔ **Project manager:** The person ultimately responsible for the successful completion of the project

✔ **Project team members:** People responsible for successfully performing individual project activities

✔ **Functional managers:** The team members' direct-line supervisors

✔ **Upper management:** People in charge of the organization's major business units

## Project manager

If you're the project manager, you're responsible for all aspects of the project. (See Chapter 8 for definitions of authority, responsibility, and accountability.) This doesn't mean you have to do everything yourself, but it does mean that you have to see that it all gets done satisfactorily. In this role, you're specifically responsible for:

✔ Determining objectives, schedule, and resource budgets

✔ Ensuring you have a clear, feasible project plan for how you'll reach your performance targets

✔ Creating and sustaining a focused and committed team

✔ Selecting or creating your team's operating practices and procedures

✔ Accomplishing objectives, within time and budget targets

✔ Monitoring performance against plans and dealing with any problems that arise

✔ Resolving priority, work approach, or interpersonal conflicts

✔ Controlling project changes

✔ Reporting on project activities

✔ Keeping your clients informed and committed

✔ Contributing to your team members' performance appraisals

On occasion, you may hear people use the terms *project director* and *project leader,* both of which sound similar to "project manager." Check with your organization, but usually project manager and project director describe the same position. Project leader, however, is a different story. People often think of management as focusing on things and leadership as focusing on people, or management as dealing with established procedures and leadership as dealing with change. Therefore, using the term "project leader" emphasizes that the person responsible for project success should stimulate a shared vision and positive interpersonal relationships as key factors in achieving project success. But again, check with your organization to be sure they are using the term "project leader" in this way. Often it, too, is just used as another term for project manager!

## Team members

Team members must satisfy the requests of both their functional managers and their project manager. As a team member, your responsibilities related to your project assignments include the following:

✔ Ensuring that you perform your tasks in accordance with the highest standards of technical excellence in your field

✔ Performing your assignments on time and within budget

✔ Maintaining the special skills and knowledge you need to do your work

In addition, you're responsible for working with and supporting your team members' project efforts. Such help may entail the following:

✔ Considering the effect your actions may have on your team members' tasks

✔ Identifying situations and problems that may affect team members' tasks

✔ Keeping your team members informed of your progress, accomplishments, and any problems you encounter

# Functional managers

Functional managers are responsible for orchestrating their staff's assignments among different projects, as well as providing the resources to allow their staff to perform their assignments in accordance with the highest standards of technical excellence. Specifically, they are responsible for the following:

✔ Developing or approving plans that specify the type, timing, and amount of resources needed to do tasks in their area of specialty

✔ Ensuring team members are available to perform their assigned tasks when needed and for the amount of time promised

✔ Providing technical expertise and guidance to help team members solve problems related to their project assignments

✔ Providing the equipment and facilities for a person to do his or her work

✔ Helping people maintain their technical skills and knowledge

✔ Ensuring consistent methodological approaches on all projects throughout the organization dealing with a particular area

✔ Completing team members' performance appraisals

✔ Recognizing performance with salary increases, promotions, and job assignments

✔ Approving team members' requests for annual leave, administrative leave, training, and other activities that will take time away from the job

# Upper management

Upper management creates the organizational environment; oversees the development and use of operating policies, procedures, and practices; and funds and encourages the development of required information systems. More specifically, they're responsible for

✔ Setting policies and procedures for addressing resource priorities and conflicts

✔ Creating and maintaining labor and financial information systems

✔ Providing facilities and equipment to support the performance of project work

✔ Defining the limits of managers' decision-making authority

# Working Successfully in a Matrix Environment

Avoiding the pitfalls of a matrix environment requires that you recognize the diverse cast of characters that play a role in your project and develop ways of focusing and supporting a team of players who haven't worked extensively together before (and may feel organizational pressures pulling them in different directions).

The following tips can help you successfully navigate the waters:

✔ **Create and continually reinforce a team identity.**

- **Clarify team vision and working relationships.** As soon as your team is formed, work with the members to develop a clear picture of your project's mission that people understand and support. Give people an opportunity to become familiar with each other's work styles.

- **Define team procedures.** Encourage your team to develop its own work procedures, rather than to allow people to use the approaches of their respective functional groups.

- **Clarify each person's authority.** Team members may have to represent their functional areas when making project decisions. Clarify the level of authority they have and who has the authority they don't have.

- **Be aware of and attend to your team's functioning.** Help people establish comfortable and productive interpersonal relationships. Continue to support these relationships throughout your project.

- **Be sure one person is assigned as project manager — with overall coordinative responsibilities.** The project manager will encourage all team members to keep the overall goals of the team in mind and focus attention on the interfaces between activities being handled by different team members.

✔ **Create team member buy-in.**

- **Get commitment.** In a matrix environment, team members most often have no line authority over each other. Therefore, the only reason people do the work you want is to respond to the request of someone else whom they think does have the power, or because they've made a personal decision to do it. Work with people initially and throughout your project to encourage them to commit to achieving your project's goals.

- **Get to know other people's styles.** The more comfortable you make the work environment for others, the more they'll want to spend time in that environment.

✔ **Elicit support from others in the environment.**

- **Get a champion.** Because you don't have authority over the people who can affect your chances for success, get an ally who does — or who at least is at a similar level — as soon as possible.

- **Ask for and appreciate your team members' functional manager's support.** Thanking a functional manager for supporting his or her staff and allowing the staff to honor their project commitments encourages the manager to provide similar support for you again in the future.

✔ **Develop procedures to address the more common problems.**

- **Plan in sufficient detail.** Work with team members to clearly and concisely define the required work to be performed and the specific roles and responsibilities for all activities, in order to estimate how much effort people will have to invest in their assignments and when.

- **Identify and address conflicts promptly.** Conflicts arise frequently in a matrix environment, given people's diverse responsibilities, different styles, and lack of experience working together. Encourage people to identify and discuss conflicts as soon as they occur. Develop systems and procedures to deal with conflicts promptly, before they get out of hand.

- **Encourage open communication among team members, especially regarding perceived problems and frustrations.** The earlier you hear about problems, the more time you'll have to deal with them. Also, the more comfortable team members are working in your project's environment, the more time they'll want to spend there.

- **Establish an upper management oversight committee to monitor project performance and address conflicts that arise.** Project and functional managers are concerned with meeting their individual organization commitments. Unfortunately, these diverse commitments often result in conflicting demands on people's time and effort. An upper-management oversight committee ensures that the overall impact on the organization is considered when deciding how to resolve such conflicts.

# Chapter 7

# Involving the Right People in Your Project

• • • • • • • • • • • • • • • • • • • • • • • • • • • • • • • • • • • • • • • • • • • • • • •

## In This Chapter

▶ Understanding your project's diverse audiences

▶ Creating a project audience list

▶ Identifying drivers, supporters, and observers

▶ Determining who has authority in your project

• • • • • • • • • • • • • • • • • • • • • • • • • • • • • • • • • • • • • • • • • • • • • • •

*O*ften, a project is like an iceberg: Nine-tenths of it lurks below the surface. You receive an assignment and you think you know what it entails and who has to be involved. Then, one by one, new people emerge as the project unfolds — people who will affect what you need to accomplish and how you approach the project.

You run two risks when you don't involve key people or groups in your project in a timely manner. First, you may miss important information that could affect the project's performance and ultimate success. Second, and sometimes more painful, you may insult someone. You can be sure that when someone feels slighted or insulted, he or she will take steps to make sure you don't do it again in the future!

As soon as you begin to think about your project, start to identify people who may play a role. This chapter shows you how to identify these candidates; decide whether, when, and how to involve them; and determine who has the authority to make critical decisions.

# Understanding Your Project's Audience

A *project audience* is any person or group that supports, is affected by, or is interested in your project. Your project audiences can be inside or outside your organization, and should be identified in a written *project audience list.* Knowing your project's audiences helps you to:

> ✔ Plan if, when, and how to involve them.

> ✔ Determine whether the scope of the project is bigger or smaller than originally anticipated.

You may hear other terms used to refer to project audiences, but each term addresses only some of the people you would include on your complete project audience list. Here are some examples:

> ✔ A *stakeholder list* identifies people and groups who'll support or be affected by your project. The stakeholder list most often doesn't include people outside of your organization or those who are merely interested in your project.

> ✔ A *distribution list* identifies people who receive copies of written project communications. Distribution lists are often out of date. Sometimes people are on the list because no one thought to remove them; other times, people are on the list because no one wants to run the risk of insulting them by removing them. In either case, their presence doesn't ensure that they actually support, are affected by, or are interested in your project.

> ✔ *Team members* are people whose work is directed by the project manager. All team members are part of the project audience, but the audience list includes more than just the team members.

## Using categories to create an audience list

Start to develop a project audience list as soon as you begin to think about your project. Continue to add and subtract names until the project is finished. To increase your chances of identifying all appropriate people, develop your audience list in categories — you're less likely to overlook people if you consider exactly who from the accounts payable group in the finance department should be included than if you try to determine all of the people from the entire organization at the same time.

A client of mine asked me to review an audience list he had prepared for a multiyear project that would touch every aspect of his organization. He handed me a list that included over 300 names, organized alphabetically, and he asked me if I thought anyone was missing. The problem was, I had no way of knowing, by looking at an uncategorized list of 300 names, whether anyone was missing. I had no idea why the people in the list had been included or what areas they were supposed to represent.

Start your audience list by developing a hierarchical grouping of categories that covers the major areas from which audiences would be identified. I often use the following list:

- ✔ **Internal:** People and groups inside your organization, such as the following:

  - **Upper management:** Executive-level management responsible for the general oversight of all organization operations

  - **Requester:** The person who came up with the idea for your project and all of the people through whom the request passed before it was given to you

  - **Project manager:** Person with overall responsibility for successfully completing the project

  - **Team members:** People whose work is directed by the project manager

  - **Groups normally involved:** Groups typically involved in most projects in the organization, such as human resources, finance, contracts, and the legal department

  - **Groups needed just for this project:** Groups or people with special knowledge related to this project

- ✔ **External:** People and groups outside your organization, such as the following:

  - **Clients or customers:** People or groups that buy your organization's products and services

  - **Collaborators:** Groups or other organizations with which you may pursue joint ventures related to your project

  - **Vendors, suppliers, and contractors:** Organizations that provide human, physical, or financial resources to help you perform your project's work

  - **Regulators:** Government agencies that establish regulations and guidelines that govern some aspect of your project work

  - **Professional societies:** Groups of professionals that may influence or be interested in your project

  - **The public:** The local, national, and international community of people who may be affected by or interested in your project

## Dealing with reality rather than ignoring it

A number of years ago, I ran into a woman who had attended my project management training session some months earlier. After initial pleasantries, she said the training session had been very helpful and that she had already put into practice several techniques I had discussed. However, she said that she had tried to develop an audience list and had found that it was of no use at all.

She then explained to me what had happened. Her boss had assigned her a project that had to be finished in two months. Remembering the training session, she immediately set out to develop an audience list. But much to her horror, her initial audience list included over 150 names! How, she wondered, was she supposed to involve over 150 people in a two-month project? She concluded that the audience list was clearly useless.

In fact, her audience list had fulfilled its purpose perfectly. Apparently, she felt that each of the people on her list would in some way affect the success of her project. Identifying them at the start of her project gave her three options.

✔ She could plan how and when to involve each person during the project.

✔ She could assess whether the potential consequences of not involving one or more of her audiences would be acceptable.

✔ If she felt she couldn't ignore any of the audiences identified, she could discuss with her boss extending the project deadline or reducing its scope.

You can develop your audience list further by identifying groups or people within each of these categories, continuing in this way until you have identified specific audiences in each area by name and position.

As you develop your audience list, be sure not to overlook the following potential audiences:

✔ **All support groups:** These people don't tell you what you should do; instead, their job is to help you accomplish the goals of the project. If support groups know about your project early, they can fit you into their work schedules more readily. They may also be able to tell you information about their capability or the processes they manage that may influence what you can hope to accomplish. Such groups include:

  • Human resources

  • Quality

  • Legal services

- Procurement or contracting

- Finance

- Security

- Facilities

- Information services

✔ **End users of your project's products:** In some cases, you may omit end users on your audience list because you're not aware of who they are. In other situations, you may think you have taken their concerns into account through the use of *liaisons* — people who represent the interests of the end users.

A major international bank had spent millions of dollars revising and upgrading its information system. The people in charge of the project had worked closely with special liaisons in Europe, who were chosen to represent the interests of the local bank personnel — the people who would enter and retrieve data from the system. When the system was turned on, a fatal problem was immediately identified: Over 90 percent of the local bank personnel in Europe were non-English speaking, but all of the system documentation had been written in English. The entire system was unusable!

The system designers had spent substantial time and money working with the liaisons to ensure that the interests and needs of the system users would be identified and addressed. However, the liaisons had apparently misinterpreted their roles: They thought they were to identify issues from their own experience rather than to identify and share issues raised by the local bank personnel. It turned out that English was the primary language of all the liaisons, so the issue of language was never identified. Putting both the liaisons and the local bank personnel on the audience list would have reminded the project staff to be sure that the concerns of the local bank personnel had been considered.

✔ **People who will maintain or support the final product:** People who will service your project's products will affect the continuing success of these products after they are introduced. Involving them throughout your project gives them a chance to offer suggestions to make your project's products easier to maintain and support. It also allows them to become familiar with the products and see how best to include their maintenance in existing procedures.

Suppose you're asked to coordinate your organization's annual blood drive. Table 7-1 illustrates some of the groups and people you may include in your project's audience list.

| Table 7-1 | | A Portion of an Audience List |
|-----------|--|-------------------------------|
| *Category* | *Subcategory* | *Audiences* |
| Internal | | |
| | Upper management | Executive oversight committee<br>Vice president of sales and marketing<br>Vice president of operations<br>Vice president of administration |
| | Team members | Customer service representative<br>Community relations representative<br>Administrative assistant |
| | Groups normally included | Finance<br>Facilities<br>Legal |
| | Groups or people with special knowledge or interest | Project manager and team from last year's blood drive<br>Public relations |
| External | | |
| | Clients, customers | Donors from prior years<br>Potential donors |
| | Regulatory agencies | Local Board of Health |
| | Vendors, contractors | Nurses who will be in attendance<br>Food service provider<br>Landlord of facility where the drive will be held |
| | Professional societies | American Medical Association<br>American Association of Blood Banks |
| | Public | Local community<br>Local newspapers<br>Local television and radio stations |

# Improving the completeness and utility of your audience list

To ensure your audience list is most useful and complete, consider the following guidelines as you develop your list:

✔ **Eventually identify each audience by position description and name.** You may, for example, initially identify people from sales and marketing as an audience. Eventually, however, you want to specify the particular people to be considered from the sales and marketing group, such as the brand manager for XYZ product, Sharon Wilson.

✔ **Speak with a wide range of people.** Check with people in different organizational units, from different disciplines, and with different tenures in the organization. Ask every person if he or she can think of anyone else with whom you should speak. The more people you speak with, the less likely you'll overlook someone important.

✔ **Allow sufficient time to develop your audience list.** Start to develop your list as soon as you're assigned the project. The longer you think about your project, the more potential audiences you'll identify. Continue to check with people throughout the project to find out more about additional audiences they may identify.

✔ **Include audiences who may play a role at any time during your project.** Your only job at this stage is to identify names so that you won't forget them. At a later point, you'll decide if, when, and how to involve them (see the "Identifying the Driver, Supporters, and Observers in Your Audience" section, later in this chapter).

✔ **Include team members' functional managers.** Include each team member's *functional manager* (that is, the person to whom the project manager or team member directly reports) on your audience list. Even though functional managers don't directly perform project tasks, they can help to ensure that the project manager and team members devote all the time they originally promised to the project.

✔ **Separately include a person's name on the audience list for every different role he or she will play.** Suppose your boss will also be providing expert technical advice to your project team. Include your boss's name twice — once as your direct supervisor and once as the technical expert. If your boss is subsequently promoted or leaves the company, listing him or her twice reminds you that a new person is now fulfilling the role of your direct supervisor and must be brought up to speed accordingly.

✔ **Continue to add and remove names from your audience list throughout your project.** Your audience list evolves as you learn more about your project and as your project changes. Encourage people involved in your project to continually identify new candidates as they think of them.

✔ **When in doubt, write down a person's name.** Your interest is to avoid overlooking someone who may play an important part in your project. Identifying a potential audience doesn't mean you have to involve them; it means that you must consider them. It's a lot easier to eliminate a name when you determine that the person isn't part of your audience than it is to add a name (that you initially overlooked) later in the project.

## Developing an audience list template

An *audience list template* is a predesigned audience list that contains audiences typically included for projects similar to yours. An audience list template reflects the cumulative experience gained from doing numerous projects of a particular type. As you perform more projects, you add audiences to the template that you overlooked in earlier projects and remove ones that proved not to be needed. Using templates can save you time and improve your accuracy.

Suppose you prepare the budget for your department each quarter. After doing a number of these budgets, you know most of the people who'll give you the necessary information, draft and print the document, and have to approve the final budget. Each time you finish another budget, you revise your audience list template to include any new information you learned from your recently completed project. The next time you prepare your quarterly budget project, you begin your audience list with the audience list template that you've been developing from your past projects. You then add and subtract names as appropriate for this particular budget preparation.

Templates can save time and improve accuracy. However, don't inhibit people's active involvement in the development of the audience list by using a template that's too polished. Lack of involvement by certain key people can lead to lack of commitment to the project's success.

When using templates, keep the following in mind:

- ✔ **Develop templates for frequently performed tasks, as well as for entire projects.** Templates for kicking off the annual blood drive or submitting a newly developed drug to the Food and Drug Administration are valuable. But so are templates for individual tasks that are part of these projects, such as awarding a competitive contract and having a document printed. Templates for tasks can be incorporated into a larger audience list for an entire project for which these tasks will be performed.

- ✔ **Focus on position description rather than name of prior audience.** Identify an audience as "accounts payable manager" instead of "Bill Miller." People come and go, but functions endure. For each specific project, you can fill in the appropriate names.

- ✔ **Develop and modify your audience list template from previous projects that actually worked, not from plans that looked good.** Often, you develop a detailed audience list at the start of your project but you don't revise the list during the project to add audiences that you overlooked in your initial planning. If you only update your audience list template with information from the audience list that you prepared at the start of your project, your template won't reflect what you learned during the actual performance of the project.

✔ **Use templates as starting points, not ending points.** Make clear to those involved that the audience list template is the start of your audience list for your project, not the final list. Every project differs in some ways from similar ones in the past. If the template isn't critically examined, you may miss people who weren't involved in previous projects but who need to be considered for this one.

✔ **Continually update your templates to reflect the experience gained from performing different projects.** The post project evaluation (see Chapter 15) is an excellent time to review and critique your original audience list. At the end of your project, take a moment to revise your audience list template to reflect the lessons learned.

# Image is everything

Two sales representatives for the same company had very different experiences when trying to develop an audience list for their new projects. Each had just signed a contract with a customer to deliver and install some complex computer equipment. Both realized that identifying and involving the right people would be critical to ensuring their projects' success. So each immediately started to prepare an audience list.

✔ The first representative put her audience list template on a set of overheads, using a commercially-available graphics package. When she introduced the template to the staff of her client company, they were impressed with the high quality of the overheads and her entire presentation. However, despite her repeated questions, not one person could think of any people to add or remove. Although she was uncomfortable using her template as the project audience list with no input from the company staff, she had no choice. Throughout the entire project, staff from the company continually identified other people who were in some way involved in the project, often causing considerable delays and

duplication of work. The project came in late and over budget.

✔ The second representative handwrote her audience list template on several sheets of chart paper. As soon as she began her presentation to her client, participants began to offer suggestions for additional people to include and some to remove. After a brief but intense session, she and the participants had developed an entirely revised and much more comprehensive audience list. As the project unfolded, she was able to anticipate and plan for the involvement of all key personnel. The project was completed on time and within budget.

Why the different results? Both sales representatives were honestly interested in getting their respective clients involved in the development of their audience lists. However, the first person's presentation was so polished that her client didn't believe she really wanted their comments and suggestions. The second person's presentation convinced her audience that she really wanted their involvement. And the results reflected the difference.

# Identifying the Drivers, Supporters, and Observers in Your Audience

After identifying everyone in your project audience, determine which of the following groups they fall into, to decide whether, how, and when to involve them.

- ✔ **Drivers:** People who have some say in defining the results that your project is to achieve. These are the people for whom you're performing your project.

- ✔ **Supporters:** The people who help you perform your project. Supporters include those who authorize the resources for your project as well as those who actually work on it.

- ✔ **Observers:** People who are interested in the activities and results of your project. Observers have no say in what your project is to accomplish and they're not actively involved in supporting it. However, your project may affect them at some point in the future.

Consider that an information technology group has just been assigned a project to modify the layout and content of a monthly sales report that's prepared for all sales representatives. The project was requested by the vice president of sales and approved by the chief information officer (CIO), the boss of the head of the information technology group.

- ✔ **Drivers:** The vice president of sales is a driver for the project, because he has specific reasons for asking that the report be revised; the CIO is a potential driver, because she may be looking to achieve certain capabilities through the performance of this project; individual sales representatives are all drivers for this project, because they are looking to get certain specific capabilities from the redesigned report.

- ✔ **Supporters:** The systems analyst who will design the revised report, the training specialist who will train users in how to use it, and the vice president of finance who authorizes the funds for printing the changes in the system operating manual are all supporters.

- ✔ **Observers:** The head of the customer service department, who is curious how your project will affect the chances that an improved problem-tracking system will be developed this year, is a potential observer.

Beware of supporters who try to act like drivers. As in the previous example, the analyst responsible for finalizing the content and format of the revised monthly sales report may try to include certain additional data items that she thinks may be helpful. However, the drivers determine whether they want specific data to be in the report. The analyst determines only whether it's possible and what it will cost.

## Finding a project champion

A *project champion* is a person in a high position in the organization who strongly supports your project; advocates for your project in disputes, planning meetings, and review sessions; and takes whatever actions are necessary to help ensure the successful completion of your project.

As soon as you start your planning, find out if your project has a champion. If it doesn't, try to recruit one. An effective champion should have the following characteristics:

✔ Sufficient power and authority to be able to resolve conflicts over resources, schedules, and technical issues

✔ A keen interest in the results your project will produce

✔ A willingness to have his or her name cited as a strong supporter of your project

Keep in mind that the same person can be both a driver and a supporter. The vice president of sales is a driver for the project to develop a revised monthly sales report. The vice president of sales is also a supporter if he has to transfer funds from the sales department budget to pay for developing the report.

## Deciding when to involve them

Projects pass through the following five stages as they progress from an initial idea through completion (see Chapter 1 for detailed explanations of these phases):

✔ Conceive

✔ Define

✔ Start

✔ Perform

✔ Close

Plan to involve drivers, supporters, and observers in each phase of your project, depending on the roles they'll play.

### Drivers

Involve drivers from the start to the finish of your project.

✔ **Conceive phase:** Heavy involvement. Identify and speak with as many drivers as possible in this phase. Their desires and your assessment of feasibility will influence whether your project should be pursued. If you uncover additional drivers later in your planning or while performing project tasks, be sure to explore with them the issues that led to the creation of your project and to identify and assess any special expectations they may have.

✔ **Define phase:** Moderate to heavy involvement. Consult with drivers during this phase to ensure that your project plan addresses their needs and expectations. Have them formally approve your plan before you proceed to start the actual project work.

✔ **Start phase:** Moderate involvement. Announce and introduce the drivers to the project team. Having the drivers talk about their needs and interests reinforces the importance of the project and helps team members form a more accurate picture of what needs to be accomplished. Having the drivers meet team members increases the drivers' confidence that the project will be successfully completed.

✔ **Perform phase:** Moderate involvement. Keep drivers apprised of project accomplishments and progress to sustain their ongoing interest and enthusiasm. Involving drivers during this phase also ensures that the results being achieved are meeting their needs.

✔ **Close phase:** Heavy involvement. Have drivers assess the project's results and determine whether their needs and expectations were met. Identify any recommendations they may have for improving performance on similar projects in the future.

### Supporters

Just as with drivers, involve supporters from the start to the finish of your project.

✔ **Concept phase:** Moderate involvement. Wherever possible, have key supporters assess the feasibility of meeting the expectations of the drivers. If key supporters are identified later in the project, have them confirm the feasibility of meeting the expectations that have been set.

✔ **Definition phase:** Heavy involvement. Supporters are the major contributors to the project plan. Because they do or facilitate all of the work, have them determine technical approaches, schedules, and resources required. Also have them formally commit to all aspects of the plan.

✔ **Start phase:** Heavy involvement. Familiarize all supporters with the planned project work. Clarify how the supporters will work together to achieve the project results. Have the supporters decide how they'll communicate, resolve conflicts, and make decisions throughout the project.

✔ **Perform phase:** Heavy involvement. By definition, supporters will be performing the work of the project at this time. Keep them informed of project progress, encourage them to identify any performance problems encountered or anticipated, and work with them to develop and implement solutions to these problems.

✔ **Close phase:** Heavy involvement. Have the supporters conclude their different tasks. Inform them of project accomplishments and recognize their role in the project's achievements. Elicit their suggestions for how future projects can be performed even more effectively.

### Observers

Choose those observers with whom you want to actively share information about your project. Involve them minimally throughout.

✔ **Concept phase:** Minimal involvement. Inform observers that your project exists and tell them what it'll produce.

✔ **Definition phase:** Minimal involvement. Inform observers about the planned outcomes and timeframes.

✔ **Start phase:** Minimal involvement. Tell them that the project has started and confirm the dates for planned intermediate and final milestones.

✔ **Performance phase:** Minimal involvement. Inform observers of key achievements during the project.

✔ **Close phase:** Minimal involvement. When the project is completed, inform observers about the project's products and results.

# Using different methods to keep them involved

Keeping drivers, supporters, and observers informed as you progress in your project is critical to the project's success. Choosing the right method can stimulate a group's continued interest and encourage them to actively support your work. Consider the following approaches for keeping your project audiences involved throughout your project:

✔ **One-on-one meetings:** Formal and informal discussions with one or two other people about project issues. One-on-one meetings are particularly useful for interactively exploring and clarifying special issues of interest to a small number of people.

✔ **Group meetings:** Planned sessions for some or all project team members or audiences. Smaller meetings are useful to brainstorm project issues, reinforce team-member roles, and develop mutual trust and respect among team members. Larger meetings are useful to present information of general interest.

✔ **Informal written correspondence:** Notes, memos, letters, and e-mail. Informal written correspondence helps you document informal discussions and share important project information.

✔ **Written approvals:** Formal, written agreement about a project product, schedule, or resource commitment or a technical approach to project work.

---

# Tips for effective involvement

Plan to involve drivers, supporters, and observers so they can make the greatest contribution to your project.

✔ **Involve people early in planning if they will have a role later on.** Give your audience the option to participate in planning, even if they won't perform their work until later in the project. Sometimes they can share information with you early on that will make performing their tasks easier. At the very least, they can reserve time to provide you the services you anticipate needing.

✔ **If you're concerned with the legality of involving an audience, check with your legal department or contracts office.** Suppose you're planning to award a competitive contract to buy certain equipment for your project. You'd like to know whether prospective bidders typically have this equipment on hand and how long after the contract is awarded it would take for you to receive it. However, you're afraid that speaking to potential contractors while you're still planning your project may tip them off that the procurement is coming and give rise to charges of favoritism by the unsuccessful bidders who didn't know

about the procurement in advance. Rather than just ignoring this important audience, check with your contracts office or legal department to determine how you can get the information you want and still maintain the integrity of the bidding process.

Remember to do the following:

✔ **Develop a plan with each key audience to meet their information needs and interests, as well as yours.** Determine what information they want and you feel they'll need, when you'll provide it to them, and in what format. In addition, clarify what you want from them, how they'll provide it to you, and when.

✔ **Always be sure you understand each audience's WIIFM (What's In It For Me).** Clarify why it's in each audience's interest to see your project succeed. Throughout your project, keep reminding them of the benefits they'll realize when your project is completed and the progress your project has made towards achieving those benefits. See more about identifying project benefits for different audiences in Chapter 12.

---

# Getting People with Sufficient Authority

*Authority* is the right to make project decisions that others must follow. Having opinions about how an aspect of the project should be addressed is different from having the authority to decide how it will be addressed. Mistaking a person's level of authority can lead to wasted time and money, as well as to frustration.

When determining your project's audiences, confirm that the people you've identified have sufficient authority to make the decisions necessary to perform their assigned tasks. If they don't, find out who does and how to bring those people into the process.

A client of mine attended a meeting to reach a final decision about the color that his group's new offices would be painted. All of the people working on the project to renovate and upgrade his group's offices were present. After intense discussions, all present agreed that the walls for the new office space would be painted a light gray.

One week later, the team member from the facilities department informed the rest of the team that his boss decided the color the group had chosen was too expensive and that they would have to choose another color. The entire meeting a week earlier had been a complete waste of everyone's time. Each person at that meeting had assumed that the others in attendance had the necessary authority to support whatever decision the group made. Had they realized beforehand that the facilities department representative didn't have this authority, they could have:

✔ Asked the representative from the facilities department to find out the criteria that would be considered when deciding whether particular colors could be used

✔ Developed and prioritized two or more alternatives and asked the representative from the facilities department to present them to his boss for final approval

✔ Invited the person who did have the authority to attend

✔ Postponed the meeting until the right people could attend

In your own projects, take the following steps to define each person's authority:

1. **Clarify each person's tasks and decisions.**

   Define with each person in the project audience what his or her tasks will be and what his or her role in the task will be. Will she just be working on it? Will she be asked to approve schedules, resource expenditures, or work approaches?

2. **Ask each person what authority he or she has regarding each decision and task.**

   Ask the person about her authority for individual tasks, rather than for all issues in a particular area. It's easier for a person to know with confidence that she can approve supply purchases for up to $5,000 than that she can approve all equipment purchases, no matter what type and how large.

   Clarify decisions that the person can make herself. For decisions needing someone else's approval, find out whose approval they need. (Just be sure to ask and not assume!)

3. **Ask people how they know what authority they have.**

   Does a written policy, procedure, or guideline confirm the authority? Did the person's boss tell her in conversation? Is the person just assuming?

**4. Check the history.**

Have you or others worked with this person in the past? Has she been overruled on decisions she said she was authorized to make?

**5. Has anything changed recently?**

Is the person new to the organization? To her current group? To her current position? Has the person recently started working for a new boss?

Reconfirm the information in these steps when the audience's decision-making assignments change. Suppose, for example, that you initially expect that individual purchases on your project will all be at or under $2,500. Bill, the team representative from the finance group, assures you that he has the authority to approve such purchases for your project without checking with his boss. You now find that you have to purchase a piece of equipment for $5,000. Be sure to verify with Bill that he can personally authorize this larger expenditure. If he can't, find out whose approval is also required.

# Chapter 8

# Defining Team Members' Roles and Responsibilities

### In This Chapter

▶ Defining authority, responsibility, and accountability

▶ Clarifying what you can and can't delegate

▶ Holding people accountable when you don't have direct authority over them

▶ Developing and using a Linear Responsibility Chart

▶ Understanding and dealing with a micromanager

*Y*our project team typically includes people from different parts of the organization, with different skill sets and operating styles. You may not have worked extensively with these people before. Your project usually has a tight time schedule, and your team members most likely are working on several other projects at the same time.

Success in this environment requires that you reach agreements about how you'll work with your team members to maximize everyone's contribution and minimize wasted time and mistakes. You need to develop an approach that gives you and others confidence that everyone will live up to their commitments. You need to understand the planned roles, and you need to be comfortable with them.

## Defining the Key Concepts

Use the following concepts to define and clarify how team members should relate to each other and to their assigned tasks:

> ✔ **Authority:** The ability to make binding decisions about your project's products, schedule, resources, and activities. Examples include your ability to sign purchase orders not to exceed $3,000 and your ability to change a scheduled date by no more than two weeks.

- ✔ **Responsibility:** The commitment to achieve specific results. An example is your promise to have a draft report ready by March 1.

- ✔ **Accountability:** Bringing consequences to bear based on people's performance. Having your boss reflect in your annual performance appraisal that you solved a difficult manufacturing problem is an example of accountability.

Many people think of accountability as a negative concept — if you foul up, you pay the price. This fear often causes people to shun positions in which they would be held accountable for performance. Paying a price when you foul up is certainly half of the concept. The other half, however, is that when you do a good job, you're rewarded. This positive reinforcement is a far more effective way to encourage high-quality results.

These three terms address similar issues. However, each one is a distinct element that's required to define and reinforce team relationships.

Consider authority and responsibility, as follows:

- ✔ **Similarity:** Both authority and responsibility are upfront agreements. Before you start your project, you agree who can make which decisions and who will ensure that particular results are achieved.

- ✔ **Difference:** Authority focuses on process, while responsibility focuses on outcomes. Authority defines the decisions you can make but does not mention the results you have to achieve. Responsibility addresses the results you will accomplish, with no mention of the decisions you can make to reach your desired outcomes.

Consider responsibility and accountability, as follows:

- ✔ **Similarity:** Both responsibility and accountability focus on results.

- ✔ **Difference:** Responsibility is a before-the-fact agreement, while accountability is an after-the-fact process.

People who make promises, fail to keep their promises, and experience no resulting consequences create some of the worst frustrations in a project environment. It's essential that you keep in mind the following guidelines for accountability:

- ✔ **If you're responsible, you should be held accountable.** In other words, if you make a promise, you should always face consequences based on how well you honor your promise.

- ✔ **If you're not responsible, you shouldn't be held accountable.** If something goes wrong but you weren't responsible for ensuring that it was handled correctly, you shouldn't face negative consequences. (Of course, you shouldn't receive positive accolades if things go well in this case, either.)

Holding people accountable when they aren't responsible is called *scapegoating*. This process of assigning blame to the closest person when things go wrong only encourages people to avoid dealing with you in the future.

# Assigning Project Roles

*To delegate* is to give away something you have. (I know that many other definitions of delegating exist, but I'll keep it simple; to delegate is to give away.) You delegate for three reasons:

✔ To free yourself up to do other tasks

✔ To have the most qualified person make decisions

✔ To develop another person's ability to handle additional assignments prudently and successfully

## Determining what you can and can't delegate

Follow these two guidelines when assigning project roles:

✔ You can delegate authority, but you can't delegate responsibility.

✔ You can share responsibility.

Remember, too, that you can choose to transfer to another person the right to make decisions that you are empowered to make, but you can't rid yourself of the responsibility for the results of those decisions.

Suppose you have the authority to sign purchase orders for your project not to exceed $5,000. Suppose further that you aren't told not to give this authority to someone else, and no policy specifically prevents you from giving it to someone else. You could delegate some or all of this authority to Matt if you wanted to. That is, you could give Matt the authority to sign purchase orders for your project not to exceed $5,000. However, if Matt mistakenly bought ten reams of specialty paper for $3,000 instead of the five that he really needed, you would be responsible for the poor decision.

You can always take back authority that you delegated to someone else, but you can't blame the person for exercising that authority while he or she has it.

It's critical that you actively reinforce and support your delegations of authority. Suppose you've been the leader of a project team for the past two months, and Mary has been your assistant. Mary has been helping to deal with people's technical issues as follows:

- ✔ When someone runs into a technical problem, he or she discusses it with Mary.

- ✔ Mary analyzes the problem and decides how to address it.

- ✔ Mary discusses the problem with you and explains her proposed solution.

- ✔ If you agree with Mary's proposed solution, you ask her to implement it.

- ✔ If you don't agree with Mary's suggestion, you work with her to develop a more acceptable approach.

Yesterday, you told Mary that you wanted to change the way she deals with technical issues. You explained that, from now on, she won't have to pass her proposed solutions by you before implementing them. After discussing this with her, you told the other team members about the new procedure.

This morning, Joe came to Mary to discuss a problem he was having with a contractor. After listening to the problem, Mary gave Joe very specific instructions for how to deal with it. As soon as Joe left Mary's office, however, he called you on the phone. He recounted the problem he had discussed with Mary and her proposed solution, and he asked you if you agreed with the approach Mary had recommended.

You now have a dilemma. On the one hand, you want to support Mary's newly delegated authority to develop and implement solutions to technical problems on her own. On the other hand, you want to ensure that things go smoothly and successfully on your project. What should you do?

The only response you can make to Joe that will support your delegation of authority to Mary is this: "Do whatever Mary told you to do."

What if you responded to Joe, "Yes, Mary's solution sounds good to me"? That won't do it. By declaring that you like Mary's solution, you undercut Mary's authority to make the decision on her own! Perhaps you just wanted to tell Joe that you had full confidence in Mary's ability to develop an appropriate solution, and the one she proposed was an example of her good judgment. However, in reality, your response suggests to Joe that you are still in the approval process, because you just gave your approval to Mary's *decision* rather than to her authority to make whatever decision she felt was appropriate.

You want to support your delegation of authority, but you also want to ensure your project's success. So how do you deal with the following situations?

✔ **You don't agree with Mary's recommendation.** If you fear that following Mary's recommendation will have catastrophic consequences, you must suggest to Joe that he wait until you can discuss the issue with Mary. In this instance, protecting your project and your organization is more important than supporting your delegation of authority.

In all other instances, though, you should tell Joe to follow Mary's suggestion, because she has the authority to make that decision. Here are several reasons to do so even if you don't agree with her choice:

- She may know more about the situation than you've learned from your conversation with Joe.

- Maybe she's right and you're wrong.

- Suppose your approach is better than Mary's. How will she learn to make better choices in the future if you don't discuss with her why you don't agree with her decision?

- If Mary believes that you'll jump in to save her every time she makes a bad decision, she'll be less concerned about making the correct decision the first time.

You can always ask Mary later to explain privately the rationale for her decision and you can offer your thoughts and opinions, if you feel it's necessary.

✔ **Joe's call indicates a more general problem with the team's procedures and working relationships.**

- Perhaps you weren't clear when you explained the new working procedures to your team member. Explain and reinforce the new procedures to Joe.

- Perhaps Joe didn't like Mary's answer and is trying to go behind her back to get his way. Again, you must reinforce that the decision is Mary's to make.

- Perhaps Mary wasn't clear enough in her explanation to Joe why she recommended what she did. Suggest to Mary that she explain the reasons behind her solutions more clearly and that she probe to make sure people understand and are comfortable with the information she shares.

- Perhaps some interpersonal conflict exists between Joe and Mary. Talk with both Joe and Mary to determine whether such a conflict exists and, if it does, how it came about. Work with Joe and Mary to help them address and resolve the conflict.

## Delegating with confidence

Delegation always involves some risk — you have to live with the consequences of someone else's decisions. Take the following steps to increase your comfort level and improve the person's chances for successful performance:

- ✔ **Clarify what you want to delegate.** Describe in unambiguous terms the work you want the other person to perform; also explain what you *don't* want the person to do.

- ✔ **Choose the right person.** Determine the skills and knowledge you feel a person must have to perform the task successfully, and don't delegate the task to a person who lacks these skills and knowledge.

- ✔ **Make the delegation correctly.** Explain the work to be done, how much effort you expect the person to expend, and the date by which the work is to be completed.

- ✔ **Monitor performance.** Set up frequent, well-defined checkpoints at which you can monitor performance; monitor according to that schedule.

Delegation doesn't have to be an all-or-nothing proposition where you either make the decision yourself or withdraw from the situation entirely. Consider the following six degrees of delegation, each of which builds on and extends the ones that come before it:

- ✔ **Get in the know:** Get the facts and bring them to me for further action.

- ✔ **Show me the way to go:** Develop alternative actions to take based on the facts you've found.

- ✔ **Go when I say so:** Be prepared to take one or more of the actions you have proposed, but don't do anything until I say so.

- ✔ **Go unless I say no:** Tell me what you propose to do and when; take your recommended actions unless I tell you otherwise.

- ✔ **How'd it go?** Analyze the situation, develop a course of action, take action, and let me know the results.

- ✔ **Just go!** Here's a situation; deal with it. I don't want to hear about it again.

Each level entails some degree of independent authority. If I ask you to find the facts about a situation, you choose what information sources to consult, which information to share with me, and which to discard. The primary difference between the levels is the degree of checking before taking action.

## Sharing responsibility

The decision to delegate authority is unilateral; it doesn't require the agreement of both parties. You can choose to give someone the authority to make a decision whether or not he or she wants it. Once you give your authority to another person, he or she is free to pass it on to someone else (if you haven't specifically told him or her not to).

Responsibility, however, is a two-way agreement; you ask me to respond to a customer inquiry, and I agree that I will. Because you and I agreed that I would handle the inquiry, I can't decide to give the assignment to someone else and not worry about whether he or she accomplishes it. I committed to you that the inquiry would be addressed; the only way I can free myself from this responsibility is to ask if you would agree to change our original understanding.

Suppose Alice, your boss, asks you to prepare a report highlighting the latest sales figures for your organization. You figure that you can prepare the text of the report in Microsoft Word and any necessary graphics in Microsoft PowerPoint. You know where to get the raw sales data, and you know how to use Word, but you don't know how to use PowerPoint. However, Bill, a member of your staff, does know how to use PowerPoint. So you accept Alice's assignment, figuring that you'll ask Bill to prepare any required graphics. When you ask Bill if he'll help you, he says that he will.

A week later, Alice asks how you're doing on the report. You tell her that you've completed the text, but Bill hasn't finished the graphics. You suggest that she check with Bill to find out how he's doing and when he'll be finished. How do you think Alice will respond to your suggestion?

After a moment's silence, Alice reminds you that *you* agreed to prepare the report and, therefore, ensuring that all parts of the work are completed is your responsibility, not hers. In other words, because you accepted the responsibility for completing the report, you can't choose to give away part of that responsibility to someone else.

By the way, Alice was correct in refusing to deal directly with Bill for a couple of other reasons:

- ✔ If Alice had agreed to check directly with Bill, she would've been doing you a disservice. She would have tacitly been telling Bill that whenever you give him assignments in the future, he should be concerned about satisfying her rather than you. In other words, she would've undermined your leadership position.

- ✔ It would have been difficult for Alice to follow up with Bill, even if she had wanted to, because she didn't know exactly what you asked him to do or when you asked him to do it.

The only way you can relieve yourself of some or all of the responsibility you accepted is to ask Alice if she will agree to a revised plan.

## *Holding people accountable when they don't report to you*

What happens when people who don't report to you agree to help you? Can you hold people accountable for their performance if you have no direct authority over them?

Suppose you were recently assigned to a new inventory control system project — an effort to design, develop, test, and implement an upgraded inventory control system for your organization. It's Monday morning, and you just learned that your friend Eric had been working on this project until a month ago.

You call Eric and ask him to fill you in on the project's history. After a few minutes, you realize that he knows more about your project than anyone else with whom you've spoken to date. You then make an unusual request. You explain to Eric that you and three other team members are developing a users' manual for the new system. You explain further that Chapter 1 of the manual will recount the history and development of the new system. You ask him if he would be willing to do you a favor and write a draft of Chapter 1 for you and your three colleagues by a week from Friday. Eric agrees, and you both hang up the phone.

Suppose that a week from Friday comes and goes, and you never receive the draft of Chapter 1 from Eric. He never calls you to explain why he didn't submit the draft, and you never check with him to see what's happening. Does this situation sound familiar? You probably make and receive requests like this several times each day. And, unfortunately, there have probably been times when people promised to help you out but didn't deliver. What, if anything, can you do?

You should always hold people accountable if they accept the responsibility to complete an assignment. Further, you shouldn't hold people accountable if they didn't accept responsibility. Therefore, the first question is this: After your phone call, was Eric responsible for writing a draft of Chapter 1 for you and your colleagues?

Very simply, the answer is yes. Why? Because he made the commitment. I'm not suggesting that Eric is responsible for preparing the draft of Chapter 1 and that you and your colleagues are off the hook. Your responsibility to ensure that the user's manual is prepared hasn't changed, but Eric accepted the responsibility to prepare this draft for you. It makes no difference that Eric is no longer assigned to work on the project or that he doesn't report to your boss. He's responsible because he said that he would be.

Eric may try to distinguish between "ethical responsibility" and "organizational responsibility." He may argue that he has a personal obligation to complete the draft because he said he would, but he has no organizational obligation because nothing was in writing and he hadn't been formally assigned to your project team. That argument doesn't hold up. There should be no difference between personal and organizational commitments. If he didn't want to accept the obligation, all he had to do was say no.

The second question is: Did you hold Eric accountable for his failure to perform in accordance with his promise? The answer is no. No consequences resulted from his failure to deliver a draft of Chapter 1 as promised.

Suppose you hadn't received the draft because he hadn't sent it to you. What messages does your behavior (or, in this case, your lack of behavior) give to Eric?

> ✔ **The assignment wasn't that important.** What a terrible message. You asked Eric to take time from his busy day to do something for you, and you didn't even care whether he completed the task? He's probably happy that he decided not to spend time on the task, because apparently it wouldn't have made any difference anyway.

> ✔ **Eric's behavior was okay.** This is an even worse message; it confirms that making promises, not performing, and not explaining your behavior to anyone is okay. Situations could arise that would make it impossible for Eric to honor a commitment he made, but does that justify not calling to tell you about the situation? Unfortunately, this type of behavior, multiplied many times every day, defines an organizational environment where promises mean little and breaking them becomes an accepted element of business as usual.

Most likely, these messages are not the ones you intended to convey. You probably figured that Eric had gotten swamped with work, and you didn't want to make a big deal out of it because he agreed to go out of his way to help you. Unfortunately, he has no way of knowing what's in your mind, because you chose not to tell him.

Maybe he didn't just decide not to prepare the draft of Chapter 1. Consider some other possibilities:

> ✔ **He sent you the draft but it got lost in the delivery system.** Among other things, accountability is a feedback process. Unfortunately, most people figure that no news is good news. When Eric didn't get a call from you, he assumed that you'd received the draft and found it acceptable. Certainly, he figured, you would've called if you had any questions!

> ✔ **He misunderstood you initially; he thought you needed the draft by a month (rather than a week) from Friday.** Maybe he's still working on the draft and plans to give it to you on the date he thought you needed it.

You may not try to hold people accountable when you have no authority over them because you don't think it's appropriate (after all, you're not their boss) or because you don't know how. But remember what I said earlier: Holding people accountable is appropriate and necessary if they've accepted the responsibility to perform. Accountability helps people know that they're on the right track and enables you to formally acknowledge when they complete the promised assignments. You don't need authority to hold people accountable; they just must accept the responsibility.

Use the following approaches to hold people accountable if you have no direct authority over them:

- ✓ **Find out who does have direct authority over the person and bring that supervisor into the process.** Consider soliciting the approval of the person's boss. If you do so correctly and at the right time, you can improve the chances for success. In the example of Eric, suppose you considered passing your request by Eric's boss in addition to asking Eric personally. Before you end your phone call, you might ask Eric if he would mind if you passed the request by his boss. Most likely he would say, "Thanks!"

- ✓ **Put it in writing.** Have you ever noticed how strangely people react when you put an informal agreement in writing? All of a sudden, they act as if you don't trust them. Put your agreement in writing to clarify the terms, to serve as a reminder, and to formalize the agreement. If they ask, explain to them that it has nothing to do with lack of trust. If you didn't trust them, you wouldn't work with them at all!

- ✓ **Be specific.** The clearer you make your request, the easier it is for the person to estimate the effort needed to respond to the request and to produce the right result the first time.

  You may be uncomfortable being too specific because you feel that giving the person "orders" is inappropriate (after all, you have no direct authority over him or her). But your being specific makes it easier for the person, not harder.

- ✓ **Follow up.** Negotiate a schedule to monitor the person's performance and to address any issues or questions that arise. Be sure to

  - Negotiate a follow-up schedule at the outset. If you call unannounced at random times, it appears that you're checking up because you don't trust the person.

  - Base your follow-up schedule on when the person plans to achieve certain intermediate milestones, giving yourself more objective criteria for assessing how things are going.

- ✓ **Make the person accountable to the team.** Your most valuable professional asset is your reputation. When a person promises to do something for you, let others on your team know about the promise. When the person lives up to that promise, acknowledge it in front of his or her colleagues. If the person fails to live up to the promise, let him or her know that you'll share that information with others, too.

✔ **Get commitment.** When a person indicates that he or she will help you out, be sure to get a firm, specific commitment that the desired result will be achieved by this time for this cost. Beware of declarations like "I'll give it my best effort" or "You can count on me."

✔ **Create a sense of urgency and importance.** You may want to minimize any pressure the person feels by saying, in essence, that you'll understand if he or she doesn't perform to your expectations because he or she has so many other things going on. Unfortunately, this approach suggests to the person that his or her work is really not that important and actually increases the chances that you won't get what you want. Instead, let the person know how his or her work will influence other activities and people on the project. Let the person know why it's important that he or she does perform to expectations and what the consequences to the project and the organization will be if he or she doesn't.

# *Illustrating the Relationships*

Defining and sharing team roles and responsibilities upfront can improve performance and help to identify and head off potential difficulties during a project. Figure 8-1 illustrates how these relationships can be described in a Linear Responsibility Chart.

|  | Project Manager | Task Leader | Project Staffer A | Group Director | Purchasing |
|---|---|---|---|---|---|
| **Design questionnaire** | A | S, A | P |  |  |
| **Select respondents** |  | P |  |  |  |
| **Conduct pretest** |  | P | S |  |  |
| **Print questionnaires** | A | P |  | A | A |

P = Primary responsibility     S = Secondary responsibility     A = Approval

**Figure 8-1:**
A Linear Responsibility Chart describes relationships.

A Linear Responsibility Chart is a matrix that depicts the role that each project audience (see Chapter 7) will play in the performance of different project activities. As Figure 8-1 illustrates:

✔ Project activities are listed in the left-hand column.

✔ Project audiences are identified in the top row.

✔ The role that each audience will play with respect to each activity is specified in the intersections of the table's rows and columns.

Figure 8-1 illustrates a portion of a Linear Responsibility Chart for designing and conducting a customer needs survey. This chart defines three roles that you can have with regard to project activities:

✔ **Primary responsibility (P):** You have committed to ensure that the results are achieved.

✔ **Secondary responsibility (S):** You have committed to achieve some portion of the results.

✔ **Approval (A):** You're not actually doing work on the activity, but you will approve what has been done.

A Linear Responsibility Chart is a format; you can define whatever roles you feel are appropriate for your project. As examples, you might consider using the following roles in addition to the three already defined:

✔ **Review (R):** You will review and comment on the results of an activity, but your formal approval is not required.

✔ **Output (O):** You will receive products from the activity.

✔ **Input (I):** You will provide input for the work performed on the activity.

Your only limit is your creativity!

To illustrate how you read a Linear Responsibility Chart, consider the activity "Design questionnaire" in Figure 8-1. The chart suggests that three people will work together as follows:

✔ Primary responsibility for the questionnaire's content, format, and layout rests with Staffer A. On this project, Staffer A reports to the task leader who, in turn, reports to the project manager.

✔ The task leader will perform selected parts of the questionnaire design under the general coordination of Staffer A. The task leader must approve all aspects of the questionnaire design before work can proceed to the next step.

✔ The project manager must approve the entire questionnaire, even though he or she isn't doing any of the actual design and layout.

Analyze this chart vertically by audience and horizontally by activity to identify situations that may give rise to problems. After you identify these situations, you can decide whether and how to address them. Table 8-1 presents some observations and potential issues.

**Table 8-1      Situations and Issues Suggested in the Linear Responsibility Chart in Figure 8-1**

| Situation | Possible Issues |
|---|---|
| The team leader is heavily committed. | The task leader will not have enough time to handle all these duties. |
| | The task leader is making all key decisions. |
| | What if the task leader leaves during the project? |
| The group director doesn't get involved until he or she is asked to approve the funds for printing the questionnaires. | The group director will slow down the approval process by asking questions about the purpose of the project, the use of the results, and so on. |
| The project manager has no direct responsibilities for individual project activities. | Will the project manager fully understand the substance and status of project work performed? |
| The task leader is the only person involved in selecting the respondents. | Do you want a key decision that can determine the value of the entire pretest made with only one person's input? |
| The activity called "print questionnaires" requires three approvals. | Does anyone else have to approve the questionnaire before it can be used? |
| | Are too many people approving the questionnaire? Would it be acceptable to notify just one or two of these people? |
| | The activity may take longer than its estimates because this approval process is out of your control. |

After you identify a possible issue, you can choose how you want to deal with it. Possibilities include

- ✔ **Ignoring it.** As an example, you may decide that three approvals are necessary, even though the number is high.

- ✔ **Taking simple steps to minimize the risk of a problem occurring.** For example, you may ask the task leader to thoroughly document all important information in case he or she leaves the project unexpectedly.

- ✔ **Addressing it further in a formal risk-management plan.** See Chapter 14 for a discussion of how to analyze and plan to manage project risks.

## Being sure everyone's on the same page

A while back, a client of mine was preparing to start a large project. I asked if he had prepared a Linear Responsibility Chart, and he responded that, although nothing had been written down, each of the ten team members knew what everyone's roles and responsibilities were. I tried to convince him that putting the chart in writing would be helpful, but he initially thought that his team had more important things to do with their time. Finally, he said he would prove to me that writing things down wasn't always necessary.

He asked each of his ten team members to prepare a chart that represented his or her understanding of everyone's roles and responsibilities. All the team members completed their charts in less than an hour. However, when my client reviewed the results, he found that each chart portrayed a different view of what people's roles and responsibilities were! If people had tried to do their work without going through this exercise, they would have encountered frustration and conflict throughout the project.

## *Developing a Linear Responsibility Chart*

Develop your Linear Responsibility Chart as follows:

1. **Identify all people who'll participate in or support your project.**

   See the discussion of audiences in Chapter 7 for details.

2. **Develop a complete list of activities to be performed on your project.**

   See the discussion of a Work Breakdown Structure in Chapter 3 for details.

3. **Consult with all team members and draft a Linear Responsibility Chart.**

   If specific people haven't yet been identified for certain activities, consult with people who have done those types of activities before.

4. **Ask all people with whom you spoke to review and approve your draft chart.**

5. **If some people don't approve the draft chart, incorporate their recommended changes into a second draft and again ask all people with whom you spoke to review and approve the chart.**

6. **Continue until all people approve the chart.**

# Improving the quality of your chart

Take the following steps to improve the quality of your Linear Responsibility Chart:

✔ **Develop a hierarchy of charts for larger projects.** Including 50 or more activities on the same Linear Responsibility Chart can be cumbersome. Consider developing a series of nested charts for larger projects. Prepare a high-level chart that identifies responsibilities for work assignments or tasks in your Work Breakdown Structure, and develop separate charts for individual work assignments or tasks in the main chart that detail responsibilities for associated lower-level activities. (See Chapter 3 for the definition of work assignments, tasks, and lower-level activities in a Work Breakdown Structure.)

Figure 8-2 illustrates a simple example. Suppose you're planning a project to design and conduct an information system. Prepare a high-level Linear Responsibility Chart that details the roles people will play for major work assignments, such as "finalize requirements," "design system," and "test system." Display in a second chart the roles that the team leader and his or her group will play on the lower-level activities that comprise "finalize requirements."

**Design and Conduct a Customer Needs Survey**

| People / Activities | Project Manager | Team Leader A | Team Leader B | Team Leader C |
|---|---|---|---|---|
| **Finalize requirements** | A | P | | |
| **Design system** | A | | P | S |
| **Test system** | A | S | S | P |

**Finalize Requirements**

| People / Activities | Team Leader A | Staffer A | Staffer B | Staffer C |
|---|---|---|---|---|
| **Review literatrure** | A | P | S | |
| **Conduct focus groups** | P | S | | S |
| **Prepare report** | A | S | S | |

**Figure 8-2:**
A hierarchy of Linear Responsibility Charts.

✔ **Involve the entire team when developing your chart to ensure accuracy and buy-in.** It's unreasonable to expect the project manager will know exactly how experts and technical representatives from different groups should perform tasks in their areas of specialty. Further, people have a greater commitment to a plan if they participate in developing it.

✔ **Put your chart in writing.** People have to think about the issues addressed in the Linear Responsibility Chart as they plan and perform their project work. So, to save time, you may feel that putting the chart in writing is not necessary because you all know what's in it anyway. Putting the chart in writing is essential for two reasons:

- You see things you wouldn't have realized if you had thought about individual pieces of information separately.

  Refer to the Linear Responsibility Chart in Figure 8-1. Before the chart was prepared, the task leader knew that he or she was primarily responsible for selecting respondents for pretesting the questionnaire, and others knew that they were not involved in the activity but probably assumed that someone else was. Writing down this information in the table highlighted that the task leader was, in fact, the only one who would be involved in the activity.

- You ensure that people have a common understanding of their roles and relationships.

✔ **Review and update your chart throughout your project.** The longer your project, the more likely that activities will be added or deleted, that people will leave the team, and that new people will join the team. Periodically reviewing and updating your Linear Responsibility Chart enables you to:

- Assess whether the current assignments of roles and responsibilities are working out and, if not, where changes may be needed

- Clarify the roles and responsibilities for new activities

- Clarify the roles and responsibilities for people who join the team

- Clarify how you'll handle the roles and responsibilities of someone who leaves the team

If you join a project and find that no Linear Responsibility Chart exists, develop one. You can develop a Linear Responsibility Chart at any time during a project. If the project is already underway, develop a chart to clarify the roles and responsibilities from the current point forward.

# Dealing with Micromanagement

*Micromanagement* is a person's excessive, inappropriate, and unnecessary involvement in the details of a task that he or she asks another person to perform. Whatever the reasons for micromanagement, it can lead to inefficient use of personal time and energy, as well as tension and low morale among staff.

## Figuring out why you're being micromanaged

Someone may micromanage for a variety of reasons. Following are several possible situations, along with suggestions for how you can deal with them.

- ✔ **The person is interested in and enjoys the work.** Set up times to discuss interesting technical issues with the person.

- ✔ **The person is a technical expert and feels that he or she can do the job best.** Review your technical work frequently with that person; give the person opportunities to share his or her technical insights with you. Encourage the micromanager to remember why he or she assigned the task to you in the first place.

- ✔ **The person may feel that he or she didn't explain the assignment clearly or that uncertainties may crop up.** Set up a schedule to discuss and review your progress frequently so that the micromanager can promptly uncover any mistakes and help you correct them.

- ✔ **The person is looking for ways to stay involved with you and the team.** Set up scheduled times to discuss project activities. Provide the micromanager with periodic reports of project progress, and make a point to stop by and say hello periodically.

- ✔ **The person feels threatened because you have more technical knowledge than he or she does.** When talking about your project in front of others, always give the micromanager credit for his or her guidance and insights. Share key technical information with the person on a regular basis.

- ✔ **The person doesn't have a clear understanding of how he or she should be spending his or her time.** Discuss with the person the roles he or she would like you to assume on your project activities. Explain how the person can provide you with useful support as you perform your work.

- ✔ **The person feels that he or she has to stay up on the work you're doing in case anyone else asks about it.** Discuss with the person what type of information he or she needs and how frequently he or she needs it. Develop a schedule to provide progress reports that include this information.

## There's a difference between interference and interest

During the summer after my first year of graduate school, I worked for a large manufacturer of electronic equipment. I was very excited about this job because it was the first time I was regarded as a real member of a technical staff. I was looking forward to using my skills and knowledge to contribute to a project that would produce a real-world result.

I showed up for work the first day eager to jump into my initial assignment. My boss told me how pleased he was that I would be working in his group for the summer and how he wanted to be sure that he made my stay enjoyable and productive. During that first week, my boss stopped by my office several times each day to talk. He would come in, turn over my garbage can, and sit down (because the only chair in my office was the desk chair in which I was sitting and, thankfully, the garbage can was empty!) and discuss the project he had assigned to me. By the end of the week, I was demoralized and depressed. Every time I would start to read the background information for my project, my boss would come into my office to talk. I was convinced that he felt I didn't have the necessary skills to do a good job and that he was hanging over my shoulder to ensure that I didn't make any big mistakes.

As I got to know my boss better, I realized that I had misread his intentions. First, he was excited to have someone on his staff who had been studying the latest developments in a technology that was important to his project. Rather than thinking that I was incapable, he wanted to learn from me what I knew so that he could improve his own knowledge. Second, he was a thoughtful and considerate person. He knew how daunting it could be for a young person to come into an established group and try to get to know everyone. He came around frequently to get to know me, to allow me to get to know him, and to help me feel comfortable in my new environment. My insecurities led me to believe that his complimentary and considerate actions were meant as criticisms and expressions of distrust!

## Helping a micromanager gain confidence in you

For whatever reason, your boss may be micromanaging you because he or she doesn't yet have full confidence in your ability to perform. Rather than being angry or resentful, take the following steps to help the person develop that confidence:

> ✔ Don't be defensive or resentful when the person asks you questions; doing so will make it appear as though you were hiding something and will make the person worry even more.

✔ Thank the micromanager for his or her interest, time, and technical guidance. Complaining about what you perceive to be excessive oversight will only strain your relationship, increase the person's fears and insecurities, and most likely cause the person to micromanage you in even more detail. After you make it clear to the micromanager that you value his or her input and will take it into account, you can try to develop a more acceptable working relationship.

✔ Offer to explain to the person how you will approach your tasks.

✔ Work with the person to develop a scheme for sharing progress and accomplishments. Develop meaningful and frequent checkpoints. Frequent monitoring early in your work will reassure you both that you are successfully performing your assignments.

## *Working with a micromanager*

You can reduce or even eliminate most micromanagement by improving your communication and strengthening your interpersonal relationships. Consider taking the following steps:

✔ **Don't assume.** Don't jump to conclusions. Examine the situation, get to know the person who's micromanaging you, and try to understand his or her motivations. Expect that you'll be able to develop a working relationship with which you're both comfortable.

✔ **Listen.** Listen to the micromanager's questions and comments; see if patterns emerge. Try to understand the person's real interests and concerns.

✔ **Observe the person's behavior with others.** If the person micromanages others, too, it's likely that the micromanagement stems from what he or she is feeling rather than something you are or aren't doing. Try to figure ways to address the person's real interests and concerns.

✔ **If at first you don't succeed, try, try again.** Draw your first conclusion and take steps to address the situation. If that approach doesn't work, reassess the situation and develop an alternative strategy. Keep at it until you succeed.

# Part III
# Steering the Ship

The 5th Wave    By Rich Tennant

"Telephone—check, file folders—check, ruler—check, pneumatic jack hammer—check, index... WAIT A MINUTE! What am I doing?! I don't need a RULER to manage this project!"

## In this part . . .

The farther in the future you try to plan, the more likely things will change. Successful project management requires that you start off strong, keep moving in the right direction, and make required changes in a timely manner.

In this part, I describe steps that you can take to start your project off on the right foot. I suggest different information systems that you can use to track your project's performance and expenditures. I show you approaches to track, analyze, and report on project activities, and I suggest techniques for bringing your project to a successful close.

# Chapter 9

# Starting Off on the Right Foot

• • • • • • • • • • • • • • • • • • • • • • • • • • • • • • • • • • • • • • • • • • •

### In This Chapter

▶ Finalizing team member assignments

▶ Reaffirming your project plan

▶ Creating your team's identity

▶ Developing your team's operating procedures

▶ Setting up your tracking systems

▶ Scheduling your regular reports and meetings

▶ Setting your project's baselines

▶ Announcing your project

• • • • • • • • • • • • • • • • • • • • • • • • • • • • • • • • • • • • • • • • • • •

*A*fter intense work on a tight schedule, you submit your project plan for review and approval. A few days later, your boss comes to you and says, "I have some good news and some bad news for you; which would you like to hear first?" "Tell me the good news," you respond. "Your plan has been approved." "So," you ask, "what's the bad news?" "Now you have to do the project!"

Starting off your project correctly is a key to ultimate success. Your project plan describes what you propose to produce, the work you'll do, how you'll do it, when you'll do it, and the resources you'll need. You based your plan on the information available to you when you prepared it; if information was unavailable, you made assumptions. The longer the time between when you finished your plan and when you received approval to proceed, the more likely that some of the information on which your plan is based has changed.

As you prepare to start your project, you need to reconfirm or update the information in your plan, determine or reaffirm which people will play a role in your project, and prepare the systems and procedures that will support your project's performance.

# Finalizing Your Project's Participants

A *project audience* is a person or group who will support, be affected by, or be interested in your project. (See Chapter 7 for a detailed discussion of how to identify project audiences.) In your project plan, you describe the roles you anticipate people will play and the amount of effort team members will have to invest. You identify the people by name, by title or position, or by the skills and knowledge they would need.

As you start your project, confirm the identities of the people who'll work to support your project, either by verifying that the specific people included are still able to uphold their promised commitments or by recruiting and selecting new people to fill the remaining needs.

## Confirming your team members' participation

Contact all people you identified by name in your plan to do the following:

- ✔ **Inform them that your project has been approved and when work will start.** Not all project plans are approved. You rarely know in advance how long the approval process will take or how soon after approval your project will start. Tell people of your project's approval and planned start date as soon as possible so that they can reserve the necessary time in their schedules to provide the support they promised to you.

- ✔ **Confirm that they're still able to support your project.** People's workloads and other commitments may change between the time you prepare your plan and the time your project is approved. Confirm that people who promised to support your project are still available to do so. If a person is no longer able to provide the promised support, recruit a replacement as soon as possible.

- ✔ **Reconfirm the work you're expecting people to perform, when they are to do it, and the amount of time you expect they will spend on it.** Clarify with all persons the specific activities they will perform and the nature of the work they will do. Depending on the size and formality of your project, you can do so with anything from a quick e-mail to a formal work-order agreement.

- ✔ **Explain what you'll do to develop the project team and start the project work.** Tell people who'll be actively involved as project team members who else will be on the team and the steps you'll take to introduce the team members to one another and kick off the project.

A *work-order agreement* is a written description of work that a person agrees to perform on your project, the dates the person agrees to start and finish the work, and the number of hours the person agrees to spend on it. You (the project manager), the person who'll be doing the work, and that person's supervisor should approve the work-order agreement.

As Figure 9-1 illustrates, a typical work-order agreement includes the following information:

- **Identifiers:** Include the project name, project number, activity name, and Work Breakdown Structure code. The project name and number confirm that your project is now official. You use the activity name and Work Breakdown Structure code number to record work progress, as well as time and resource charges.

- **Work to be performed:** Describe the different activities and procedures to be done, as well as outputs to be produced.

- **Activity start date, end date, and number of hours to be spent:** Including this information reaffirms

  - The importance of doing the work within the established schedule and the budgeted effort

  - The person's feeling that it's possible he or she can do the described work within these time and resource constraints

  - The criteria you'll use to assess the person's performance

- **Written approvals from the person who'll do the work, his or her supervisor, and the project manager:** Including these written approvals increases the likelihood that the people have read and understand the elements of the agreement and commit to support it.

**Figure 9-1:**
A typical work-order agreement.

| Work-Order Agreement | | |
|---|---|---|
| Project name: | Project number: | |
| Activity name: | Work Breakdown Structure code: | |
| Description of work to be performed: | | |
| Start date | End date | Number of hours to be spent |
| Approvals | | |
| Project manager: | Team member: | Team member's supervisor: |
| Name_____ Date_____ | Name_____ Date_____ | Name_____ Date_____ |

If you're missing any of this information when you're ready to reconfirm a person's commitment to your project, do whatever you can to develop or find it. The longer you wait to specify any of this information, the greater the chances that people will not provide the support you had hoped for.

Whether or not you choose to reconfirm people's participation with a formal work order, be sure to take these steps:

- ✔ **Write down all key information.** If your project is informal, you may not have an official project number, people may not record on time sheets the time they spend working on it, and you may not have a separate project budget. Still, write down whatever information you have to clarify the agreements between you and the people doing the work.

- ✔ Get signed approvals from the person who will do the work and his or her supervisor.

## Assuring that others are on board

Other people may play a role in your project's success but will not directly charge time to it. Such people may include drivers and supporters:

- ✔ **Drivers** are people who have some say in defining the results that your project is to achieve. These are the people for whom you are performing your project.

- ✔ **Supporters** are people who help you to perform your project. They include the people who authorize the resources for your project as well as those who work on it.

A special audience is your *project champion,* a person in a high position in the organization who strongly supports your project; will advocate for your project in disputes, planning meetings, and review sessions; and will take whatever actions are necessary to help ensure the successful completion of your project. (See Chapter 7 for a detailed discussion of the different types of project audiences.)

Contact your project champion and all other drivers and supporters who are identified by name in your plan to

- ✔ Inform them that your project has been approved and when work will start

- ✔ Reaffirm what you're planning to produce

- ✔ Clarify with identified drivers that the project's planned results still address their needs

✔ Clarify with identified supporters exactly how you want them to help your project

✔ Develop specific plans for involving each audience throughout the project and keeping them informed of progress

In addition, some people will be interested in your project but will not define what it should accomplish or directly support your efforts. As you identify these observers, choose those you wish to keep informed of your progress and prepare a plan for how you'll do so.

## Filling in the blanks

If your plan identifies proposed project team members by job title, position description, or skills and knowledge, you have to find actual people to assume the specified roles. You can do so by assigning to your project a person who's already on your organization's staff, recruiting a person from outside your organization, or contracting with an external organization to provide the necessary support.

Whichever method you choose, you'll find it helpful to prepare a written description of the activities you want each person to perform. This description can range from a simple memo for informal projects to a written job description for more formal ones.

Prepare a separate description of your needs for each category of personnel you're looking to recruit. At a minimum, include the following information in your description:

✔ Project name, number, and start date

✔ Skills and knowledge that the person or people must have

✔ Description and start and end dates of activities to be performed

✔ Anticipated level of effort needed to perform the described work

If you plan to look inside your organization, do the following:

✔ Identify potential candidates by working with your human resources department and with area managers.

✔ Meet with the candidates to discuss your project, describe the work they will be doing, and assess their qualifications.

✔ Choose the best candidates and extend an offer for them to join your team.

✔ Document the agreement of the work they'll do.

If you're looking outside the organization, identify potential resources by working with your organization's human resources office to recruit new hires. Provide your human resources office with a detailed description of the qualifications, skills, and knowledge the people should have, the tasks they'll perform, and the level of effort they'll have to invest. Participate in the interview and assessment process.

Also, work with your organization's contracts office to obtain the support of external consultants. Provide the contracts office with a detailed description of the tasks to be performed, the level of effort you estimate they will require, and the qualifications, skills, and knowledge that the consultants should have. Participate in the review of potential contractors and review the contract before it's signed.

In addition, work with people in key organizational units to identify other individuals who should be involved throughout your project. After you identify these people:

- Meet with them to clarify your project's goals and anticipated outputs and the ways in which they will support your performance.

- Develop plans for involving them and keeping them informed of progress throughout your project.

# Reviewing the Approved Project Plan

As soon as people are assigned to the team, have them review the approved project plan.

- Team members who contributed to the proposal can remind themselves of the project's background and purpose, their planned roles, and the work to be done. They can also identify situations and circumstances that may have changed since the proposal was prepared and review and reassess project risks and risk-management plans.

- New team members can learn about the project's background and purpose, learn about their planned roles and assignments, raise any concerns they have about how they will meet established time frames and budgets, and identify questions and issues they feel might affect the project's chances for success.

# Developing Your Team

Merely assigning people to perform selected tasks on a project does not create a project team. A *team* is a collection of people who are committed to common goals and who depend on one other to do their jobs. Project teams are based on the premise that every member can and must make a valuable and unique contribution to the project.

A team is different from other associations of people who work together.

- A *group* is comprised of people who are assigned to a common task and work individually to accomplish their particular assignments.

- A *committee* is comprised of people who come together to review and critique issues, propose recommendations for action, and, on occasion, implement those recommendations.

# If you're not sure, ask!

A while back, I met a person at one of my training sessions who had been with his organization for only a short time. Upon joining his company, he was immediately assigned to his current project team. The project was just starting, but because he was new to the organization, he hadn't participated in the development of the project plan.

He told me that he could see no way to perform his assignments within the established schedule and budget constraints. He was especially frustrated that his managers had never asked him whether he thought he could accomplish his assignments; they just expected him to do it.

I asked him if he'd raised his concerns to his managers by noting specific issues, their potential impact on project performance, and possible ways of addressing them. He admitted that he had not. He felt that the people who had prepared the plan knew more about the organization than he did, so his opinions would be of no consequence. Furthermore, he figured that the project's schedule and budget had already been approved, so changing things would be impossible at this time. Finally and most important, he noted that his boss hadn't asked for his opinions.

Unfortunately, this person didn't realize that his failure to raise his concerns to his managers actually increased the chance that his project

would fail. First, if the project plan indeed had flaws, the fact that it had already been approved wouldn't make those flaws go away. The sooner the flaws were identified, the more time people would have to figure out how to correct them.

On the other hand, suppose he misunderstood parts of the plan, or perhaps his lack of experience with the organization prevented him from seeing how certain tasks could be accomplished. Instead of changing the plan, perhaps he just needed a clearer explanation of the plan so that he could better understand how to perform his assignments. Complaining about perceived flaws and management's perceived indifference to his opinions wouldn't help him perform his tasks more effectively. In fact, this complaining would only lower his morale and that of his teammates, which, in turn, would increase the chances of failure.

Successful project leaders and team members don't wait to be asked for their opinions; they proactively raise issues and suggest possible solutions. Questions and concerns are not presented as criticisms of the people who prepared the plans. Instead, they're raised and addressed in a continuing attempt to reflect the greater insight and understanding that comes with time and the benefit of diverse perspectives.

Teams entail commitment to common goals, mutually dependent work, and vital and unique contributions from all members.

A number of years ago, I presented a project management training session to employees from a cross section of departments at a large consumer products company. Our session started on a Monday morning and, by coincidence, the company had issued a directive on the preceding Friday that, starting Monday morning, all people working on projects would from that time forward be members of officially designated project teams.

When I arrived at the training session, I overheard people discussing in disbelief how the company had handled the transition to the new "team environment." Apparently, the company had sent a series of memos to all staff on Friday afternoon, telling them the teams of which they were members. People in the training room were having an informal contest to see who had been assigned to the most teams. The winner had been notified that he was a member of 16 teams!

I asked the "winner" how he could be a contributing member of 16 different project teams. He explained that, in most instances, being a "team member" just meant receiving memos that described project status once a month or so. He rarely, if ever, attended project meetings, and he had no specific assignments to perform for the majority of the projects. He was just there to provide support if it was needed. Although this company may have decided to refer to its people as team members, the people were clearly not working together in a committed, coordinated way to achieve specified end results.

As soon as you identify your project team members, take steps to define and establish your team's identity and operating practices. At the earliest possible time, start to discuss and develop the following, making sure they're well-defined and accepted:

- ✔ **Goals:** What the team as a whole, as well as each member individually, hopes to accomplish
- ✔ **Roles:** Each member's individual assignments
- ✔ **Processes:** The techniques that team members will use to help them perform their project tasks
- ✔ **Relationships:** The feelings and attitudes of team members toward each other

## Developing team and individual project goals

Team members commit to your project when they believe that their participation can help them achieve worthwhile professional and personal goals.

Help team members develop and buy into a shared sense of the project goals by doing the following:

- Discussing the reasons for the project, who is supporting the project, and the impact of the planned results. (See Chapter 2 for a discussion of how to identify the needs your project will address in the background portion of the purpose section in the Statement of Work.)

- Clarifying how the project results may benefit the organization's client populations.

- Emphasizing how the results of your project may support your organization's growth and viability.

- Exploring how the project results may impact each team member's job.

Encourage people to think about how their participation in your project may help them to achieve personal goals, such as acquiring new skills and knowledge, meeting new people, increasing their visibility in the organization, and enhancing their opportunities for job advancement. Projects aren't performed solely to help team members achieve personal benefits; however, if team members can realize personal benefits and, at the same time, perform valued services for the organization, their motivation and commitment to project success will be greater. See Chapter 12 for more on how to create and sustain team member motivation.

## Defining team member roles

Nothing can cause disillusionment and frustration faster than bringing motivated people together and giving them no guidance about how to work with each other. Two or more people will start doing the same activities without coordinating with each other, while other activities will be overlooked entirely. Eventually, people will either define tasks that they can perform by themselves without having to coordinate with anyone else, or they'll gradually withdraw from the project and work on more rewarding assignments.

To prevent this frustration, work with team members to define the roles that each member will play. Specify which activities they'll work on and define the nature of the roles they'll play. Possible roles include the following:

- **Primary responsibility:** Has the overall obligation to complete an activity.

- **Secondary or supporting responsibility:** Has the obligation to complete a part of an activity.

- **Approval:** Must approve the results of an activity before work can proceed.

- ✔ **Available for consultation:** Can be called on to provide expert guidance and support if needed.

- ✔ **Must receive output:** Is to receive either a physical product produced in an activity or a report of the results of an activity.

If you prepared a Linear Responsibility Chart as part of your project plan, use it as a starting point in your discussions of project roles with your team members. (Chapter 8 discusses how to use a Linear Responsibility Chart as an effective vehicle for defining and sharing project roles and responsibilities.) However, encourage people to raise any questions or concerns about roles portrayed so they're comfortable that the roles are feasible and appropriate.

## Defining your team's operating processes

Develop the procedures that you and your team will use to support your day-to-day work. At a minimum, develop procedures for the following:

- ✔ **Communication:** Sharing project-related information in writing and through face-to-face interactions. Such procedures might include when and how to use e-mail to share project information, which types of information should be in writing, when and how to document informal discussions, how to set up regularly scheduled reports and meetings to record and review progress, and how to address special issues that arise.

- ✔ **Conflict resolution:** Resolving differences of opinion between team members regarding project work. You want to develop both *standard approaches,* or steps that you'll normally take to encourage people to develop a mutually agreeable solution; and *escalation procedures,* or steps that you'll take if the people involved can't readily resolve their differences.

- ✔ **Decision making:** Deciding among alternative approaches and actions. Develop guidelines for choosing the most appropriate decision-making approaches for the situation, including consensus, majority rule, unanimous agreement, and decision by technical expert; and escalation procedures — steps you'll take if the normal decision-making approaches get bogged down.

## Supporting the development of team member relationships

In high-performance project teams, members trust each other and have cordial, coordinated working relationships. Developing trust and effective work practices takes time and concerted effort. Begin to help your team members get to know and be comfortable with one other as soon as your project starts. Do so by encouraging them to do the following:

✔ Work through conflicts together.

✔ Brainstorm challenging technical and administrative issues.

✔ Spend informal personal time together, such as having lunch or participating in non-work-related activities after hours.

# Helping your team to become a smooth-functioning unit

Work with your team to help them successfully develop through each of the following stages:

✔ **Forming:** Identifying and meeting team members, politely discussing project objectives, work assignments, and so forth. Share the project plan, introduce people to each other, and discuss each person's background, organizational responsibilities, and areas of expertise.

✔ **Storming:** Raising and resolving personal conflicts and feelings about the project or other team members. Encourage people to discuss any questions or concerns they have about the project plan's feasibility and work with them to address their concerns. Encourage people to discuss any reservations they have about working with other team members and about other team members' abilities to complete their assigned tasks. Keep these discussions focused on ways to ensure successful task performance — you don't want them to turn into unproductive personal attacks.

✔ **Norming:** Developing the standards and operating guidelines that will govern each team member's behavior. Encourage team members to establish the norms that will guide their behavior. Doing so is particularly important because team members most likely will come from different areas of the organization, all of which have their own procedures and practices. Examples of behavioral norms include the following:

   • **How people present and discuss different points of view:** Some people present points of view politely, while others aggressively debate their opponents in an attempt to prove their point.

   • **Timeliness of meeting attendance:** Some people always show up for meetings on time, while others are habitually 15 or more minutes late.

   • **Participation in meetings:** Some people sit back and observe, while others actively participate and share their ideas.

✔ **Performing:** Doing the project work required to produce the desired products and results, monitoring the conformance of work with established schedules and budgets, making changes to existing plans (as needed), and sharing information about project progress and issues with the appropriate people.

Keep the following in mind as you guide your team through its developmental phases:

- **If everything goes smoothly on your project, whether or not you have completed the forming, storming, and norming stages will make no difference.** Only if you hit problems will your team become dysfunctional if it hasn't progressed through every stage. Suppose, for example, that the team misses a major project deadline. If team members have not developed mutual trust for one another, they are likely to spend their time searching for someone to blame instead of working together to fix the situation.

- **On occasion, you may have to revisit a stage you thought the team had completed.** Be aware of occurrences that may make it necessary to revisit one or more completed stages. For example, a new person may join the team, or a major aspect of the project plan may change.

- **Your team will not automatically pass through these stages; you have to guide them through them.** Left to their own, teams often fail to move beyond the forming stage. People don't like to confront thorny interpersonal issues, so they tend to ignore them.

- **Periodically assess how you all feel you're performing and where, if at all, you need to work through some issues.** Managing your team is a project itself! As such, you want to periodically assess how you're doing and whether you need to take any corrective actions to bring the team back on course.

# Setting Up Your Tracking Systems

As your project unfolds, you'll track its performance in terms of the following:

- **Schedule achievement:** How well you're meeting established dates
- **Personnel resource use:** The levels of effort people are spending on their assignments
- **Financial expenditures:** Cash expenditures made for project resources

See Chapter 10 for a detailed discussion of the information systems you can use to track your project's progress.

If you'll use existing systems to track your project's schedule performance and resource use, set up and register your project on these systems as follows:

- **Obtain your official project code number.**
- **Finalize your project's Work Breakdown Structure.** Have team members review the Work Breakdown Structure included in your project plan and make any necessary changes or additions. Assign identifier codes to all Work Breakdown Structure elements.

✔ **Set up charge codes for your labor tracking system.** If your organization has a system for recording labor hours by project, and if project team members will record their hours in that system, set up the codes for all Work Breakdown Structure activities to which people will be allowed to charge time. Also, if the system can accept upper limits to the number of hours individuals are allowed to charge to specific activities, enter those limits for each activity you plan to track.

✔ **Set up charge codes for your financial system.** If your organization has a financial system that can track expenditures by project, set up the codes for all Work Breakdown Structure activities to which people will be allowed to charge expenditures. If the system can accept upper limits to the amount of expenditures team members are allowed to charge to specific activities, enter those limits for each activity you plan to track.

# Setting Up Schedules for Reports and Meetings

Meet with the appropriate project audiences and team members to develop a schedule for regular project meetings and progress reports. Confirm these things:

✔ What reports will be issued

✔ What meetings will be held and their specific purposes

✔ When the reports will be issued and when the meetings will be held

✔ Who will receive the reports and attend the meetings

✔ The format and content of the reports and meetings

See Chapter 13 for a discussion of the reports and meetings you can use to support ongoing project communications.

# Setting Your Project's Baseline

Your *baseline* is the plan you use to guide project activities and support performance assessments. Formally establish the plan that you and your team members have reviewed and revised (if necessary) as your baseline before you start project work. Use this baseline as your basis for comparison when you routinely assess performance during the project.

# Announcing Your Project

By the time you're ready to announce your project, you'll have notified your key project audiences (that is, team members, drivers, and supporters) that the project has been approved and when it'll start. Consider one or more of the following approaches to tell others in the organization who may have interest in your project:

- An e-mail message to selected individuals or departments in your organization
- An announcement in your organization's newsletter
- A flyer on a prominent bulletin board
- A formal kickoff meeting (if your project is large or will have a broad organizational impact)

In each instance, tell people the purpose and scope of your project, your intended outcomes and results, and the key dates. Your intention is to let people know that your project exists. Tell them how they can get in touch with you directly if they have questions or would like detailed information.

# Laying the Groundwork for Your Post-Project Evaluation

A *post-project evaluation* is a meeting in which you review the experience gained from your project, recognize people for their achievements, take steps to ensure that good practices will be repeated on future projects, and develop plans to correct in future projects any performance problems the team encountered. (See Chapter 15 for a detailed discussion of how to design and conduct a post-project evaluation.)

Start laying the groundwork for your post-project evaluation as soon as your project starts, as follows:

- Tell all team members that you'll hold a post-project evaluation when the project is over.
- Encourage team members to keep records of problems, ideas, and suggestions throughout the project.
- Clarify the criteria you'll use to assess project success.

✔ If the project is designed to change or improve a situation, take measures to describe the situation before you begin project work to enable you to assess the change in these indicators from the start to the end of the project.

✔ Maintain a *project log* (a narrative record of project issues and occurrences) for yourself and encourage other team members to do the same.

# Chapter 10

# Tracking Progress and Maintaining Control

## In This Chapter

▶ Reconfirming your project plan

▶ Preventing expenditures from exceeding your budget

▶ Setting up a schedule tracking system

▶ Setting up a labor hours tracking system

▶ Setting up expenditure tracking systems

▶ Pulling it all together

▶ Managing change

*I*t's a sad reality that projects born amid high hopes and expectations often die in frustration and disappointment. Your project plans represent visions of what you believe will work; however, they don't implement themselves automatically, and they can't predict the future with certainty.

Successful projects require continued care and management to ensure that plans are followed correctly and, when implemented, lead to the anticipated results. When the unexpected occurs, you need to react promptly to keep your project on track and redirect your efforts as needed.

## Controlling Your Project

*Project control* is the set of activities you perform to ensure that your project proceeds according to plan and produces the desired results. You perform the following activities throughout the life of a project:

✔ **Reconfirming the plan:** At the beginning of each performance period (the interval for which you review and assess your project work), reaffirm with team members their project responsibilities and commitments for the coming period.

✔ **Assessing performance:** Collect information during the period about what was produced; when activities started and finished; when milestones were reached; and what work effort, money, and other resources were used. Compare your team's performance with the plan and determine the reasons for any differences between planned and actual performance.

✔ **Taking corrective action:** If necessary, take steps to bring your project's performance back into conformance with your plans or, if doing so isn't possible, to change the existing plans to reflect a new set of expectations.

✔ **Keeping people informed:** Share information with selected audiences about your achievements, problems, and future plans.

Although you may choose to monitor selected project activities on a daily basis in certain situations, you never want to go for more than one month without assessing overall project performance. Assess your project's ongoing performance by considering the same three elements that you addressed in your plan:

✔ **Outcomes:** Products or results

✔ **Schedule:** The dates on which project work begins and ends

✔ **Resources:** The people, funds, equipment, facilities, and information that support or that are used in your project work

Figure 10-1 illustrates the cyclical nature of project control. At the start of each performance period, you reaffirm the following with team members:

✔ The activities they've committed to perform during the coming period.

✔ The dates on which these activities are scheduled to start and end.

✔ The number of work hours they estimated that they would need to perform the promised work.

**Figure 10-1:**
Controlling
a project
during
performance.

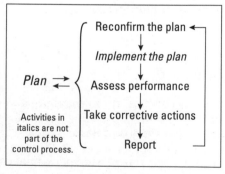

Plan $\underset{\leftarrow}{\rightarrow}$ {
Reconfirm the plan
Implement the plan
Assess performance
Take corrective actions
Report
}

Activities in
italics are not
part of the
control process.

If a person reaffirms his or her existing commitments for the coming performance period, the chances that you'll get the desired results on time and within budget increase. If not, you can work with the person to develop revised plans for how he or she will support your project.

Initially, you may be uncomfortable reconfirming commitments that people have made for an upcoming performance period because you feel that doing so

✔ **Suggests that you don't trust the person.** After all, the person has made a commitment to do the specified work; wouldn't he or she tell you if he or she was unable to live up to that commitment?

✔ **Increases the likelihood that the person will say he or she can't live up to the original promise.** Your raising the topic might actually encourage the person to tell you that he or she won't be able to honor commitments.

In most cases, though, neither of these situations proves to be true. First, your raising the issue does not suggest a lack of trust; if you didn't trust the person, you wouldn't be talking with him or her at all! Instead, it reflects your appreciation that the person may not have had a chance to tell you about new circumstances that make it difficult to honor commitments. Second, your raising the issue doesn't increase the chances that the person will opt out of a commitment. If the person wasn't going to perform as promised, you'd find out at the end of the performance period when the promised work was unfinished. Instead, you've gained an entire performance period to develop alternative ways of dealing with the new restrictions on the person's availability to your project.

Project team members work on their assigned activities during the performance period. Throughout the period, they record the following information to describe project performance:

✔ Products produced and acceptance tests passed

✔ The dates on which milestones were met

✔ The dates on which activities were started or completed

✔ The number of hours worked on each task

✔ The resources used in support of each task

✔ The funds spent in support of each task

At the end of the performance period, collect this information and compare it to the existing project plan. If actual performance conforms to the plan, share the results of your project's activities with selected project audiences and begin the process again for the next performance period. If actual performance differs from the plan, take steps to resolve the differences. First, see if you can do anything to get the project back on track. If doing so proves to be impossible, work with the appropriate project audiences to change the plan so that it contains acceptable and feasible results, schedules, and budgets.

# Preventing Resource Expenditures from Exceeding Your Budgets

Great project plans often fall by the wayside when well-intentioned people start to do what they feel is necessary to achieve the best possible results. They may spend more hours than were allotted because they feel that the additional work will produce better results. They may ask people to work on the project who were not included in the original plan because they feel that these people's expertise will improve the quality of the project results. They may spend more than the amount budgeted to buy an item they believe to be of higher quality. And they may overspend their budgets because they aren't keeping track of how much they're spending.

If possible, set up procedures that prevent people from exceeding established budgets without prior approval. For example, if people record the number of hours they spend on each project activity:

- ✔ Confirm the number of hours they'll be allowed to charge to each activity before they start to work on it.

- ✔ Arrange for the time-recording system to reject attempts to charge more than the number of hours originally agreed to unless the person has your prior written approval.

- ✔ Arrange for the time-recording system to reject any hours charged to the project by people not currently authorized to do so.

For purchases of equipment, materials, supplies, and services:

- ✔ Confirm what's to be purchased, the upper limits to be spent on individual items, if any, and the upper limit on the total expenditures allowed.

- ✔ Arrange for the procurement office or financial system to reject attempts to overspend these limits without your prior written approval.

A change to your project's budget may be necessary and desirable. However, you want to make that decision with full awareness of the change's impact on other aspects of the project.

# Establishing Project Management Information Systems

A *project management information system* (PMIS) is a set of procedures, equipment, and other resources for collecting, analyzing, storing, and reporting on information that describes project performance. To support your ongoing management and control of the project, you want to collect and maintain information about activity status, labor hours spent, and funds expended.

In some situations, you can use existing systems to track, analyze, and report on this information. In others, you may have to design, develop, and maintain your own systems. In either case, the system must include the following three components, as Figure 10-2 illustrates:

✔ **Inputs:** Raw data collected to describe selected aspects of project performance

✔ **Processes:** Storage and analysis of the data collected to compare actual performance with planned performance

✔ **Outputs:** Reports presenting the results of the analyses performed

**Figure 10-2:**
Three elements of a project management information system.

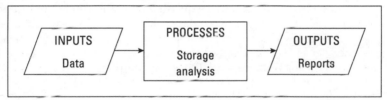

In addition to defining the data items to collect, specify how the data will be collected, by whom it will be collected, when it will be collected, and how it will be entered into the system. All of these factors can affect the timeliness and accuracy of the data and, therefore, of your project performance assessments.

Many information systems are supported by computers, scanners, printers, and plotters. However, an information system can consist of manual processes and physical storage devices as well. You might record your project activities in your notebook calendar and keep records of your project budgets in your file cabinet. You still need to monitor your procedures for collecting, storing, analyzing, and reporting your information because they affect the accuracy and timeliness of your project performance assessments.

## Monitoring schedule performance

Few organizations have established interdepartmental systems to track project schedule performance. Instead, each project team must develop its own systems.

### Defining the data to collect

Collect either or both of the following pieces of data to track schedule performance:

- ✔ The dates on which each lowest-level activity in your project's Work Breakdown Structure starts and ends
- ✔ The dates on which selected events are reached

See Chapter 3 for a discussion of the Work Breakdown Structure and Chapter 4 for the definitions of an activity and an event.

Be careful if you decide to use percentage completed to indicate an activity's progress. Most often, this measure represents only a guess because there is no clear way to determine what percentage of the activity has been completed. Saying that your new product design is 30 percent complete is virtually meaningless; there's no way to determine how much of the thinking and creating is actually done. Suggesting that you have completed 30 percent of your design because you have expended 30 of the 100 hours budgeted for the task or because three of the ten days allotted for its performance have passed is equally incorrect. The first indicator is a measure of resource use, and the second is a measure of elapsed time. Neither indicates how much of the activity's substantive work has been completed.

On the other hand, if you're performing an activity that is clearly segmented into parts that take roughly the same amount of time and effort, you may be able to determine a meaningful value of percentage completed. For example, if you planned to conduct telephone interviews with 20 different people and you have completed 10, you could argue that the activity is 50 percent complete.

### Analyzing schedule performance

Assess your project's schedule status by comparing the actual dates on which activities start and end or on which events are reached to the planned dates. Figures 10-3, 10-4, 10-5, and 10-6 present formats that support ready comparisons of these data.

Figure 10-3 depicts a key-events report. The following information in this report comes from your project plan:

- ✔ The key event identifier and description
- ✔ The person responsible for ensuring that the event is reached
- ✔ The date on which the event is supposed to be reached

These data describe performance during the period covered by the report:

- ✔ The date on which the event is actually reached
- ✔ Relevant comments about the event

| Key Event | Person Responsible | Date Due | Date Done | Comments |
|---|---|---|---|---|
| KE 2.1.1 Questionnaire design approved | F. Smith | Feb 28 | Feb 28 | |
| KE 2.2.2 Questionnaire pilot test completed | F. Smith | Apr 30 | Apr 25 | |
| KE 2.2.1 Instructions printed | R. Harris | May 15 | | |

**Figure 10-3:** A key-events report.

Figure 10-4 illustrates an activities report. Once again, the majority of the information in this report comes from your project plan. Particular data from your project plan include an activity identifier and description, the person responsible for ensuring that the activity is performed, and the dates on which the activity is supposed to start and end.

| Activity | Person Responsible | Start Date Planned | Actual | End Date Planned | Actual | Comments |
|---|---|---|---|---|---|---|
| 2.1.1 Design questionnaire | F. Smith | Feb 14 | Feb 15 | Feb 28 | Feb 28 | |
| 2.2.2 Pilot test questionnaire | F. Smith | Apr 20 | Apr 21 | Apr 30 | Apr 25 | Critical path |
| 2.2.1 Print instructions | R. Harris | May 6 | May 6 | May 15 | | |

**Figure 10-4:** An activities report.

These data describe performance during the period covered by the report:

 ✔ The dates on which the activity actually starts and ends

 ✔ Relevant comments about the activity

A combined activities and key-events report, as Figure 10-5 illustrates, presents information for both activities and events. This report uses the same format as the activities report; however, you enter the planned and actual event achievement dates in the "End Date" columns.

| Activity | Person Responsible | Start Date | | End Date | | Comments |
|---|---|---|---|---|---|---|
| | | Planned | Actual | Planned | Actual | |
| 2.1.1<br>Design questionnaire | F. Smith | Feb 14 | Feb 15 | Feb 28 | Feb 28 | |
| 2.2.2<br>Questionnaire design approved | F. Smith | - | - | Feb 28 | Feb 28 | |
| 2.2.1<br>Pilot test questionnaire | F. Smith | Apr 20 | Apr 21 | Apr 30 | Apr 25 | Critical path |

**Figure 10-5:**
A combined activities and key-events report.

Figure 10-6 illustrates a progress Gantt chart. You shade an appropriate portion of each bar to represent activity progress. This sample chart presents project performance as of June 30. According to the chart, the design phase is complete, the develop phase is one month behind schedule, and the conduct test phase is one month ahead of schedule.

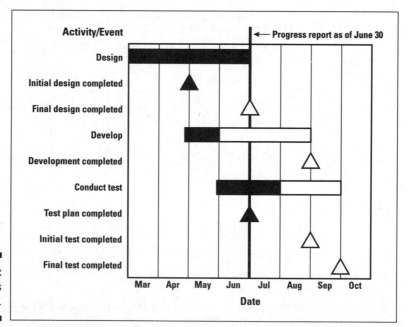

**Figure 10-6:**
A progress Gantt chart.

The most meaningful way to assess activity progress is to consider the events associated with the activity that you've achieved to date. The progress Gantt chart in Figure 10-6 really says that you've achieved by June 30 all the intermediate events associated with Task 2 that you'd planned to reach by May 31.

One final note: You might think that I violated my own guideline by reporting on four-month activities (I suggest in Chapter 3 that you want your lowest-level activities to be no more than two weeks in duration). However, you can prepare these reports with any level of detail you choose, depending on your audiences' interests and needs. This high-level report presents information for four-month activities, but the detailed plan would break these activities into subelements of no more than two weeks' duration.

Not everyone reads a progress Gantt chart in the same way. I intended the chart to suggest that Task 2 is one month behind schedule. However, people have told me that they interpret the report to mean that Task 2 is 25 percent complete because one of the four segments for Task 2 is shaded. I even had a person tell me that he thought the chart indicated that Task 2 had been finished on June 30, although I never was able to figure out how he justified that interpretation. The message is to be sure that you teach people how they should interpret the information you present graphically.

### Collecting schedule performance data

Develop a standard format and process for recording your work accomplishments; doing so will improve the accuracy of your information and take less time. I frequently use the combined activities report and key-events report format.

- At the beginning of a performance period, I print separate reports for each team member that include their activities and events for the period.

- I ask team members to record in the appropriate columns on their reports when they start or end an activity during the performance period or when they reach an event, together with any comments they want to share.

- I ask them to send me a copy of the report by the close of the first business day following the end of the performance period.

Recording and reporting on progress this way has several advantages:

- The common format for collecting and submitting data makes it easier and less time-consuming for them to use and easier for me to read.

- Recording achievements at the time they occur increases the likelihood that the data will be accurate.

- The agreed-upon schedule for submitting information to me minimizes the chances that I'll have to surprise people with unexpected requests for progress data.

- Having people continuously review their proposed schedules and record their accomplishments heightens their awareness of how well they're meeting their promises and increases the chances that they will meet their commitments.

Remember, the purpose of control is to encourage people to perform according to your plan, not just to collect data on how people are doing. The more involved and aware the people performing the work are of how they're proceeding in relation to the schedule, the greater the likelihood that they'll hit the schedule. If they don't know or care what the target date is, they're unlikely to hit it.

I also use the combined activities and key-events report format to reaffirm people's commitments at the start of a performance period. When I give them the report detailing their activities and events for the coming period, I ask them to verify the information and reaffirm their commitments. We discuss and resolve any issues that they identify.

Consider the following factors when choosing the performance period for which to monitor schedule accomplishment:

- ✔ **Is the activity on a critical path?** Activities on a critical path will delay your overall project schedule if they're delayed (see Chapter 4 for a detailed discussion of critical paths). Therefore, consider monitoring critical path activities more often to identify potential problems as soon as possible so that you can minimize their impact on the project schedule.

- ✔ **Is the activity on a path that is close to being critical?** Activities on noncritical paths can be delayed by some amount before the situation becomes critical; further delays then push back the project schedule. The maximum you can delay noncritical activities is called *slack time* or *float* (see Chapter 4). If an activity's slack time is very short, a small delay will cause the path to become critical. Therefore, consider monitoring activities with very small slack times more often, again to identify potential problems as soon as possible.

- ✔ **Is the activity risk high?** If you feel that an activity is very likely to encounter problems, consider monitoring it more frequently to identify those problems as soon as they occur.

- ✔ **Have you already encountered problems with this activity?** Consider monitoring more frequently activities with which you've had problems already. All things being equal, if you've had problems with an activity in the past, you're more likely to have them again.

Never monitor schedule performance less frequently than once a month. Experience has shown that waiting longer does the following:

- ✔ Allows people to lose focus and commitment to the activity and increases the chances that it won't be finished according to schedule

- ✔ Provides more time for small problems that may arise to go undetected longer and thus evolve into bigger problems

### Improving the accuracy of your schedule performance data

Do the following to improve the accuracy of your schedule performance data:

- ✔ **Tell people from whom you request schedule performance data how you plan to use the data.** People are always more motivated to perform a task if they understand the reasons for it.

- ✔ **Provide schedule performance reports to the people who give you the data.** People are even more motivated to perform a task if they get direct benefits from it.

- ✔ **Publicly acknowledge those people who give you timely and accurate data.** Positive reinforcement of desired behavior confirms to people that they're meeting your expectations and emphasizes to others what constitutes desirable behavior.

- ✔ **Clearly define activities and events.** Doing so helps you to understand where a project stands, when a milestone is achieved or missed, and when an activity is or isn't performed.

- ✔ **Don't collect more data than you'll use and use all the data that you collect.** Collect only the data that you know you'll use to assess schedule performance.

### Choosing a vehicle to support your schedule tracking system

You most likely will have to develop your own system to track schedule performance for your project. You can use either a manual system or a computer-based system; both offer advantages and disadvantages.

Manual systems include day planners, personal calendars, and handwritten project logs. If you use any of these systems to record your activities and achievements, you don't need special computers or software, which may save you money.

However, manual systems come with these disadvantages:

- ✔ Storing your data requires space. The more data you have, the more space you need.

- ✔ Comparing and analyzing the data by hand can be time-consuming, and the chances for errors creeping in are greater.

- ✔ Preparing reports by hand is time-consuming.

You can also use the following types of software, all of which may be available on your organization's personal computers:

- ✔ Database software such as Microsoft Access
- ✔ Spreadsheet software such as Microsoft Excel

    ✔ Word processing software such as Microsoft Word

    ✔ Project management software such as Microsoft Project

Many manufacturers offer software packages in these categories. However, I'd estimate that over 80 percent of the organizations with which I've worked have chosen Microsoft software as the company standard for these functions. Therefore, I've noted examples of Microsoft software packages in the different categories, because there's a good chance you've heard of them before and that you can easily get them installed on your computer (if you don't already have them).

See Chapter 16 for a discussion of the potential uses and benefits of software to support project management.

## Monitoring work effort expended

Monitoring work effort expended requires you to collect the actual number of hours spent working on each lowest-level Work Breakdown Structure activity. (See Chapter 3 for a discussion of the Work Breakdown Structure.)

### Analyzing labor hour expenditures

Assess your project's work effort expenditures by comparing the actual expenditures with those planned. Figure 10-7 depicts a typical labor report that describes the work effort expended by each team member working on each lowest-level project activity. The following information in this report comes from your project plan:

    ✔ An activity identifier and description

    ✔ The total hours budgeted for each team member to spend on each activity

    ✔ The hours budgeted for each team member to spend on each activity every week

You obtain or derive the following information from data submitted during the period covered by the report:

    ✔ The actual number of hours spent by each team member on each activity

    ✔ The total number of hours remaining to be spent by each team member on each activity

    ✔ The running difference between the total number of hours budgeted to be spent and those actually spent by each team member on each activity

| WBS Code | Description | Employee | | Work Effort Expended (Person-hours) | | | | | |
|---|---|---|---|---|---|---|---|---|---|
| | | | | Budget | Week 1 | Week 2 | Week 3 | Week 4 | ... |
| 3.1.2 | Design questionnaire | H. Jones | Planned | 130 | 20 | 40 | 20 | 30 | ... |
| | | | Actual | 0 | 10 | 30 | 5 | 25 | ... |
| | | | Remaining | 130 | 120 | 90 | 85 | 25 | ... |
| | | | Difference | 0 | +10 | +20 | +35 | +40 | ... |
| | | F. Smith | Planned | 70 | 0 | 20 | 20 | 15 | ... |
| | | | Actual | 0 | 0 | 25 | 10 | 15 | ... |
| | | | Remaining | 70 | 70 | 45 | 35 | 20 | ... |
| | | | Difference | 0 | 0 | -5 | +5 | +5 | ... |

**Figure 10-7:**
A labor
report.

Don't expect that actual expenditures will always agree with those planned. (In fact, if the number of hours spent on each task each month is identical to the number planned for several months, you might wonder whether people are copying the numbers from the plan onto their time sheets!) Typically, variances of 10 percent above or below the expected numbers in any month are normal.

Consider the labor charges presented for two team members in the labor report in Figure 10-7. Smith appears to be working in accordance with the plan. He charged more hours in Week 2 than planned, less in Week 3, and the same as planned in Week 4.

Jones's situation is very different. Each week, Jones is spending less time on the project than planned, and the total shortfall of hours is building steadily. It's not clear whether this shortfall indicates a problem, but the systematic undercharging does point to a situation that should be investigated further.

### Collecting work effort expenditure data

Having people fill out time sheets is the most effective way to collect work effort expenditure data. Figure 10-8 illustrates a typical time sheet.

A time sheet includes the following data:

- ✔ The number of hours you spent working on each activity during your day
- ✔ Your signature verifying that the recorded information is correct
- ✔ An approval signature verifying that the time charges made are valid and appropriate

| Activity | | | Sun | Mon | Tue | Wed | Thu | Fri | Sat | Total |
|---|---|---|---|---|---|---|---|---|---|---|
| Project No. | WBS Code | Description | Apr 3 | Apr 4 | Apr 5 | Apr 6 | Apr 7 | Apr 8 | Apr 9 | |
| | | | | | | | | | | |
| | | | | | | | | | | |
| | | | | | | | | | | |
| | | | | | | | | | | |
| | | | | | | | | | | |
| | | | | | | | | | | |
| | | | | | | | | | | |
| | | | | | | | | | | |
| **Total Hours** | | | | | | | | | | |

*Employee: Name       Signature       From _____ to _____       Approval: Name       Signature*

**Figure 10-8:**
A typical weekly time sheet.

In most instances, recording the time you spend on an activity to the nearest half hour is sufficient.

Some people may have to record their time in intervals smaller than half an hour. Lawyers, for example, often allocate their time on different jobs in six-minute segments. Their clients would have it no other way, given that a lawyer might charge $300 per hour.

A *time log* is a form that breaks the day into intervals and enables you to record the specific activity on which you worked during each interval. If you wanted to record your time in half-hour intervals and you began work at 8:30 a.m., the first interval on your log would be 8:30 to 9:00 a.m., the second would be 9:00 to 9:30 a.m., and so on.

If you fill out a time log conscientiously, it provides more accurate data because it forces you to account for what you were doing every moment of the day. However, maintaining a time log is far more time-consuming than filling out a time sheet. You don't normally need to record when during the day you performed an activity to keep track of your project work effort expenditures — just the total time you spent on it.

### *Improving the accuracy of your work effort expenditure data*

Take the following steps to increase the accuracy of the work effort expenditure data that you collect:

- ✔ **Make sure people understand that the purpose of your time-recording system is to enable you to compare actual performance with planned performance and to help you determine when aspects of the plan need to be changed.** When you ask people to detail the hours they spend on specific assignments, they often fear that you're looking to criticize them for not spending time exactly in accordance with the plan, no matter what the reason, or for not spending enough hours on project work as opposed to other administrative duties. If they believe that these are your motives, they'll allocate their work hours among activities to show you what they think you want to see rather than what's really happening.

- ✔ **Encourage people to record the actual hours they work during the period rather than requiring their total hours recorded for a week to equal 40.** If people must record a total of 40 hours per week and they work overtime, they'll omit hours or reduce them proportionately to ensure that their weekly total equals 40. You want them to record accurate data.

- ✔ **Include categories for time spent on nonproject work activities, such as "unallocated," "administrative overhead," and so on.** If you want people to honestly record the activities on which they work, you must provide them with appropriate categories.

- ✔ **Encourage people to fill out their own time sheets.** Some people ask a third person, such as a secretary, to fill out their time sheets for them. It's hard enough for you to remember what you did during the day or during the past week; it's virtually impossible for someone else.

- ✔ **Collect time sheets weekly if possible, and no less often than once every two weeks.** No matter how often you ask people to fill out their time sheets, many will wait until the sheet is due to complete it. If you collect time sheets once a month, those people will be sitting there at the end of the month trying to remember what they did four weeks ago!

- ✔ **Don't ask people to submit their time sheets for a performance period before the period is over.** On occasion, people are asked to submit time sheets by the end of the day Thursday for the week ending on Friday. First, this practice immediately reduces the accuracy of the data because it's impossible to know with certainty what you'll be doing tomorrow. More important, though, it suggests to people that, if it's okay to estimate their time for Friday, perhaps they don't have to be too concerned with the accuracy of the rest of the week's data, either.

### Choosing a vehicle to support your labor hour tracking system

First, check to see if your organization has a time-recording system in place, if it can record data in the way you need it, and if the data recorded are sufficiently accurate. When assessing an existing time-recording system, consider the following:

- Time-recording systems are typically designed to identify the portions of a person's pay that are allocated to regular work, vacation time, sick leave, and holiday leave. As such, the system may require that exempt employees (that is, employees who don't get paid for overtime) record no more than 40 hours per week. Additionally, they often lack the capability to track regular work by detailed Work Breakdown Structure categories.

- People are often uncomfortable recording the hours they spend on different assignments because they aren't sure how the information will be used.

- Standard reports available from the system may not present information in the ways you need it to support your project work effort tracking.

If you decide to create your own system, you can develop a manual one or one that is computer based. Manual systems typically involve noting in your daily calendar or personal diary hours spent on activities. Not only are the data often incomplete and of questionable accuracy, but you'll also have difficulty pulling the data together to perform organized assessments or to prepare meaningful reports. You can support a computer-based system with the following software:

- Project-management software such as Microsoft Project
- Database software such as Microsoft Access
- Spreadsheet software such as Microsoft Excel

See Chapter 16 for a discussion of the potential uses and benefits of software to support project management.

## Monitoring expenditures

You monitor your project's financial expenditures to verify that they're in accordance with the project plan and, if not, to determine how to address any deviations. You might think that determining project funds used to date and, correspondingly, the amount of funds remaining requires only reading the balance in your project's "checkbook" (that is, the financial account from which expenditures are made). However, planning for and ultimately spending project funds entails several steps. At each step, you have a better sense of whether you will order the item, whether it will be received, and what it will cost.

The process leading up to the payment of funds for goods and services received includes the following steps:

1. **You develop an initial estimate of the rough cost of the item, usually without checking with specific vendors or suppliers.**

2. **You submit a written, approved request for the item to your organization's procurement department.**

3. **The procurement department asks the vendor for the item.**

   The formal submission usually includes their understanding of the most recent price of the item and, possibly, taxes and associated shipping costs.

4. **The vendor agrees to provide the item you requested and reconfirms the price, with taxes and estimated shipping charges.**

   The purchase order signed by your procurement department and the vendor constitutes a contract for the procurement of the item.

5. **You receive the item and confirm that it works.**

6. **You receive a bill that details the final cost of the item, together with associated discounts, taxes, and shipping and handling charges.**

7. **You pay for the item.**

As you proceed from the first step to the last, the accuracy of the projected expenditure improves, and the likelihood that you'll actually make the purchase increases.

In some instances, you may want to solicit bids from several different vendors before you sign a contract to ensure that you're getting the highest quality for the best price. A *request for proposals* (RFP) asks vendors who may be interested in providing the good or service to submit formal proposals that describe exactly what they will provide, when, and for what price. If you've defined clearly and specifically the good or service you're seeking, you might issue an RFP that asks interested vendors to submit only the price they would charge for the item.

After reviewing the proposals you receive and getting vendors' answers to any questions you have, you select the offer you want to accept, negotiate the final details of the agreement, and draft a written contract to buy the item that both you and the vendor sign.

This list identifies every possible step in the procurement process. Depending on the size of your purchase and the size and formality of your organization, you may not formally go through each step for each purchase.

Suppose you identified in your plan that you need to buy a new computer as soon as possible after the project starts. Based on your prior experience and your familiarity with the marketplace, you budgeted $2,000 to purchase this computer. As soon as your project starts, you write a purchase requisition for the computer and send it to the procurement department. You describe the characteristics the computer should have and put down an estimated price of $2,000. At this point, you have $2,000 less to spend on other purchases because, as far as you know, you will have to pay this $2,000 to a computer vendor at some point in the future.

After receiving your purchase request, your procurement department checks with different vendors, selects one, and issues a purchase order for $1,920 (which includes the vendor's confirmed cost for the computer as well as associated taxes and estimated shipping charges). At this point, the procurement department has confirmed that a vendor can fill your request and has improved the accuracy of the estimate of the total cost of the computer.

As a result, you have more confidence that you'll receive the computer and a better sense of what you'll pay for it. The vendor signs the purchase order, which confirms that the vendor intends to deliver the computer and specifies its total cost.

After you receive the computer and check it out, you'll have virtually erased all doubts about whether or when you'll get it. And when you receive the bill for the computer, you will know the cost. It's still possible that the computer will malfunction or that a hidden cost will crop up, but the likelihood is very low.

Finally, after you pay the bill for the computer, you're almost certain that no portion of those funds will be available for other purchases. It's always possible that you might choose to return the computer at some point in the future and receive a partial refund, but the chances of that happening are slight.

Responsive project monitoring requires you to have a picture of the amount of project funds available at each stage of the process. To do so, you typically want to monitor purchase requisitions, purchase orders, commitments (that is, purchase orders or contracts agreed to by you and the contractor or vendor), accounts payable, and expenditures.

### Analyzing expenditures

You assess your project's work expenditures by comparing the actual expenditures with those planned. Figure 10-9 depicts a typical cost report that presents project expenditures individually for lowest-level activities and summed to provide totals for higher-level activities for the current period and for the entire project to date. The following information in this report comes from your project plan:

✔ Activity identifiers and descriptions

✔ The total funds budgeted for the performance period for each activity

 ✔ The cumulative funds budgeted to date for each activity

 ✔ The total budget for each activity

| WBS Code | Activity | Performance Period | | To Date | | Total Budget |
| --- | --- | --- | --- | --- | --- | --- |
| | | Budget | Actual | Budget | Actual | |
| | Total | $8,500 | $8,200 | $15,500 | $15,100 | $200,000 |
| 1.0 | Finalize requirements | 5,000 | 4,400 | 12,300 | 11,400 | 45,000 |
| 1.1 | Conduct focus groups | 3,000 | 2,900 | 7,500 | 7,100 | 10,000 |
| 1.2 | Review documents | 1,500 | 1,200 | 4,000 | 3,800 | 5,000 |
| 1.3 | Prepare report | 500 | 300 | 800 | 500 | 4,000 |
| | ⋮ | | | | | |

**Figure 10-9:** A cost report.

The actual numbers for the period are derived from data submitted during the period covered by the report. Because no definition is given, "actual" in this illustration may mean the value of purchase requisitions, purchase orders, commitments, accounts payable, and/or expenditures.

*Earned Value Analysis* is a method of determining from resource expenditures alone not only whether you're over or under budget but also whether you're ahead of or behind schedule. On complex projects, it's a useful way to identify areas where you should investigate further for possible current or potential problems. See Appendix B for further discussion of Earned Value Analysis.

### Collecting expenditure data and improving its accuracy

Typically, you obtain your expenditure data from purchase requisitions, purchase orders, vendor bills, and written checks. You normally see all purchase requisitions because you probably have to approve them. The procurement department typically prepares purchase orders, and you may be able to get copies. Vendor bills are usually sent directly to the accounts payable group in the finance department, and these people pay the checks. You may be able to have them send copies of bills to you so that you can verify the amounts and so forth, and you can request reports of all checks written with funds from your project if the finance department tracks expenditures by project code.

Take the following steps to increase the accuracy of your project's expenditure data:

 ✔ Check to see that purchase orders are removed from your totals after a bill has been received (or a check has been written) to avoid double-counting the expenditure.

 ✔ Be sure to include the correct Work Breakdown Structure charge code on each purchase requisition.

> ✔ Verify that the purchase order includes the correct Work Breakdown Structure charge code.
>
> ✔ Periodically remove from your lists old purchase requisitions and purchase orders that have been voided or cancelled.

### *Choosing a vehicle to support your expenditure tracking system*

First, check the nature and capabilities of your organization's financial tracking system. Most organizations have a financial system that maintains records of all expenditures. Often, the system also maintains records of accounts payable. Unfortunately, many financial systems categorize expenses by cost center but don't have the capacity to classify them by project or activity within a project.

If you have to develop your own system for tracking project expenditures, consider using the following types of software:

> ✔ Project-management package such as Microsoft Project
>
> ✔ Accounting package such as QuickBooks
>
> ✔ Database package such as Microsoft Access
>
> ✔ Spreadsheet package such as Microsoft Excel

See Chapter 16 for more information on the potential uses and benefits of software to support project management.

Even if your organization's financial system can classify expenditures by activity within a project, you'll probably have to develop your own system for tracking purchase requisitions and purchase orders. Consider using a spreadsheet program or database software to support this tracking.

# *Pulling It All Together*

Develop a set of procedures to collect and submit the required information and to analyze work and results. Follow these procedures throughout your project's life.

1. **At the start of a performance period, reconfirm with people the activities you expect them to perform during the period, the start and end dates they agreed to for these activities, the dates on which they agreed to achieve key events, and the work effort they'll have to spend to complete their activities.**

   If any people disagree with you about any of this information, work with them to come up with an acceptable modification to the existing plan.

2. **During the period, have people record the following performance data:**

   - The dates on which activities start and end and on which events are reached

   - The work hours they spend on individual project activities

   - Purchase requisitions they submit and purchase orders they send out

3. **At agreed-upon intervals during or at the end of the period, have people submit the following data either to all relevant organizational systems or to systems specially maintained for your project:**

   - Their activity achievement data

   - Their work hour records

   - Their purchase requisition and purchase order information

4. **At the end of the period, do the following:**

   - Confirm that all acceptance tests, peer reviews, and other assessments of work produced during the period have been successfully passed.

   - Enter schedule and resource information into the appropriate information systems.

   - Produce reports from project-specific systems or obtain reports from organizational systems that compare planned and actual schedule and resource performance for the period.

   - Identify differences between planned and actual performance and determine the reasons for those variances.

   - Formulate corrective actions to get back on track or, as needed, to change selected aspects of the existing plan.

   - Obtain all required approvals to make needed changes to existing plans.

   - Take the corrective actions you developed.

   - Report on achievements, problems, corrective actions, and the results of the corrective actions taken.

5. **At the beginning of the next performance period, start the cycle again.**

A *baseline* is the current version of your project plan that you're using to guide project performance and against which you're comparing actual project performance. *Rebaselining* is officially adopting a new project plan to guide activities and serve as the comparative basis for future performance assessments.

If you feel that revising your plan and adopting a new baseline is necessary:

- ✔ Consult with key project audiences to explain why the changes are needed and to solicit their approval and support.
- ✔ Make sure that all key project audiences know about the new baseline.
- ✔ Keep a copy of your original plan and all subsequent modifications to support your final performance assessment when the project is over.

Rebaselining is a last resort when project work is not going according to plan. Exhaust all possible strategies and approaches to get back on track before you attempt to change the plan itself.

Monitoring project performance doesn't identify problems; it identifies symptoms. When you identify a symptom, you must investigate the situation to determine the nature of any underlying problems, the reasons for the problems, and how to fix the problems.

You can't get an accurate picture of where your project stands by monitoring only one or two aspects of your project. You must consider performance in all three dimensions at the same time to determine the reasons for any inconsistencies you identify.

Suppose a member of your project team spent half as much time working on a project activity during the period as you had planned at the beginning of the month. Does this mean that there's a problem? You really can't tell. If he or she accomplished all the events that were planned, perhaps not. If some events were not accomplished, perhaps there is. You must consider both resource expenditures and schedule achievements.

Suppose all the events were reached. You still don't know whether there was a problem — you have to confirm that the quality of the products produced during the month meet the established standards.

## Identifying possible causes of delays and variances

If an activity is running behind schedule, it may be due to one or more of the following reasons:

- ✔ People are spending less time on the activity than was budgeted.
- ✔ The activity is taking more work effort than you figured.
- ✔ People are expanding the scope of the activity.
- ✔ Work you hadn't identified is required to perform the activity.

- ✔ The people working on the activity have less experience with similar activities than you anticipated.

- ✔ People are not accurately recording their schedule performance.

The following situations may result in people charging more or less time to activities than you'd planned:

- ✔ The person performing the work is more or less productive than you assumed when you developed the plan.

- ✔ You allowed insufficient time for becoming familiar with the activity before starting to work on it.

- ✔ The person is more or less efficient than you considered.

- ✔ The activity is requiring more or less work than you anticipated.

- ✔ People are recording their time incorrectly.

Spending more or less to support your project activities than you'd planned could occur because

- ✔ The bills for goods or services were received late.

- ✔ You prepaid for certain items to receive special discounts.

- ✔ You didn't need certain goods or services that you had included in your plan.

- ✔ You needed goods or services that you hadn't included in your plan.

- ✔ Expenditures were allocated to the wrong accounts.

## Identifying possible corrective actions

If your actual performance deviates from your plan, consider doing the following:

- ✔ **If the variance results from a one-time difficulty, try to take steps to get back on the plan.** Suppose you'd planned to spend 40 hours to buy a piece of equipment. You figured you'd have to visit four stores before you found the equipment, but you found exactly what you wanted for the price you wanted to pay at the first store. Don't change your plan, because most likely you'll wind up requiring slightly more time on some future activities and it'll tend to even out.

- ✔ **If the variance suggests a situation that will lead to similar variances in the future, consider modifying your plan accordingly.** Suppose you finished your task with half the allotted work effort because you're more experienced than the person anticipated. If your experience enables you to be more efficient on future assignments, revise the plan to reduce the amount of effort you plan to spend on those assignments.

# Managing Change

No matter how carefully you plan, things will happen during your project that you hadn't anticipated. Perhaps an activity will turn out to be more involved than you figured, client needs and desires will change, or new technology will evolve. When such things occur, you may need to modify your project to respond to these new situations.

Even though change is necessary and desirable, it always comes at a price. Furthermore, people may have different opinions about which changes are important and how to implement them.

On large projects, formal change-control systems govern how requests for changes are assessed and acted upon. Whether you handle change requests formally or informally, always follow the steps illustrated in Figure 10-10.

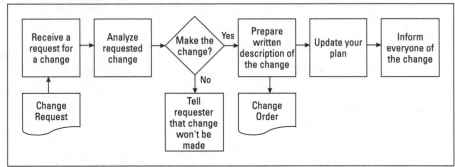

**Figure 10-10:**
A change-control system.

✔ When you receive a request for a change to some aspect of your project, clarify exactly what you're being asked to do. If possible, ask that the request be submitted to you in writing, or confirm the request by putting in writing what you understand the requester is asking you to do. In a formal change-control system, all changes must be submitted in writing on a change-request form.

✔ Determine the potential impact of the change on all aspects of your project. Also consider what would happen if you didn't make the requested change.

✔ Decide whether you'll implement the change. If this change will impact others as well, involve them in the decision, too.

✔ If you decide not to make the change, tell the requester and explain why.

✔ If you decide to make the change, prepare written instructions for taking the steps required to implement the change. In a formal change-control system, all aspects of the change are described in a written change order.

✔ Update your plan to reflect any changes in schedules, outcomes to be produced, or resource budgets as a result.

✔ Tell team members and appropriate audiences about the change and its expected impact on your project.

Observe the following guidelines to ensure that changes are smoothly incorporated into your project:

✔ **Don't use change as an excuse for inadequate planning.** Be as accurate and complete as possible when you prepare your project plan; doing so will save you time and money in the future.

✔ **Remember that change always has a cost.** Don't ignore the cost because you figure that you're going to have to make the change anyway; determine the cost so that you can plan for it and, if possible, minimize it.

✔ **Assess the impact of change on all aspects of your project.** Maintain a broad perspective; a change early in your project may impact your project from beginning to end.

*Scope creep* is the gradual expansion of project work without formal acknowledgment and acceptance of these changes and the associated costs and impacts. Scope creep can occur due to

✔ Lack of clarity and detail in the original description of project scope, objectives, and work to be done

✔ Willingness to make "small" changes to a project without formal review and approval

✔ Allowing people who will not do the work associated with the changes themselves to decide whether to make changes

✔ Feeling that you should never say "no" to a client

✔ Personal pride that encourages you to believe that you can do anything

Control scope creep by doing the following:

✔ Identifying all project objectives in your project plan and describing them in sufficient detail

✔ Always assessing the impact of requested changes on project products, schedules, and resources

✔ Sharing your true feelings about whether you can implement the requested changes

✔ Developing positive, mutually trusting relationships with your clients so that they will be more receptive when you raise issues that you feel will be associated with the requested changes

# Chapter 11

# Keeping Everyone Informed

· · · · · · · · · · · · · · · · · · · · · · · · · · · · · · · · · · · · · · · ·

## In This Chapter

▶ Sharing information in writing

▶ Sharing information through meetings

▶ Preparing a project progress report

▶ Conducting upper management progress reviews

· · · · · · · · · · · · · · · · · · · · · · · · · · · · · · · · · · · · · · · ·

A key to successful projects is effective communication — sharing the right messages with the right people in a timely manner. Informative communications support the following:

✔ Continued buy-in and support from key audiences and team members

✔ Prompt and responsive problem identification and decision-making

✔ A clear project focus

✔ Ongoing recognition of project achievements

✔ Productive working relationships among team members

Planning your project communications upfront enables you to choose the appropriate media for sharing different messages.

## Choosing the Medium that Fits Your Needs

Project communications can be both formal and informal. *Formal* communications are preplanned, conducted in a standard format in accordance with an established schedule. *Informal* communications occur as people think of information they want to share.

# An unusual way to encourage people to read your reports

A number of years ago, I spoke with a client who had been managing a large project with the federal government. He explained that, at the end of each month, he would submit an extensive report of the work performed, issues encountered, and actions recommended, as required by the terms of the contract. However, after he submitted a report, his government project officer would routinely call to ask for information that he had included in the report, never comment on issues raised, and never take action on any of the proposed recommendations. My client strongly suspected that the government project officer never read the reports!

Becoming increasingly frustrated, my client finally came up with a novel idea that he incorporated into his latest monthly report. A few weeks after submitting this report, he stopped by to pay a courtesy call on his project officer.

In the course of their conversation, my client offhandedly asked if the project officer had read his most recent monthly progress report. The project officer assured him that he had. My client then asked the project officer if he had noticed anything unusual in the report. The project officer said that he didn't remember, but that he would check it again. After several minutes of searching, he retrieved the report from the bottom of a large stack of papers that obviously hadn't been moved in weeks and started to thumb through it. When he arrived at page ten, he found a $100 bill clipped to the page! My client expressed tremendous relief as he retrieved the $100 from the report. "Thanks," he exclaimed. "I knew I must have left that $100 bill somewhere; I just couldn't remember where!"

At least my client could be sure that his project officer would check all paper-clipped pages in future progress reports.

Informal communications occur continuously in the normal course of business. However, you must take care not to rely on these informal interchanges to share thoughts about all aspects of your project, because they often tend to involve only a small number of the people who may benefit from the topics being addressed. To minimize the chances for misunderstandings and hurt feelings:

- ✔ Confirm in writing the important information that you share in informal discussions.

- ✔ Avoid having an informal discussion with only some of the people who are involved in the topic being addressed.

## *Sharing information in writing*

Written reports enable you to present factual data more efficiently, choose your words to minimize misunderstandings, provide a historical record of the information you shared, and share the same message with a wide audience. However, written reports don't

- ✔ Allow your intended audience to ask questions to clarify the content, meaning, and implication of the message you're trying to send

- ✔ Enable you to verify that your audiences received and interpreted your message in the way you intended

- ✔ Enable you to pick up nonverbal signals that suggest your audience's reactions to the message

- ✔ Support interactive discussion and brainstorming about your message

Most important, you may never know whether your audience even read the reports you sent!

Take the following steps to improve the chances that people will read and understand your written reports:

- ✔ Prepare regularly scheduled reports in a standard format. Doing so makes it easier for your audience to know where to look for specific types of information.

- ✔ Stay focused. Preparing several short reports to address different topics is better than combining several topics into one long report.

- ✔ Minimize the use of technical jargon and acronyms.

- ✔ Use written reports to share facts, and identify a person for people to contact to clarify or discuss further any information included in those reports.

- ✔ Clearly describe any actions you want people to take based on the information in the report.

- ✔ Use novel approaches to emphasize key information, such as printing key sections in a different color or on colored paper, or mentioning particularly relevant or important sections in a cover memo.

- ✔ After you send your report, discuss with the people who received it one or two key points that you addressed in the report. Doing so will tell you quickly whether they've read it.

- ✔ Keep your reports to one page if possible; if not, include a short summary (one page or less) at the beginning of the report.

Be careful of the "yes, but" syndrome, which basically says that you think an idea sounds great, but your special situation requires a different approach. A number of years ago, I shared in a training program my suggestion to keep project reports to one page or less if possible. Most people agreed that doing so made sense, but one participant rejected the notion. He proceeded to explain that his project was so important and so complex that he sent his boss monthly project reports that were a minimum of ten pages in length, and that his boss read every word.

I had the opportunity to speak with this participant's boss a few weeks after the training session about a totally unrelated matter. In the course of our conversation, he happened to mention his frustration with a person on his staff who felt his project was so important that he had to submit monthly progress reports that were no less than ten pages long. He said that he usually read the first paragraph of these reports, but he rarely had time to review them thoroughly. He said that he hoped this person had listened carefully when I suggested in my training session that reports should be kept to one page or less!

## Sharing information through meetings

Few words can elicit the emotional reactions of anger and frustration that the word *meeting* can. People view meetings as being anything from the last vestige of interpersonal contact in an increasingly computer and technology-focused society to the biggest time-waster in business today. Here are some of the most common frustrations about meetings that people express:

- Not being given sufficient advance notice
- Not having the right people attend
- Not starting on time
- Not having an agenda
- Not sticking to the agenda if one exists
- Having no actions result from the meeting
- Discussing issues that you thought had been resolved at a previous meeting
- Having people represent that they have the authority to make a decision and then having their decision reversed after the meeting
- Reading written material aloud that people could've read themselves beforehand
- Having 95 percent of the meeting deal with issues in which you're not interested or involved
- Knowing that the next meeting will be no better than the last one

Meetings can be valuable, though, if you plan and manage them effectively. When handled correctly, meetings can help you learn about other team members' backgrounds, experience, and styles; stimulate brainstorming, problem analysis, and decision-making; and provide a forum for people to explore the reasons for and interpretations of a message.

You can improve your meetings by taking the following steps.

### Premeeting preparation

✔ Clarify the purpose of the meeting.

✔ Decide who needs to attend and why. If you need information, decide who has it. If you want to make decisions at the meeting, decide who has the necessary authority and make sure that that person attends.

✔ Give plenty of advance notice of the meeting.

✔ Tell others the purpose of the meeting.

✔ Prepare a written agenda that includes topics and times. Doing so helps people to see why attending is in their interests. The agenda is also your guideline for conducting the meeting.

✔ Circulate the written agenda and any background material in advance so that people can prepare for the meeting.

✔ Keep meetings to one hour or less. You can force people to sit in a room for hours, but you can't force them to keep their minds on the activities and information discussed. If necessary, schedule several meetings to discuss complex issues or multiple topics.

### Meeting conduct

✔ Start on time, even if people are absent. Once people see that you'll wait for latecomers before starting, everyone will come late!

✔ Assign a "timekeeper" — someone who will remind the group when allotted times for topics have been exceeded.

✔ Take written minutes of who attended, what items were discussed, and what decisions and assignments were made.

✔ Keep a list of action items to be explored further after the meeting, and assign responsibility for all entries on that list.

✔ If you don't have the right information or the right people in attendance to resolve an issue, stop your discussion and put it on the action item list.

✔ End on time.

*Follow-up*

✔ Promptly distribute meeting minutes to all attendees.

✔ Monitor the status of all action items to be performed.

✔ Don't just think about these suggestions; act on them!

# Preparing a Written Project-Progress Report

The most common regularly-scheduled, written project communication is the project-progress report. A *project-progress report* reviews what has happened during a performance period, describes problems and the corrective actions needed, and previews what is planned for the next period.

A project-progress report is a convenient way to keep key audiences involved in your project and informed of anything they have to do to support your ongoing performance. In addition, preparing the report gives you an opportunity to step back and review all aspects of your project so that you can recognize accomplishments and identify situations that may require your early intervention.

Decide to whom you will give regularly scheduled project-progress reports by answering the following questions:

✔ Who needs to know about your project?

✔ Who wants to know about your project?

✔ Whom do you want to know about your project?

At a minimum, consider providing project-progress reports to your supervisor, upper management, your client or customer, project team members, others who will be helping you on the project, and others who are interested in or will be affected by the project's results.

Be sure to include some or all the following information in your project-progress report:

✔ **Performance highlights:** Always begin your report with a summary of highlights. (Keep it to no more than one page!)

✔ **Performance details:** Describe in detail the outcomes produced, activities performed, milestones reached, labor hours worked, and funds expended.

✔ **Problems and issues:** Highlight special issues or problems that you encountered during the period and propose any needed corrective actions.

✔ **Approved changes to the plan:** Report all approved changes made to the existing project plan.

✔ **Risk-management status:** Update your project risk assessment by reporting on changes in project assumptions or the likelihood that they will come to pass, as well as their impact on existing project plans.

✔ **Plans for the next period:** Summarize major work and accomplishments planned for the next performance period.

Use the following tips to improve the quality of your project-progress reports:

✔ **Tailor your reports to the interests and needs of your audiences.** Provide only the information that your audience wants and/or needs. If necessary, prepare separate reports for different audiences.

✔ **If you're preparing different progress reports for different audiences, prepare the most detailed one first and extract information from that report to produce the others.** This approach ensures consistency among the reports and reduces the likelihood that you'll perform the same work more than once.

✔ **No matter what your audiences request, produce a project-progress report no less often than once per month.**

✔ **Make sure that all the product, schedule, and resource information you include in your report is for the same time period.** Doing so may not be easy if you depend on different organization systems for your raw performance data. For example, if you track project schedule performance on a system that you maintain yourself, you may be able to produce a status report by the end of the first week after the performance period ends. However, your organization's financial system, which you use to track project expenditures, may not generate performance reports for the same period until a month after the period ends.

✔ **Always compare actual performance with respect to the performance planned.** Presenting the information in this format highlights issues to be addressed.

✔ **Include no surprises.** If something significant occurs during the period that requires prompt action, tell all the people involved immediately and work to address the problem. Mention the occurrence and any associated corrective actions in the progress report to provide a record.

✔ **Use your regularly scheduled team meetings to discuss issues and problems raised in the project-progress report.**

# Holding Key Project Meetings

Active, ongoing support from all major project audiences gives you the greatest chance for achieving project success. Continually reinforce your project's vision and how you're progressing toward it and help your project's audiences understand when and how they can most effectively support your efforts.

Consider using some or all of the following types of meetings during your project:

- **Regularly scheduled team meetings:** Opportunities for team members to share progress and issues and to sustain productive and trusting interpersonal relationships.

- **Ad hoc team meetings:** Special sessions for team members to address problems and issues as they arise.

- **Upper-management reviews:** Periodic summary of project status, major accomplishments, and issues with which you need upper management's help. This type of meeting enables you to keep the project fresh in their minds and note ways to keep it in line with major organization initiatives.

The following sections cover each meeting type in detail.

## Regularly scheduled team meetings

Project teams should have the opportunity to meet periodically to reaffirm the project's focus and keep abreast of activities within and outside the project that will affect their work and the project's ultimate success. Recognizing that most people work on several projects at the same time, these meetings can reinforce the team's identity and working relationships.

Consult with team members to develop a meeting schedule that is convenient for as many people as possible. If some people can't attend in person, try to have them participate in a conference call. (See Chapter 16 for more about how you can use technology to support your project.)

In addition to the general suggestions for ensuring productive meetings that I presented earlier in this chapter, observe the following guidelines when planning and conducting team meetings:

- Even though the meetings are regularly scheduled, always prepare a specific agenda, distribute it beforehand, and solicit comments and suggestions.

- Distribute your progress report for the most recent performance period before the meeting.

✔ Distribute beforehand any other background information related to topics that will be discussed at the meeting.

✔ Limit discussions that require more in-depth consideration; deal with them in other forums.

✔ Start on time and end on time (there, I said it again!).

✔ Prepare and distribute brief minutes of the meeting.

## Ad hoc team meetings

Hold ad hoc team meetings to address specific issues that arise during your project. An ad hoc meeting might involve some or all of your team's members, depending on the issues to be addressed. Because issues often arise unexpectedly, it's important that you do the following:

✔ Clarify the issue and what you hope to achieve at your meeting.

✔ Identify and invite all people who may be interested in, affected by, or working on the issue.

✔ Clearly explain the meeting's purpose to all invitees.

✔ Carefully document all action items developed at the meeting and assign responsibility for their completion.

## Upper-management progress reviews

Take every opportunity to help upper management remember why your project is important to them. They may have approved your project months ago, but chances are it's now only one of many things going on in a busy organization.

An upper management progress review is typically presided over by a senior manager and run by the project manager. Team members and representatives from all functional areas attend. This meeting provides an opportunity to highlight the progress and status of your project, acknowledge any support that functional managers have provided, remind upper management of future project plans, determine whether major priorities that initially led to the creation of your project have changed and whether your project should change accordingly, and discuss specific ways in which upper management can support your project to ensure its continued successful performance.

Make your upper management progress review effective by observing the following tips:

✔ Identify the interests of your audience and explain how your project is meeting those interests.

- Keep your presentation short; choose a few key messages and emphasize them.

- Highlight your key information, but be prepared to go into more detail on issues if you're asked to do so.

- Allow time for questions.

- Present updated information on project risks and how you're addressing them.

- Distribute a brief handout at the meeting that summarizes the key points of your presentation.

- After the meeting, distribute notes that highlight issues raised and actions agreed upon at the session.

## Talk only when you have something to say

Several years ago, I started the first morning of a three-day project management training session by asking participants to share their expectations for the program. One gentleman informed me that he knew all about project management and that, as far as he was concerned, the session was a complete waste of time. He noted that he was attending the session at his manager's direct request, but he expected to learn nothing of value that he would want to use on the job.

I asked him why he felt this way, and he told me of an experience he had had a year earlier. He had been a team member on a major project for his organization. The project was going poorly, and his organization had hired a consultant to determine why. After a series of interviews and several days of observation, the consultant concluded that the people on the team just weren't communicating. Everyone was overworked and never took a moment to share their thoughts, activities, or frustrations with their team members.

Upon hearing the assessment, the organization's upper management directed the project team to start holding one-hour project meetings first thing every Monday morning. At first, the team members complied. Even though Monday morning was a time when people normally rushed to start a busy week, they changed their schedules to attend the one-hour meeting. Despite their initial misgivings, people thought the first meeting was productive because it was the first time in months that they had spoken with one other. People had little new to say at the second meeting, however, because only a week had passed since the preceding session. By the third meeting, people were so frustrated at having to waste an hour of their packed days in a meaningless activity that they went en masse to management and declared that if the meetings continued, they all would resign! The meetings were cancelled immediately.

Not only did I understand why the person felt the way he did, but I totally agreed with him. Never hold meetings because someone else says you should; hold them because you believe that they meet an important need. Specify that need clearly and design the meetings to address it effectively. If the meetings stop being productive, cancel them.

# Chapter 12

# Encouraging Peak Performance

## In This Chapter

▶ Clarifying the difference between management and leadership

▶ Tapping into the different types and sources of power

▶ Taking four steps to create and sustain motivation

*Y*our project's success depends on your ability to organize, coordinate, and support a diverse team working toward a common goal. Often, these people come from different areas of your organization, have different operating styles, and don't report to you administratively. Successfully guiding such a group of people requires both vision and structure.

## Practicing Both Management and Leadership

Leadership and management are two related but distinct sets of behaviors for guiding and supporting people through the stages of a project. Management focuses on creating plans and assessing performance; leadership emphasizes defining a vision and taking actions to increase the chances that your vision will become reality. Management focuses on systems, procedures, and information; leadership focuses on people. Management creates order and predictability; leadership helps people to address change.

Table 12-1 illustrates leadership and management approaches to support the key stages of a project. Practice both management and leadership to maximize your chances for achieving project success, as follows:

✔ In your project's planning stages, explore the "why" of the project (a leadership issue) to help elicit people's buy-in and commitment, as well as the "what," "when," and "how" (management issues).

✔ When preparing to begin project work, assign people to the team and explain their roles and responsibilities, and also get their personal commitments that they'll perform their assignments to the best of their abilities.

✔ Throughout your project, track your progress and deal with any problems you encounter, and also encourage people to sustain their ongoing commitment to achieving project success.

| Table 12-1 | Comparison of Leadership and Management Approaches to Project Activities | |
|---|---|---|
| **Activity** | **Leadership** | **Management** |
| Planning | Creating and sharing visions and strategies | Specifying objectives, schedules, and budgets |
| Organizing | Eliciting commitments from team members | Assigning people to the team and defining their roles |
| Performing | Motivating team members | Monitoring and reporting on progress and dealing with problems |

# Developing Personal Power and Influence

*Power* is the ability to influence the actions of others. Establishing effective bases of power enhances your ability to coordinate your project team and other key audiences to achieve project success.

## Looking at the reasons people will do what you ask

People respond to your requests and direction for different reasons:

✔ **Rewards:** People will do what you ask because they want the benefits that you can give them. Examples of rewards include raises, bonuses, and recognition.

✔ **Punishments:** People will do what you ask because they *don't* want what you can give them. Examples of punishments include poor performance appraisals and undesirable job assignments.

✔ **Your position:** When you're the project manager, your team members will take your requests more seriously because they feel that it's appropriate for the project manager to direct team members. You can lose this power if you behave inappropriately, but you have it initially.

✔ **What you stand for:** People will do what you ask because they agree with what you're trying to accomplish. They know that your requests and actions are attempts to achieve the results that they too want to achieve.

✔ **Who you are:** People will listen to you because they appreciate and respect who you are, as reflected by your sensitivity, your loyalty to others, your sense of humor, or other characteristics of your behavior.

✔ **Your expertise:** People will listen to you because they respect the skills and knowledge that you bring to your job. They'll listen to you because they believe that you're probably right.

You don't have to be the technical expert on your project to command the respect of your team members. You do need to be an expert in the skills and knowledge that you'll be called upon to use on the project. Because you're the project manager, these skills and knowledge include your ability to plan and control the project, your ability to encourage effective communication, your ability to encourage a positive and productive work environment, and your understanding of the political environment in the organization in which your project is being performed.

Being both the technical expert and the project manager on your project can work against you. If you're not careful, you can inhibit others' willingness to accept responsibility and perform their work independently because

✔ They feel that their work will never be as good as yours.

✔ You keep the challenging and important assignments for yourself because you like the work and think that you can do the best job.

✔ You resist approaches that differ from the ones you normally take.

✔ You tend to micromanage people to ensure that they're performing their assignments just as you would.

Of course, your technical expertise can be a significant asset if you use it correctly. Praise from you for a job well done will mean a lot more than praise from someone who is less qualified to assess the work.

While many factors can contribute to your ability to influence people, in general, your power over others can be

✔ **Ascribed:** Someone gives you the authority to reward and punish those whom you want to influence.

✔ **Achieved:** You earn the respect and allegiance of those whom you want to influence.

# Learning from experience

In the absence of reasons to do otherwise, people tend to believe what we say. Unfortunately, we often say exactly what we don't want people to believe or do, and then we're surprised when they listen to us.

When I was in high school, my social life wasn't all that I wanted it to be. Years later, as my sons were preparing to enter high school, I thought about my experiences and how I could help my sons to avoid the frustrations and disappointments that I experienced. The more I thought about it, the more I became convinced that my approach was a major reason for my lack of success. Here's an example of a typical phone conversation I'd have when I called a girl to ask her out on a date:

"Hi, this is Stan Portny."

"Hi, Stan."

"Say, I don't suppose you'd want to go out with me Saturday night, would you?"

"I hadn't thought about it, but I guess you're right. I don't."

I'd hang up the phone depressed, convinced that I'd never be able to get a girl to go out with me. Although I didn't realize it, I had succeeded in getting the girl to do the very thing I'd suggested to her!

I related this story to a friend a while back, and my friend immediately agreed with my observation. He then asked the key question: "Why do we say the very things we don't want people to hear?" After much discussion, we agreed that the reason is either fear of success (what would I say to the girl if I were alone on a date with her for three hours?!) or fear of failure (trying to minimize the pain of the rejection we fear). Unfortunately, by trying to minimize the pain of failure, we wind up essentially guaranteeing that we will experience it.

You frequently see this behavior at work in project management. You're assigned to a new project, and the project leader immediately tells you all the reasons why the project may not work and, even if it is completed, why the results won't be as great as everyone thinks. Then he or she wonders why the project team isn't committed to the project's success! If you want to have a chance to succeed, you have to be willing to take a risk.

Achieved power is far more effective than ascribed power. People who act in response to ascribed power usually look to do the least necessary to get the rewards they want or to avoid the consequences they fear. On the other hand, people who are motivated by achieved power work to achieve the highest possible quality of results because they have decided that doing so is in their best interests.

Whether or not you recognize and acknowledge it, you have considerable opportunity to develop and use achieved power. You can choose how you want to influence people's behavior, or you can inadvertently influence their behavior. Either way, your actions will influence people's behavior.

## Establishing the bases of your power

Take the following steps to increase your ability to influence your team members and others in your project environment:

- ✔ Determine what authority you have over the people you want to influence. Typical types of authority include the ability to give salary increases, give promotions, complete performance appraisals, and assign people to future jobs.

- ✔ Find out who else has authority over the people you want to influence.

- ✔ Clarify for yourself the reasons why successfully completing the project is in your organization's interest, and share those reasons with others.

- ✔ Get to know others and understand, appreciate, and acknowledge their special talents and strengths.

- ✔ Let others get to know your good side. Your power to influence people is based on their perceptions of your character, abilities, and authority.

- ✔ Don't condemn or complain but do give feedback when necessary.

- ✔ Become proficient in the tasks you have to perform.

Your bases of power will diminish over time if you don't consistently reinforce them. Meeting with team members at the start of your project can help them to see and appreciate your style and recognize that you're all trying to accomplish similar goals. If you don't have contact for the next six months, however, those initial positive impressions will fade, and your ability to influence people's commitment and performance will decrease as well.

# Creating and Sustaining Team-Member Motivation

Efficient processes and smooth working relationships create the opportunity for successful projects. Having team members who are personally committed to your project's success gives you the greatest chance of achieving it. Your major task as a project manager is to encourage all the people associated with your project to be motivated and committed to its success.

Motivation is a personal choice — the only person you can motivate directly is yourself. You can create the *opportunity* for others to become motivated, but you can't make the decision for them.

Four factors encourage a person to become and remain motivated to achieve a goal:

- ✔ **Desirability:** The value of achieving the goal
- ✔ **Feasibility:** The likelihood that the goal can be achieved
- ✔ **Progress:** How you're proceeding as you try to reach your goal
- ✔ **Reward:** The payoff you realize when you reach the goal

Helping others understand how your project meets their professional and personal needs in each of these areas strengthens their commitment to help your project succeed.

## Clarifying your project's benefits

While some people commit to completing an assignment because someone tells them to do so, you'll have a much more serious commitment when you personally recognize and appreciate a project's benefits. When discussing your project's benefits with your team, consider those things, such as the following, that are important to your organization, its employees, and its clients.

- ✔ Improved products and services
- ✔ Increased sales
- ✔ Improved productivity
- ✔ More efficient operations
- ✔ Better work environment

Also consider potential benefits to each of them personally, such as the following:

- ✔ Learning new skills and becoming more knowledgeable
- ✔ Working in an enjoyable environment
- ✔ Expanding your business contacts
- ✔ Enhancing your career potential
- ✔ Successfully meeting a challenge

For years, I've suggested in my training programs that helping people to identify what they personally can get by participating in a project increases their commitment to the project and, therefore, the chances that the project will succeed. Occasionally, I meet a person who reminds me that his staff receive salaries for working at their jobs. He suggests, therefore, that he doesn't have to worry that people feel they can realize personal benefits by doing their assigned tasks. As far as he's concerned, they'll perform their assignments because they want to continue receiving their paychecks. Unfortunately, relying on reward power in this way encourages people to do the least necessary to ensure they'll continue to receive their paychecks, rather than to work to achieve the highest quality results.

I'm not suggesting that your primary concern when designing and performing a project is the personal benefits that team members can realize. However, people will be more committed if they feel that they can accomplish personal goals while helping their organization achieve its goals.

You can help people to understand and appreciate the benefits that your project could achieve for the organization by

- Identifying the situation that led to your project

- Identifying your project's key drivers and clarifying what they hope that you achieve (see Chapter 7 for the definition of project drivers)

- Accepting and appreciating the worth of those benefits in your own mind

- Encouraging others to discuss the expected benefits and recognize their value

- Encouraging others to think about additional benefits that may have been overlooked

You can encourage people to identify personal benefits that they could realize from participating in your project by

- Discussing their personal interests and career goals and relating those interests and goals to aspects of the project

- Discussing past projects they have enjoyed and the reasons they have enjoyed them

- Discussing some of the benefits that you and others hope to realize by working on this project

## *Demonstrating feasibility*

A project is feasible if you think that you have a chance to accomplish it. No matter how desirable a project may be, you won't get excited about working on it if you think that accomplishing it is impossible. Success doesn't have to be guaranteed, but you must believe that you have a chance.

Of course, feasibility is a subjective assessment. What seems impossible to one person appears to be feasible to another.

Your assessment of feasibility can become a self-fulfilling prophecy. If you think that an assignment is feasible, you'll work hard to complete it, and if you encounter problems you'll try to work them out. However, if you really believe that you have no chance of succeeding, you'll give up at the first sign of difficulty. Any problems will just confirm what you already knew — that the project was doomed from the start.

Once you give up, you have no chance of succeeding. And your initial belief that the project wasn't feasible has become a self-fulfilling prophecy! Help people to believe that a project is feasible by working with them to define what will be produced, when, and how. Specifically, consider the following:

- ✔ Involving them in the planning process
- ✔ Encouraging them to identify potential concerns so that you can analyze them and develop plans to address them
- ✔ Explaining why you feel that your targets and plans are feasible
- ✔ Developing responsive risk-management plans

## Reporting progress

Appreciating your project's value and feasibility helps to create initial motivation for people. However, if the project lasts for more than a couple of weeks, the initial motivation will die out if you don't reinforce it continually. People need to know how they're doing over time for two reasons:

- ✔ Achieving each intermediate milestone provides personal satisfaction.
- ✔ Your recognizing successful performance confirms that they're on the right track, which reinforces their belief that they can and will succeed.

Have you ever seen a 12-month project in which all the major milestones occur in months 11 and 12? When do you think people get serious about working on this kind of project? Months 10, 11, and 12, if they're still around by then. Help to keep people on track and excited about your project by doing the following:

- ✔ Developing meaningful and frequent intermediate milestones in your planning process
- ✔ Continually assessing how people are doing

✔ Frequently sharing information with people about their performance and accomplishments

✔ Continually reinforcing the benefits that everyone will realize when you successfully complete your project

## Providing rewards

People need to know that what they did made a difference for two reasons:

✔ To confirm that they accomplished the correct results and met their audiences' needs

✔ To confirm that people appreciated the effort they invested

Early in my career, I worked for the federal Department of Health, Education and Welfare (HEW). HEW was headed by a cabinet-level Secretary, and major programs with HEW were headed by Assistant Secretaries. Major functional areas within each program were headed by Deputy Assistant Secretaries.

A Deputy Assistant Secretary hired me to be part of a new group he was forming to bring formalized analysis to social and health programs. My first assignment was to coordinate a congressionally mandated study of a formula for allocating federal funds among different state programs. I awarded a small contract for analytical support and completed the project in about six months. The project was straightforward, and I completed it on time, within budget, and to the audience's expectations.

When I submitted the report to my boss, he told me that a delegation from HEW would formally deliver it to congress in special hearings that were being conducted. I'd like to tell you that I led the HEW delegation and personally handed the senators the report, which had my name prominently placed on the cover. In fact, I wasn't a member of the delegation at all, and my name had been removed from the report. However, I was allowed to sit in the rear of the huge senate chamber where the hearings were being conducted, and I knew that I had prepared the report.

Although attending the hearings was exciting, the real surprise came about a week later, when I received a personal note signed by the Assistant Secretary of the department. In the note, the Assistant Secretary thanked me for my efforts in completing the study and noted that this was the first time in his recollection that the department had delivered a congressionally mandated study on time.

It's been more than 25 years since I received that note, and I'm certain that the Assistant Secretary no longer remembers who I am or that I completed that study. However, 25 years later, I still think about him and that note, which took him no more than five minutes to write!

Perhaps you're thinking that you'll write many notes as soon as you become an assistant secretary in the federal government. But do you really need to achieve that level of prominence for your notes to make a difference?

I've kept a folder over the years I've been presenting training programs. The folder has six letters in it, each written by a different person who attended one of my training programs, each sharing essentially the same message. In each letter, the author says that something I related in my training program changed his or her life. As far as I'm concerned, I can receive no greater compliment than to know I said something that changed a person's life!

I'd like to think that, of the more than 25,000 people I've trained in the past 20 years, perhaps 1,000 feel that something I said in a program they attended changed their lives. I'd like to believe that, but I can guarantee you that there are six.

These six people weren't Assistant Secretaries or presidents of organizations at the time they wrote their letters. They were just people like you and me. However, they chose to set themselves apart by taking a few minutes of their time to send me a letter. And their few minutes of effort is still paying dividends years later.

# Chapter 13

# Bringing Your Project to a Close

. . . . . . . . . . . . . . . . . . . . . . . . . . . . . . . . . . . . . . . . . . . . . . . . . . . . . .

## *In This Chapter*

▶ Planning for project termination

▶ Addressing the remaining administrative issues

▶ Helping people bring their association with the project to a close

▶ Using a novel approach to announce your project's end

. . . . . . . . . . . . . . . . . . . . . . . . . . . . . . . . . . . . . . . . . . . . . . . . . . . . . .

*O*ne characteristic that distinguishes a project from other work assignments is that it has a distinct end, a point in time at which all associated work is done and the results are achieved. However, with the intense demands pulling you on to your next assignment, it's not unusual to allow completed projects to languish and eventually fade away, instead of clearly announcing when they're done and recognizing the results and the people who made them possible.

Unfortunately, this demise hurts both the organization and the people who performed the work. If you don't assess the extent to which desired outcomes were, in fact, achieved, you're unable to determine whether the project was well conceived, well planned, or well performed. Further, people who worked on it don't have the chance to experience the sense of closure, of achievement, of a job well done.

Instead, bring your projects to a close by doing the following:

✔ Finish all substantive work.

✔ Perform required administrative tasks.

✔ Help team members complete their association with your project and move on.

This chapter shows you how.

# Finishing the Work

Closing out your project requires that you do the following:

- ✔ Complete all unfinished project activities.
- ✔ Get all required acceptances and approvals.
- ✔ Assess the extent to which the results met the expectations.

Bringing a project to an end typically entails wrapping up a multitude of small details and open issues. Dealing with numerous detailed assignments can be frustrating under the best of circumstances. However, the following unique situations and pressures make the end of a project even more difficult:

- ✔ Often you don't have a detailed, written list of all the activities that have to be performed.

- ✔ Some team members may have already begun working on new assignments, so in order to close out the project, the remaining members have to pick up new responsibilities in addition to their original ones.

- ✔ The project staff may lose motivation, as general interest in the project wanes and people look forward to new assignments.

- ✔ The project staff may not want the project to end, because they don't want to end the personal and professional relationships they've developed or they're not excited about what they're doing next.

- ✔ Your customer (internal or external) may not be very interested in completing the final details of the project.

Increase your chances for project success by approaching your closure as suggested in the following sections.

## Plan for project termination in detail

View termination (the close phase — see Chapter 1) as a separate project. Gather your remaining team members and prepare a plan for termination that clarifies your objectives, activities, and resource assignments.

Develop a project-closure checklist of all activities that you and your team must complete before your project can be over. Here are some examples:

- ✔ Products you must produce
- ✔ Acceptance tests you must pass

> ✔ Approvals you must get
>
> ✔ Final reports you must write
>
> ✔ Resources you must reassign
>
> ✔ Administrative tasks you must finish

Be sure to assign specific responsibility for each item on the project-closure checklist.

## Reestablish team identity and spirit

In order to reestablish team identity and spirit, consider doing the following:

> ✔ Call your team together and reaffirm your mutual commitment to bring the project to successful completion.
>
> ✔ Continue to focus your team's attention on the value and importance of the final product.
>
> ✔ Monitor the final activities closely and give frequent feedback on performance to each team member.
>
> ✔ Be accessible to team members.

## Finish smoothly

Observe the following tips to help your project termination go smoothly:

> ✔ **Start laying the groundwork for closure when you prepare your project plan.** Ensure that you describe your project objectives completely and clearly and identify all relevant objective measures and specifications. If your project may change one or more existing conditions, describe these conditions before you start your project so that they may serve as a comparative basis for assessment when your project is finished.
>
> ✔ **Include project closure activities in your project plan.** Specify in your project's Work Breakdown Structure all activities you'll have to perform to close out your project and plan sufficient time and resources to perform these activities.

# Handling the Administrative Issues

Before your project can be officially closed, you have to fulfill any outstanding procedural or legal requirements and close existing charge accounts, as follows:

- ✓ **Obtain all required approvals.** Obtain written approval that all required performance tests have been passed, standards and certifications have been followed, and customer or client acceptances have been obtained.

- ✓ **Reconcile outstanding transactions.** If you've made project purchases from outside sources, resolve any disputes with vendors and suppliers and pay all outstanding bills. If you've been allocating project work effort and funds expenditures to specially established project accounts, reconcile any situations in which labor charges or funds expenditures may have been allocated incorrectly.

- ✓ **Close out charge categories.** If you've been recording labor and funds expenditures in specially established project accounts, close these accounts now, so that no future time and resource charges can be made to them.

# Handling the People

Help project team members complete their project responsibilities and move on to their next assignments. In particular, do the following:

- ✓ **Acknowledge and document team members' contributions.** Express your appreciation to people for their assistance on your project and share your assessment of the quality of the work they performed. Also take a moment to thank the people's supervisors for making them available to your project and let the supervisors know your assessment of how their employees performed.

  Share positive feedback in public; share constructive criticisms and suggestions for improvement in private. In both cases, be sure to share your comments with team members personally and follow up your conversation in writing.

- ✓ **Help people plan for their transition to new assignments.** If appropriate, help them find their next project assignment. Help them develop a schedule for winding down their involvement with your project while ensuring that they fulfill all of their outstanding obligations.

  Consider holding a final project meeting or lunch to allow people to bring closure to their work and their project relationships.

# Using a Novel Approach to Announce Your Project's Closure

Announcing to your organization that your project is finished is important for two reasons:

✔ To alert people in your organization that the planned outcomes of your project are now available

✔ To confirm to people who may have supported your project at some point that their efforts led to a successful result

If your project was small, chances are that everyone who participated knows that it's over and what the results were. If it took a long time (six months or more) and involved many groups in your organization, the chances are that people who participated early on may never see the actual results of the work they invested.

A while back, I was talking with a client who had just completed a one-year project that entailed the design, development, production, and introduction into operation of a small piece of equipment to be used in the cockpit of certain aircraft. When he officially ended his project, he was reflecting on the many different people from all areas of his organization who had helped him during the year. In addition to the engineers who completed the final installation and testing of the equipment in the planes, countless others provided essential support including contract officers, procurement specialists, financial managers, human resource specialists, test lab personnel, logisticians, and others.

He realized that, if past experience was any indicator, the vast majority of these support people would never see the final result of their efforts. So he decided to do something that had never been done before in his organization. He put together a small display in his workplace that illustrated the birth, evolution, and fruition of his project. He included everything from the signed contract document and purchase orders to the initial design model and the final approved engineering drawings to pictures of the device installed in an airplane, pictures of a pilot who would be using it, and photos of the maintenance people who would be supporting it. He then sent messages to the people who had worked on the project announcing the display and inviting them to come by to visit.

The response he received was overwhelming. He estimated that more than 100 people came by to look at the display. He overheard conversations that people had with their colleagues in which they proudly declared that they had written the purchase orders for this equipment — equipment that they now could see would affect people's lives. The most poignant comment he received was from a technician who worked in the test laboratory. The technician told him this was the first time in the 11 years he had worked for the organization that he ever saw the final results of an item that he tested.

The client estimated that he spent several hours assembling the display. Yet the positive results he and his organization received from this sharing were immeasurable.

Take a moment to let people know the true results of the work they invest. Nothing can provide stronger motivation to jump into the next assignment and provide continued high-quality support.

# Conducting a Post-Project Evaluation

Lay the groundwork for repeating good practices and experiences and avoiding mistakes made by conducting a post-project evaluation. See Chapter 15.

# Part IV
# Getting Better and Better

The 5th Wave                    By Rich Tennant

"GET READY, I THINK THEY'RE STARTING TO DRIFT."

## In this part . . .

You become a truly skilled project manager by learning from your experiences and using all available tools and resources to help you responsively manage your project from start to finish.

In this part, I suggest how you can identify and deal with potential project risks. I discuss how to plan for and conduct a post-project evaluation session after the project is completed. Finally, I suggest ways to use new technologies to improve your management of projects, along with some technology pitfalls to avoid.

# Chapter 14

# Dealing with Risk and Uncertainty

### In This Chapter

▶ Clarifying the difference between risk factors and risks

▶ Identifying possible risk factors

▶ Assessing the impact of risks on your project

▶ Selecting a strategy for managing your project's risks

▶ Preparing a risk-management plan

*Y*our first step towards a successful project is to develop a plan that will allow you to do the work required to produce the desired results in the available time for the available resources. If your project will last a relatively short time, and if you were thorough and realistic in your planning, things should have a high likelihood of working out the way you figured.

However, the larger and more complex the project and the longer it lasts, the more likely that some aspects of your project will not work out as you had envisioned. Remember the best laid plans. . .? You'll give yourself the greatest chance for success if you confront head-on the possibility that some things may change, and prepare at the outset for how to minimize any associated negative consequences.

Consider potential project risks when deciding whether to undertake your project, when developing your project plan, and continually while performing your project's work. Share information about your project's risks and your plans for managing them with all appropriate audiences initially and through-out your project's life.

# Defining Risk and Risk Management

*Risk* is the possibility that you may not achieve your product, schedule, or resource targets because something unexpected occurs or something planned does not. Because it's impossible to predict the future with certainty, all projects have some degree of risk. However, project risk is greater

- ✔ The longer your project lasts

- ✔ The longer the time span between when you prepare your project plan and when you start your project work

- ✔ The less experience you, your team members, or your organization has had with similar projects in the past

- ✔ The newer the technology or work approaches you'll be using

*Risk management* is the process of identifying possible risks, assessing their potential impact on your project, and developing and implementing plans for minimizing their negative effects. Risk management won't eliminate risks, but it'll give you your best chance of successfully accomplishing your project, despite the uncertainties of a changing environment.

The following risk management strategies won't work:

- ✔ **The ostrich approach:** Ignoring risks or pretending they don't exist

- ✔ **The prayer approach:** Looking to a higher being to solve all your problems or to make them disappear

- ✔ **Denial:** Recognizing that certain situations may cause problems for your project, but refusing to accept that these situations may occur

I met a person a while ago who was preparing to start a large project that was a top priority for his organization. He mentioned that his project's success heavily depended upon one particular person who was assigned full time to the project for six months and would be doing all the technical development. I asked if he had considered what he'd do if the person left the project before it was finished. He responded that he didn't have to worry about it, because he just wouldn't allow it to happen.

It occurred to me that his approach for dealing with risk was similar to the person who cancelled her health insurance for a year, because she wasn't planning on getting sick! He may have been able to speak with top management and get their agreement that the person would be given no other assignments for the duration of his project. However, he still couldn't guarantee that the person wouldn't get sick or decide to leave the organization!

Consider the potential impact of risks on the chances for project success when you

- ✔ Decide whether to undertake the project in the first place

- ✔ Develop your project objectives, strategies, responsibility assignments, schedules, and resource budgets

- ✔ Monitor ongoing performance and respond to problems that may arise

- ✔ Consider making changes to your project after it's underway

Manage risks and minimize their negative impact on your project as follows:

- **Identify risks:** Determine which aspects of your plan or envisioned project environment may change.

- **Assess their potential impact on your project:** Assess what will happen if things don't work out the way you envision.

- **Develop plans for mitigating the impact of the risks:** Decide how you'll protect your project from the possible negative consequences of risks.

- **Monitor the status of your project's risks throughout performance:** Determine whether existing risks continue to be risks, whether the likelihood they'll occur changes, and whether other risks arise.

- **Keep others informed:** Explain to all key audiences the status and potential impact of all project risks from the exploration of the initial concept through the completion of all project work.

# Identifying Risks

Discover potential project risks by:

- Identifying conditions or situations that may lead to risks
- Determining the specific risks associated with these conditions or situations

## Recognizing risk factors

A *risk factor* is a situation that may give rise to one or more project risks. A risk factor itself doesn't cause you to miss a product, schedule, or resource target. However, it increases the likelihood that you may miss one.

The fact that neither you nor your organization has undertaken projects similar to the one you're planning is a possible risk factor. Because you have no direct prior experience, you may overlook activities you'll need to perform or you may underestimate the time and resources required to perform them. Just because you have no prior direct experience doesn't guarantee you'll have these problems. However, it may increase the chances that you will.

Identify possible risk factors by reviewing written materials and interviewing people who know about or were involved in the development of your project. Specifically consider

- How the different phases of your project have been handled
- The information developed in each of the phases

### Risk factors arising from your project's evolution

All projects progress through the following five phases:

- **Conceive:** An idea is born
- **Define:** A plan is developed
- **Start:** A team is formed
- **Perform:** The work is done
- **Close:** The project is ended

See Chapter 1 for a detailed discussion of these phases.

Table 14-1 illustrates possible risk factors that may arise, depending upon how you've handled your project's progression through these phases.

| Table 14-1 | Possible Risk Factors During Your Project's Evolution |
|---|---|
| *Life Cycle Phase* | *Possible Risk Factors* |
| All | Insufficient time was devoted to one or more phases |
| | Key information wasn't written down |
| | You moved to a subsequent phase without completing one or more of the earlier ones |
| Conceive | Not all background information and plans were recorded in writing |
| | No formal cost-benefit analysis was performed |
| | No formal feasibility study was performed |
| | You don't know who first came up with the idea for your project |
| Define | People preparing the plan hadn't done similar projects in the past |
| | The project plan wasn't written down |
| | Parts of the plan were omitted |
| | Some or all aspects of the project plan weren't approved by all key audiences |
| Start | The people assigned to perform the project aren't the ones who prepared the plan |
| | Members who didn't participate in the development of the project plan don't review the plan and raise any questions they may have |

| Life Cycle Phase | Possible Risk Factors |
|---|---|
| | No effort was made to help the team establish its identity and focus |
| | Project team procedures for resolving conflicts, reaching decisions, or ongoing communication weren't developed |
| Perform | The needs of your primary clients change |
| | Incomplete or incorrect information is collected regarding schedule performance and resource expenditures |
| | Project progress reporting is inconsistent |
| | One or more of your key project supporters is reassigned |
| | Project team members are replaced during performance |
| | Market place characteristics or demands change |
| | Changes are made informally, with no consistent analysis of their impact on the overall project |
| Close | One or more of your project's drivers don't formally approve the project's results |
| | People are assigned to new projects before all the work on this project is completed |

Table 14-2 suggests potential risk factors that may arise in conjunction with the different information addressed in your project plan.

| Table 14-2 | Possible Risk Factors |
|---|---|
| Planning Information | Possible Risk Factors |
| Project audiences | You haven't dealt with this client before |
| | You've had problems when you've dealt with this client before |
| | Upper management or other key drivers are only mildly interested in your project |
| | Your project has no champion |
| | You haven't specifically identified project audiences at all |

*(continued)*

**Table 14-2** *(continued)*

| Planning Information | Possible Risk Factors |
| --- | --- |
| Project background | Your project is the result of a spontaneous decision, rather than a well-thought-out assessment |
| | No one has proved conclusively that successfully completing your project will eliminate the problem it was designed to address |
| | Your project requires other planned activities to be completed before your can perform your work |
| Project scope | The project is unusually large |
| | The project will require a variety of skills and knowledge |
| | The project will involve different organizational units |
| Project strategy | There is no declared strategy at present |
| | You plan to use a new, untested technology or approach |
| Project objectives | One or more objectives are missing |
| | Performance measures are unclear or missing |
| | Performance measures are difficult to quantify |
| | Performance targets or specifications are missing |
| Constraints | No constraints are identified |
| | Constraints are vague |
| | In general, all constraints may lead to potential project risks |
| Assumptions | Assumptions are vague |
| | In general, every assumption leads to a potential risk |
| Work packages | Work packages aren't sufficiently detailed |
| | Some or all people who will be doing the work didn't participate in developing the work package descriptions |
| Roles and responsibilities | Not all supporters were involved in developing the roles and responsibilities |
| | You're overly dependent on one or more people |
| | No primary responsibility is assigned for one or more activities |

| Planning Information | Possible Risk Factors |
|---|---|
| | Two or more people have primary responsibility for the same activity |
| | No one person has overall responsibility for the entire project |
| Schedule (activity-time estimates) | Time estimates were developed by backing into an established end date |
| | Your organization has no historical database of how long it took to perform similar activities in the past |
| | Part of your project work entails procedures or technologies you haven't used before |
| | Some activities will be performed by people with whom you haven't worked before |
| Schedule (activity interdependencies) | Interdependencies aren't specifically considered when developing the schedule |
| | Partially related activities are scheduled to be done simultaneously, in the hopes of saving time |
| | No formal analytical approach is used to assess the impact of interdependencies on your schedule |
| Personnel | No estimates have been made of the actual work effort required to perform individual activities |
| | No formal consideration has been given to availability and efficiency. |
| | No plans have been prepared for when people working less than full time on your project will invest their effort |
| | New or inexperienced personnel will be performing project activities |
| Other resources | No plans have been prepared to identify the type, amount, and timing of nonpersonnel resources you'll need |
| Funds | No project budget has been prepared |

# Identifying Risks

Separately describe how each risk factor you identify may cause you to miss your product, schedule, or resource targets.

Suppose you plan to use a new technology in your project. The fact that you'll use a new technology is a risk factor. Possible product, schedule, and resource risks arising from this risk factor are as follows:

- **Product risk:** The technology may not produce the desired results.

- **Schedule risk:** Tasks using the new technology may take longer than you anticipate.

- **Resource risk:** Your existing facilities and equipment may not be adequate to support the use of the new technology.

When identifying potential risks, do the following:

- Review past records of problems encountered in similar situations

- Brainstorm with experts and people with related experience

- Be specific. The more specifically you describe a risk, the better able you are to assess its potential impact. As an example:

  • Weak: "Activities may be delayed."

  • Strong: "Delivery may take three weeks instead of two."

Try to eliminate as many potential risk factors as you can as soon as possible in your project. As an example, suppose a key audience hasn't approved your project's objectives. Rather than just noting that there's a risk that you may not correctly address the audience's needs, do whatever you can to get the audience to approve the objectives!

# Assessing the Potential Consequences of Risks

Determine the potential impact a risk poses for your project by determining the likelihood that it'll occur and the magnitude of the consequences if it does occur.

## Assessing the likelihood of a risk occurring

Consider using one of the following schemes to describe the chances that a risk will come to pass:

- **Probability of occurrence:** You can express the likelihood a risk will occur as a probability. *Probability* is a number between 0 and 1 indicating the likelihood that a given situation will come to pass. A probability of 0 means that the situation will never occur and a probability of 1 means that it will always occur. (You may also express likelihood as a percentage instead of a fraction. In this case, a likelihood of 100 percent means the situation will always occur.)

✔ **Category ranking:** Classify risks into categories that represent the likelihood they will occur. You may use "High," "Medium," and "Low" or "Always," "Often," "Sometimes," "Rarely," and "Never."

✔ **Ordinal ranking:** Order the risks so the first is the most likely to occur, the second is the next most likely, and so on.

✔ **Relative likelihood of occurrence:** If you have two possible risks, you can, for example, declare that the first is twice as likely to occur as the second.

You can estimate the likelihood that a risk will occur on your current project by comparing the number of times the risk actually did come to pass on similar projects you've performed before. As an example, suppose you've designed 20 computer-generated reports during the past year for clients with whom you hadn't worked before. Eight times, when you submitted your design for final approval, your client wanted at least one change made. If you're planning to design a computer-generated report for a client with whom you haven't worked before, you may conclude there's about a 40 percent chance that you'll have to make changes to the final report design when you submit it to your client for approval.

When using objective information to determine the likelihood of different risks occurring on your project

✔ Consider previous experience with projects similar to your current one

✔ Ensure as many as possible of the associated conditions are the same as for your current project

✔ Make sure you're drawing conclusions based on a sufficient number of prior situations

✔ Keep in mind that the more situations similar to yours you consider, the greater the confidence in any conclusions you can draw

In the absence of objective data, solicit the opinions of experts and people who have worked on similar projects in the past.

You can estimate the likelihood that a particular risk will come to pass on your project by soliciting the opinions of ten people who have worked on projects similar to yours in the past. You can, for example, ask them to estimate the likelihood of a risk as being "high," "medium," or "low." Suppose six choose "high," two choose "medium," and two choose "low." You may then develop your estimate of the likelihood as follows by assigning values of 3, 2, and 1, to "high," "medium," and "low," respectively. Determine the weighted average of your responses as follows:

$$(6 \times 3 + 2 \times 2 + 2 \times 1) \div 10 = (18 + 4 + 2) \div 10 = 2.4$$

This suggests the likelihood of occurrence is between medium and high.

To increase the accuracy of likelihood estimates based upon the opinions of others, try the following:

- **Define as clearly as possible what the category names mean.** You may suggest that "low" means the likelihood the risk will occur is between 0 and 33 percent, "medium" means it's between 33 and 66 percent, and "high" means it's between 66 and 100 percent.

- **Consider the opinions of as many people as possible.**

- **Be sure that the projects from which the people you consult draw their opinions and the conditions surrounding those projects are truly similar to yours.**

- **Don't allow people to discuss their estimates with each other before they share them with you.** Initially, you're looking for individual opinions, not a group consensus.

- **After they've submitted their initial estimates to you, consider having the people discuss with each other their reasons for their estimates and whether they would like to revise them.**

Precision is different from accuracy. *Precision* refers to the detail with which a number is expressed. *Accuracy* refers to how correct the number is. You may estimate the likelihood of a particular risk occurring on your project to be 67.23 percent. However, even though you express the risk to two decimal places, your guess will have little chance of being accurate if you've had no prior experience with similar projects in the past.

Unfortunately, people often assume that numbers expressed with greater precision are also more accurate. You can help avoid misinterpretations when you share your assessments of likelihood with others by using round numbers, categories, or relative rankings.

The more factors that suggest a particular risk may occur, the higher the likelihood that it will occur. Ordering from a vendor with whom you haven't worked before may raise the possibility that delivery times will be longer than initially promised. However, the likelihood of delays in delivery time is greater, if, in addition, this is a special order item, you're asking for delivery during a busy period for the vendor, and the vendor has to order several parts to make the item you've requested.

# Assessing the magnitude of the consequences

Determine the specific effect that each risk would have on your project's product, schedule, and resource performance. When evaluating these effects, do the following:

- **Consider the impact of a risk on the total project, rather than on just a portion of it.** Taking one week longer to complete an activity than originally planned may cause intermediate milestones to be missed and cause the personnel who were waiting for the results of this activity to start their work to sit idly. However, the impact to the project would be even greater if the delayed activity is on your project's critical path (see Chapter 4), which would mean that the one-week delay would cause the final completion date for your entire project to be delayed by one week.

- **Consider the impact of related risks when assessing their impact on the overall project.** The likelihood that you'll slip your schedule is greater if three activities on the same critical path have a significant risk of slippage instead of just one.

Be sure to describe risks and their associated consequences as specifically as possible. As an example, suppose you feel there's a risk that a key piece of equipment you ordered for your project may arrive later than expected. You can express that risk as follows:

- **Weak:** Delivery may be delayed.

- **Strong:** Delivery may be delayed by two weeks.

Just stating that delivery may be delayed doesn't give you enough information to determine the impact of that delay on the overall project. It also makes it harder to estimate the risk of that delay actually occurring. Are you talking about a delay of one day? One month?

Stating that delivery may be delayed by two weeks allows you to determine more precisely the impact on the overall project schedule and resources. It also makes it easier for you to decide how much you'd be willing to spend to avoid that delay.

Risk estimation and assessment can be supported with a variety of more formal techniques, including the following:

- **Decision trees:** Diagrams illustrating different situations that may occur as your project unfolds, the likelihood of each situation occurring, and the consequences to your project if it does.

✔ **Risk assessment questionnaires:** Formal data-collection instruments for eliciting expert opinion about the likelihood that different situations may come to pass on your project and their associated impacts.

✔ **Automated impact assessments:** Computerized spreadsheets that consider in combination both the risk that different situations will occur and the consequences if they do.

# Managing Risk

Recognizing those risks that pose a potential threat to your project's successful completion is the first step towards controlling them. You also, however, have to develop specific plans for reducing their potential impact on your project.

## Choosing the risks you want to manage

All identified risks affect your project in some way if they occur (after all, that's the definition of a risk). However, you may determine that trying to anticipate and avert problems that can be caused if a particular risk comes to pass takes more time and effort than just dealing with the problems, should they arise.

Your first step in developing a risk management strategy is to choose those risks that you feel you need to address proactively. When making this choice, do the following:

✔ **Consider together the likelihood of a risk and its potential impact on your project.** If the impact of a risk would be great and the chances it will occur are high, you probably want to develop plans to manage it. If the impact is low and the likelihood is low, you may decide not to worry about it.

When either the impact would be high but the likelihood is low or vice versa, consider the situation more carefully. A more formal approach for considering the combined effect of likelihood of occurrence and potential impact is to define the *expected value of the risk*, as follows:

Expected value of the risk = (quantitative measure of the impact, if it occurs) × (probability it will occur)

✔ **In certain instances, a potential consequence is so totally unacceptable that, even if it has a low likelihood of occurrence, you're not willing take the chance.** At a minimum in such a situation, develop a plan to manage the risk. In fact, you may actually want to reconsider whether you want to undertake the project at all.

# Developing a risk-management strategy

Choose one of the following approaches for dealing with the risks you decide you want to manage:

✔ **Minimize the chances they'll occur.** Take actions to reduce the chances that an undesirable situation will come to pass. As an example, consider that you have a person who's new to your organization assigned to a task. Consequently, you feel there's a risk the person may take longer to do the task than you've planned. Consider taking the following steps to reduce the chances that the person will require more time:

- Explain the task and the desired results very clearly to the person before he or she begins to work on it.

- Develop frequent milestones and monitor the person's performance often so that you can identify and deal with any problems as soon as they occur.

- Have the person attend training to refresh the skills and knowledge he or she will need to perform the assignment.

✔ **Develop contingencies.** Develop one or more alternative action plans you'll follow in the event an undesirable situation does come to pass.

Suppose you're counting on having your organization's publication department reproduce 100 copies of the manual you'll use in an upcoming training program. If you're concerned that the department may be working on other higher priority projects at the time you'll need them, consider locating an external vendor that can reproduce the manuals, if the need arises.

✔ **Buy insurance:** Pay a price to reduce the potential impact of an undesirable situation if it comes to pass. As an example, suppose you need a piece of equipment on a specified date. You may decide to order the same part from two different vendors to increase the likelihood that at least one of the parts will arrive on time.

# Communicating about risks

People often share information about project risks ineffectually or not at all. As a result, projects suffer problems and setbacks that may have been avoided had proper actions been taken beforehand.

You may be reluctant to deal with risk because the concept is hard to grasp. If you're only doing your project once, what difference does it make that a particular situation would occur 40 times out of 100? You may also feel that focusing on possible risks suggests that you're looking for why your project will fail rather than how to make it succeed.

Early in my career, I accepted a job with a small consulting firm. As my first assignment, the president asked me to review a Request for Proposals (RFP) he had received to develop a strategy for preparing our proposal. I spent two days reviewing the RFP and I developed a list of 20 potential risks that I thought we should consider.

When I met with the president to discuss my thoughts, I immediately began to read off the list of potential project risks. When I reached the fifth risk, the president stopped me. He said that he'd assigned me to review the RFP because he thought we should submit a bid. However, if I thought we couldn't do it, I should just tell him and he'd give the assignment to someone else. I'd spent two days identifying all the foreseeable project risks so we could figure out ways to minimize their impact on the project, but he thought I was trying to justify why we shouldn't submit a bid! I realized I should've told him why I was identifying all of these things that could go wrong instead of assuming that he knew.

Communicate about project risks early and often. In particular, share information with both drivers and supporters at the following points in your project (see Chapter 1):

- **Concept:** To support the decision whether to undertake the project
- **Definition:** To guide the development of all aspects of your project plan
- **Start:** To allow team members to discuss and understand potential risks and to encourage them to recognize and address potential problems as soon as they occur
- **Perform:** To update the likelihood identified risks will occur, to reinforce what people should do to minimize the negative impact of project risks, and to guide the assessment of whether or not to make requested changes to the project

You can improve your communications by doing the following:

- Explaining in detail the nature of a risk, how it would impact your project, and the basis on which you estimated its likelihood of occurrence.
- Telling people your most recent assessment of the current chances that risks will come to pass, what you're doing to minimize the chances of problems for your project, and what they can do to reduce the chances of negative consequences for your project.
- Encouraging people to think and talk about risks, always with an eye toward figuring out ways to minimize their negative impacts on your project.
- Documenting in writing all the information about the risk.

# Preparing a Risk-Management Plan

A risk-management plan lays out specific strategies to minimize the potential negative consequences that uncertain occurrences will have on your project. Develop your risk-management plan in the define phase of your project, refine it in the start phase, and continually update it during the perform phase (see Chapter 1 for more on these phases). Include the following in your risk-management plan:

✔ Risk factors

✔ Associated risks

✔ Your assessment of the likelihood of occurrence and the associated consequences for each risk

✔ How you plan to manage selected risks

✔ How you plan to keep people informed about the status of the selected risks throughout your project

Table 14-3 illustrates a portion of a risk-management plan.

| Table 14-3 | A Portion of a Risk-Management Plan |
|---|---|
| *Plan Element* | *Description* |
| Risk factor | You haven't worked with this client before. |
| Risks | **Product:** Chance for miscommunication, leading to incorrect or incomplete understanding of client's needs |
|  | **Schedule:** Incomplete understanding of client's business operation, leading to an underestimate of how long it'll take to survey the current operations |
|  | **Resources:** Inaccurate understanding of client's technical knowledge, leading to assigning tasks to the client that he or she won't be able to perform; the need to have additional staff assigned to the project to perform these tasks |
| Analysis | Chances of misunderstanding the client's needs = high |
|  | Chances of underestimating the time to survey operations = low |
|  | Chances of misunderstanding the client's technical knowledge = low |

*(continued)*

**Table 14-3** *(continued)*

| Plan Element | Description |
|---|---|
| Strategy | Only deal with the risk of misunderstanding the client's needs. Reduce the chances of this happening by<br><br>• Using approaches such as reviewing past correspondence or reviewing written problem reports to identify the client's needs.<br><br>• Having at least two team members present in every meeting with the client's staff.<br><br>• Speaking with different staff in the client's organization.<br><br>• Putting all communications in writing.<br><br>• Sharing progress assessments with the client every two weeks throughout the project. |

# Chapter 15

# Using the Experience You've Gained

- - - - - - - - - - - - - - - - - - - - - - - - - - - - - - - - - - - - - - - - - - - - - - - - - - - - - - - - - - -

### In This Chapter

▶ Preparing for and conducting a post-project evaluation

▶ Following up on a post-project evaluation

- - - - - - - - - - - - - - - - - - - - - - - - - - - - - - - - - - - - - - - - - - - - - - - - - - - - - - - - - - -

**P**articipants in my training programs often tell me they wish they had attended my session years ago, before they actually had to work on teams or lead projects. One of the ongoing frustrations of the project environment that I hear about most often is that you make the same mistakes over and over again. While you have a unique opportunity to learn firsthand what works and what doesn't, as you try to perform your projects, the lessons often appear to be forgotten as soon as they're learned.

Of course, you don't do this on purpose. Chances are, you're in such demand that you're off to your next assignment before you completely finish your current one. You rarely have the luxury of reflecting on your experience so that you can enhance and improve your approaches in the future.

Plan to hold a post-project evaluation, covered extensively in this chapter, after each project you perform. Learn from your successes, learn from your mistakes, and always reflect your past experiences in your future behavior.

## Preparing for a Post-Project Evaluation

A *post-project evaluation* is an assessment of project results, activities, and processes to

✔ Recognize project achievements and acknowledge people's contributions

✔ Identify techniques and approaches that worked and devise steps to ensure they're used again in the future

✔ Identify techniques and approaches that didn't work and devise steps to ensure that things are handled differently in the future

A *project postmortem* is another term that's used to refer to a post-project evaluation. I avoid using this term, however, because it conjures up an image of an autopsy being performed to determine the cause of death of a project! I prefer to have people leave with a more positive memory of their experience with a project.

## Preparing for the meeting throughout the project

Your project evolves through the stages: conceive, define, start, perform, and close, as it goes from an idea to a completed effort (see Chapter 1 for definitions of each stage). During the project, take steps in each stage to lay the groundwork for your post-project evaluation:

✔ **Conceive phase:**

- Identify key project *drivers:* the people for whom you're performing your project. (See Chapter 7 for definition and discussion of the different types of project audiences.)

- Determine the benefits that people thought they would realize when they decided to authorize your project.

- If your project is designed to change an existing situation, take "before" measures of key characteristics to compare to "after" outcomes.

- If a formal cost-benefit analysis was performed (see Chapter 1), find out which benefits people considered they would achieve through this project.

✔ **Define phase:**

- Identify any additional project drivers.

- Develop clear and detailed descriptions of all project objectives, including performance measures and performance targets to be achieved.

- Include the activity "Conduct a post-project evaluation" in your Work Breakdown structure and allow time and resources to perform it. See Chapter 3 for a discussion of a Work Breakdown Structure.

✔ **Start phase:**

- Tell team members that there will be a post-project evaluation at the end of the project.

- Encourage team members to record issues, problems, and successes throughout their project involvement.

✔ **Perform phase:**

- Maintain files of cost, labor-hour charges, and schedule performance reports throughout the project. See Chapter 10 for details on how to track and report on resource expenditures and schedule performance.

- Maintain project logs, which identify and describe situations and problems encountered, unexpected occurrences that affected project performance, and techniques or approaches that were unusually successful.

✔ **Close phase:**

- If your project is designed to change an existing situation, take "after" measures of key outcome characteristics.

- Obtain final cost, labor-hour, and schedule performance reports for the project.

- Hold a post-project evaluation session.

- Distribute minutes from the post-project evaluation session.

## Setting the stage for the post-project evaluation meeting

Prepare for your post-project evaluation meeting by collecting information on the following:

✔ Results produced

✔ Schedule performance

✔ Resource expenditures

✔ Changes during the project in project objectives, schedule, and budgets

✔ Unanticipated occurrences or changes in the environment that occurred during the project

✔ Customers' satisfaction with the project results

✔ Management's satisfaction with the project results

Collect this information from the following sources:

- Progress reports
- Exception reports
- Project logs
- Cost reports
- Schedule reports
- Project memos, correspondence, and meeting minutes
- Customer opinions
- Management opinions

# Conducting the Post-Project Evaluation

At the post-project evaluation meeting, explore the following issues:

- Did you accomplish the project objectives?
- Did you meet the project schedule?
- Did you complete the project within budget?
- With regard to problems encountered during the project
  - Could they have been anticipated and planned for in advance? If so, how?
  - Were they handled effectively and efficiently when they occurred?
- Were the project management systems and procedures used effective?

In order to set the stage to effectively obtain this information and feedback, observe the following tips:

- **Invite the right people.** Invite the people who participated in your project at all points throughout its life. If the list of potential invitees is too long, consider meeting separately with selected subgroups and holding a general session for everyone to review the results of the smaller meetings and solicit final comments and suggestions.

- **Declare at the beginning of the session that this is to be a learning experience, rather than a finger-pointing session.**

✔ **Encourage people to**

- Identify what others did well.

- Examine their own performance and see how they could've handled situations differently.

✔ **Consider holding the session away from your office.** People often feel more comfortable critiquing existing practices and thinking of new approaches when they're away from their normal work environment.

Consider running the session according to the following agenda:

✔ Introduction

✔ Overall review of performance

- Results achieved, schedules adhered to, and resources expanded

- Approaches to project planning

- Project tracking systems and procedures

- Project communications

- Team practices

✔ Discussion and recognition of special achievements

✔ Review of customer and management comments

✔ Discussion of problems and issues encountered

✔ Discussion of how to reflect the experience gained from this project in future efforts

Be sure to assign a person to take notes during the post-project evaluation meeting. These notes should recount in detail any suggestions for how to reflect the experience gained from this project in future efforts.

# Following Up on the Post-Project Evaluation

Often, your busy schedule pulls you to new projects before you've had a chance to analyze and learn from the experiences of ones completed. However, even when you manage to take even a few moments to review your experiences, the lessons learned are seldom incorporated into changed operating practices.

A participant at one of my training sessions shared her frustration about a dilemma she was facing back at her job. She explained that she had just finished working as a team member on a project that lasted for over a year. The project had achieved most of the results that were originally desired, but the success came at the cost of budget overruns, schedule slips, and team members' emotional and physical exhaustion from the pressure of working in a continual crisis mode.

A month earlier, she had attended a full-day post-project evaluation, during which team members explored in depth what went right and what went wrong on the project and how they might be able to use the lessons they learned on future efforts.

She and her former team members had since moved on to a new assignment, and she was noticing that they were all making the same mistakes they had made on the previous project — mistakes they had vowed at the post-project evaluation never to make again! She was upset and wondered what she had to do to ensure that the lessons learned from her previous experience were acted on.

After sharing a few general thoughts with her, I asked how her other team members had reacted to the report of recommendations from the post-project evaluation that was distributed after the session. She appeared stunned, and admitted no one had taken any notes at the session and no report of the session had been prepared. More than ten mid- and high-level managers had spent an entire day discussing plans and approaches for improving their organization's operations, and no one had thought to put even one of the ideas discussed down on paper. No wonder nothing had changed; no one knew specifically what he or she was to do.

As soon as practical after you hold your post-project evaluation session, prepare and distribute a report describing the following:

- ✔ Practices to be encouraged on future projects
- ✔ Steps to be taken to encourage these practices
- ✔ Practices to be avoided on future projects
- ✔ Steps to be taken to avoid these practices
- ✔ Alternative approaches to these practices that will be implemented

# Chapter 16

# With All the Great New Technology, What's Left for You to Do?

• • • • • • • • • • • • • • • • • • • • • • • • • • • • • • • • • • • • •

## In This Chapter

▶ Recognizing how software can support project planning and control

▶ Identifying the different types of software that can support project management

▶ Specifying what you'll have to do to support your software

▶ Choosing the right software

▶ Recognizing the benefits and limitations of e-mail

• • • • • • • • • • • • • • • • • • • • • • • • • • • • • • • • • • • • •

*P*roject management entails using systems and procedures to help people work together to achieve common goals. A major part of project management is information — getting it, storing it, analyzing it, and sharing it. However, the key to successful project management is using information to guide and encourage people's performance.

Technological advances provide easier and more affordable ways to handle information. Computer software allows you to enter, store, and analyze information and to present the results in professional formats. E-mail allows you to communicate in writing with people in remote locations at all hours of the day.

However, the technology alone can't encourage focused and committed team performance. In fact, excessive reliance on today's technology can actually result in poor morale, confused and disorganized team members, and lower overall performance. Successful project management requires that you use the technology for those jobs it can handle and find other appropriate ways of handling the ones it can't.

# Using Computer Software Effectively

The software available today to support special analyses and reporting that helps you plan and control your project looks so good that you may be tempted to believe that using it is all that's required to ensure your project's success. Because you're probably trying to accomplish more in less time with fewer resources, you'd like to believe that the software is the answer to your problems. Sometimes this message is actually reinforced by your managers.

A number of years ago, I met a person who had just been given his first project to manage. Wanting very much to succeed in his assignment, he asked his boss if he might receive some project management training, because he had no previous exposure to the skills and knowledge required to fulfill this role. His boss immediately agreed. He then handed him a copy of the most popular project management software package of the day and declared, "This is all you'll need. Learn how to use this package and all your projects will be successes." Scary, isn't it?

Software can help with data entry, data analysis, data storage, and report generating activities. However, it can't do the following:

✔ **Ensure that information entered is appropriately defined, timely, and accurate.** In most instances, information to support project planning or control is recorded by people and then entered into a computer. You can program the software to check for correctness of format or internal consistency, but the software can't ensure the quality and integrity of the data.

As an example, suppose you're using a computer program to maintain records of the labor hours that team members charge to your project. You can program the computer to reject hours that are inadvertently charged to an invalid project code. However, you can't program the computer to recognize that hours are charged to a wrong project that also happens to have a valid code.

✔ **Make decisions.** Software can help you determine objectively what would happen if you chose a number of different possible courses of action. However, software can't effectively take into account all the associated objective and subjective considerations associated with each course of action that you weigh, in order to decide which plan of action you should pursue.

✔ **Create and sustain dynamic interpersonal relationships.** Despite people's fascination with chat rooms, e-mail, and other types of computer-aided communication, computers don't foster close, trusting relationships between people. If anything, technology makes it more difficult for you to get to know others, because it removes your ability to see facial expressions and body language.

Incorrectly using project-management software can actually waste scarce resources and hurt team member morale. A while back, a client recounted a particularly unpleasant experience she had had with project-management software. She'd been assigned to manage a major project that her organization was planning to undertake. The project was extremely important to the organization's future, and upper management wanted to do everything possible to ensure its success. Recognizing the size and complexity of the project, upper management hired a person who had extensive experience with a popular project-management software package to prepare the project plan.

The person worked intensely, coming in before others arrived and leaving after they were gone. After three months, he emerged from his office with a completed plan. The plan included thousands of activities, detailed schedules, and resource assignments. From the start, it was a disaster. Major areas of work had been omitted, responsibilities had been assigned to inappropriate people, and schedules failed to take into account other commitments and organization activities. The expert had consulted no one on the project team during the entire development process, and people were incensed that a stranger new to the organization would presume to tell them how to do their work. The project team threatened to resign *en masse*.

Management took action in short order. They fired the expert and threw the plan in the garbage. Not only had they wasted three months of time and effort, they still had no viable project plan. Instead, they now had a disgruntled and disillusioned project team! The message was clear — the use of project-management software alone does not guarantee project success.

## How software can help

Consider using software for the following:

- ✔ Storing and retrieving important project information
- ✔ Analyzing and updating that information
- ✔ Preparing presentations and reports describing the information and the results of the analyses

Should you decide to use project-management software, two types can help you with your project-management activities:

- ✔ **Stand-alone, specialty software:** Separate packages that perform one or two functions very well that can support your project planning and performance
- ✔ **Integrated project-management software:** A single package that incorporates limited portions of the capabilities of several specialty packages to support a wider array of your project planning and performance activities

Each type offers benefits and drawbacks, discussed in the two following sections.

### Stand-alone, specialty software

The following types of specialized software can support your project planning and performance:

- ✓ **Word processing** (Microsoft Word is an example): Useful for preparing your project plans, maintaining your project log, creating progress reports, and preparing written communications

- ✓ **Business graphics and presentation** (Microsoft PowerPoint is an example): Useful for preparing overheads and slide shows for project presentations and developing charts and artwork for written reports and publications

- ✓ **Spreadsheet** (Microsoft Excel is an example): Useful for storing moderate amounts of data, performing repetitive calculations, and presenting information in a variety of chart formats

- ✓ **Database** (Microsoft Access is an example): Useful for storing and retrieving large amounts of data for subsequent analysis and presentation

- ✓ **Accounting** (Intuit QuickBooks is an example): Useful for keeping records of project income and expenses and producing a variety of descriptive and comparative reports

- ✓ **Day planner and scheduler** (Microsoft Outlook is an example): Useful for scheduling your calendar, maintaining a "To-Do" List, keeping your address book, and managing your e-mail activities

Many manufacturers offer software packages in the above categories. However, I'd estimate that over 80 percent of the organizations with which I've worked have chosen Microsoft software as the company standard for these functions. Therefore, I've noted examples of Microsoft software packages in the different categories, because there's a good chance that you've heard of them before and that you can easily get them installed on your computer, if you don't already have them.

Initially, specialty packages were designed to perform one or two functions very well. As they have evolved, however, they've been expanded to include additional capabilities that support their primary functions: Word-processing packages now possess some spreadsheet, business graphics, and database capabilities; spreadsheet packages now have some business-graphics and word-processing capabilities, and database packages now have some spreadsheet and word-processing capabilities.

# To use software or not to use software

With the array of options available, choosing the best software for your purposes can be difficult. Answering the following questions will help.

✔ **Do you need software at all?** If you're handling a single project that has fewer than 15 to 20 activities, most of which are performed one at a time, you may not need software to plan and control it. However, if you're handling several such projects, you need to perform many activities simultaneously, or your project entails more than 15 to 20 activities, you're a good candidate for using software.

✔ **Do you want an integrated project-management package or individual packages?** Consider specialized packages to support small projects that won't require extensive reporting or replanning.

In general, specialty packages offer the following strengths:

✔ They offer powerful capability in their area of specialty.

✔ You most likely have several of the packages already available on your computer, which means you could use them immediately for no additional cost.

✔ It's likely that people already know how to use many of the commonly available specialty packages, which means people will be more apt to use them and to use them correctly.

However, using them does pose some potential concerns:

✔ **They are likely to encourage piecemeal approaches to project planning and control, which may result in your omitting certain key steps.** You can use a business graphics package to draw a Gantt chart (see Chapter 4) from any data you enter. However, you have confidence that the schedule is feasible only if you consider the impact of activity interdependencies when you develop your data, which a business graphics package doesn't allow you to do.

✔ **They aren't easily integrated.** You can, for example, depict your project's schedule on a Gantt chart with a graphics package and display personnel hours over the duration of each task in a spreadsheet. However, if one of your people is unexpectedly out sick for a week, you'd have to make separate changes to each program to reflect a revised allocation of the person's hours in the spreadsheet and change the Gantt chart in the graphics package to reflect new activity start and/or end dates. Even though some programs can share data directly with others, the process is often cumbersome.

### Integrated project-management software

Integrated project-management software combines database, spreadsheet, graphics, and word-processing capabilities to support many of the activities that are normally associated with planning and performing your project. An example of an integrated package is Microsoft Project, although you can find more than 50 such packages of all shapes and sizes on the market today.

A typical integrated project-management package allows you to do the following:

- Create a hierarchical list of your project's activities and their components.

- Define and store key information about your project, activities, and resources.

- Define activity interdependencies. See Chapter 4 for more information on activity interdependencies.

- Develop schedules by considering activity durations, activity interdependencies, and resource requirements and availability.

- Display a schedule in Gantt chart and table formats (see Chapter 4).

- Assign people to work on project activities for specific levels of effort at certain times.

- Schedule other resources to be used on project activities at specified times.

- Determine your overall project budget.

- Determine the impact on schedule and resources of changes to a project plan.

- Monitor the dates on which you start or end activities or reach milestones.

- Monitor the person-hours and resource costs incurred.

- Present planning and tracking information in a wide array of graphs and tables.

A word of caution is in order here. Just because the package has a wide range of capabilities doesn't guarantee that you'll use them correctly. Remember the old adage: garbage in, garbage out? Even the most advanced software package available today won't help your project if people aren't willing to collect and submit accurate and timely data.

Many years ago, a participant in one of my training programs expressed great frustration with the integrated project-management software she was using. She said it took her almost two hours to reflect the impact on her project schedule from delays in three project activities.

## Choosing an integrated project-management package

If you decide you want to use an integrated project-management package, consider the following factors when choosing your program:

✔ **Types and formats of reports generally required.** Choose a package that supports the type of reports and reporting you'll want to use with minimum customization required.

✔ **People's general comfort and familiarity with computers and software — will they take the time and effort to learn and then use the package?** Choose a package that people will use. It doesn't help to have a package with state-of-the-art analysis and reporting capabilities if no one will take the time to learn how to use it.

✔ **What software is available and used in your organization already?** All other things being equal, it makes sense to choose an existing package because others most likely will have experience with it.

✔ **Does your organization have existing systems to record labor hours charged and expenses incurred for your project?** If your organization does have such systems, consider a package that can easily interface with them. If not, consider a package that provides you the capability to store the information you'll need.

✔ **Project environment in your organization — the size of the resource pool of people working on projects, the number and typical size of projects, and so on.** Choose a package that has the necessary capacity and speed.

Check out *Microsoft Project For Dummies* by Martin Doucette (IDG Books Worldwide, Inc.) for more information on effectively using this software's capability.

The rest of the training participants, most of whom also used an integrated project-management software package, were extremely surprised, as was I. We figured it should've taken closer to two *minutes* than two hours. We spent five minutes asking questions to understand more about her project and the information she had entered into her software. After running into a series of dead ends, I offhandedly said that I just didn't understand it. I told her I was sure that, after she entered all of her project's activities and defined their interdependencies (covered in Chapter 4), it should take just a few minutes to determine the impact of activity delays on the overall project schedule. She replied, "What's an interdependency?"

She had entered her activities, together with their associated start and end dates, into her software. However, she had never defined the interdependencies between the activities. As a result, when two activities were delayed, the software had no way of determining the impact of these delays on other project activities. Instead, she had to recalculate by hand the new start and end dates for all activities and separately enter these dates into the software.

Integrated project-management packages, therefore, offer benefits as well as drawbacks. The benefits are as follows:

- The package's different functions are linked, so, for example, if you enter personnel requirements once, they'll be considered when developing schedule and resource budgets, as well as when preparing reports of project progress.

- The packages typically come with a variety of preprogrammed report formats.

Using an integrated project-management package can also lead to the following problems:

- People may not have it immediately available to them, which means it costs money to purchase and takes time to procure and install.

- Most people require some degree of training to become comfortable with how the package works.

## Supporting your software

No matter which type of project-management software you choose, your project's ultimate success will depend upon how well you coordinate and support your project planning and control activities. Table 16-1 illustrates different activities software can support, the types of software that can provide the support, and what you'll have to do to ensure the activity is performed correctly.

| Table 16-1 | Using Software to Help Manage Your Projects | |
|---|---|---|
| **What the Software Can Do** | **Type of Software to Use** | **What You'll Have to Do** |
| Document your project objectives. | Word processing Integrated project-management package | Ensure that all project objectives have measures and performance targets. Ensure that key people approve the objectives. |
| Record project audiences. | Word Processing Integrated project-management package | Identify the audiences. |

| What the Software Can Do | Type of Software to Use | What You'll Have to Do |
|---|---|---|
| Illustrate project team roles and responsibilities. | Word Processing Spreadsheet Business graphics Integrated project-management package | Get people to agree and commit to their roles and responsibilities. |
| Develop possible schedules. | Integrated project-management package | Ensure that all required activities are included. Ensure that duration estimates are accurate. Ensure that necessary activity interdependencies are included. Explain the reasons for interdependencies and duration estimates. Ensure that project drivers and supporters buy in to the schedules. |
| Display schedule possibilities. | Word processing Spreadsheet Business graphics Integrated project-management package | Choose the actual schedule dates from among the possibilities. |
| Display the personnel needed and their required levels of effort. | Word processing Spreadsheet Business graphics Integrated project-management package | Determine the personnel needed. Estimate the required levels of effort. |
| Display planned personnel allocations over time. | Spreadsheet Business graphics Integrated project-management package | Choose when, over time, people will spend their hours on task assignments. Decide how to deal with potential resource conflicts. |
| Display funds and other nonhuman resource budgets. | Spreadsheet Business graphics Integrated project-management package | Determine the budgets. Explain the budgets to project team members. |
| Keep records of activity performance and milestone achievement. | Spreadsheet Integrated project-management package | Develop the procedures for collecting and submitting schedule-performance data (see Chapter 10). Ensure that people submit the data on time. |

*(continued)*

**Table 16-1 (continued)**

| What the Software Can Do | Type of Software to Use | What You'll Have to Do |
| --- | --- | --- |
| Keep records of the work hours that people charge to your project. | Spreadsheet Integrated project-management package | Create the charge codes. Develop the procedures for recording and submitting labor hours data. Ensure that labor hours are charged to the correct accounts. Ensure that the information is submitted and entered on time. |
| Keep records of financial commitments and expenditures. | Spreadsheet Database Accounting Integrated project-management package | Create the charge codes. Ensure that expenditures are charged to the correct accounts. Ensure that the information is submitted and entered on time. |
| Prepare reports of schedule and resource performance. | Word processing Accounting Spreadsheet Integrated project-management package | Define report formats and timetables. Select the people who'll receive the reports. Interpret the reports. Ensure that people read the reports they receive. Develop needed corrective actions. |
| Prepare presentations of project progress and accomplishments. | Word processing Spreadsheet Business graphics Integrated project-management package | Choose the information to be included. Select the people who'll receive the reports or attend the presentations. |

# Introducing project-management software into your operations

Before you rush out and buy any project-management software, plan how you'll prepare to make maximum use of its capabilities and avoid any associated pitfalls.

✔ Be sure you have a firm grasp of project planning and control approaches before you consider using any software.

✔ See what software others in your organization are using now or have used before; find out what they like, what they don't, and why.

✔ If possible, ask someone who already has a copy of the software if you can spend a few minutes exploring its operation.

✔ After you have the package installed on your computer, load a simple project or a small part of a larger project (that is, enter the activities, durations, interdependencies, resources used, and so on).

✔ Use some of the program's capabilities at first (determine the impact of small changes on your schedule, print out some simple reports, and so on); use more as you get more comfortable and feel the need.

✔ Consider a formal training program after you've become comfortable with the basics of how to access the software's different capabilities.

# Making Use of E-mail

Before the advent of e-mail, people consistently told me that the two most common frustrations in their daily routine were the number of unproductive meetings they attended and playing "telephone tag" trying to get in touch with people.

Is sharing accurate information with the right people in a timely manner essential for project success? You bet. Yet, meetings and telephones, two of the most common communication vehicles, are often ineffective for fulfilling this central need. Is it any wonder that people embraced e-mail as soon as it became common in the workplace?

---

## Preparing a communications plan

Prepare a communication plan in the start phase of your project and monitor and revise it, if needed, in the perform phase (see Chapter 1 for more on these phases). In your plan, identify the following:

✔ **The purposes of your communications:** Routine progress reporting, relationship building, problem solving, and so on

✔ **The methods you'll use:** Meetings, written reports, e-mail, and phone calls

✔ **Specific activities you'll conduct:** E-mail to announce changes to your project plan, monthly meetings to review milestones reached during the past month, and so on

Consider using several different communication approaches to address a topic that's particularly important and sensitive.

E-mail is a fast and convenient means of one-way, written communication. As such, it has many desirable qualities:

- **The sender and receiver don't both have to be present at the same time.** You can write an e-mail message whenever you want and your recipient can read it at his or her convenience.

- **The sender and receiver don't both have to be in the same place.** You can send your message from Iowa to a person in Tibet.

- **Your message is delivered quickly.** Delivery of your message doesn't depend on delivery schedules, work hours, or weather conditions.

- **E-mail serves as written documentation.** Your message can be read several times to clarify its meaning and serve as a reminder in the future that the information had been shared.

- **You can store e-mail on computer hard disks, floppy disks, Zip disks, or CDs, rather than in hard copy.** This saves you both space and money and makes retrieval easier.

Unfortunately, e-mail also has the following drawbacks:

- **People may not read it.** I often meet people who regularly receive between 50 and 100 e-mails each day! They readily admit they scan the first few lines to decide if a message is worth reading. Some just read whom it's from to decide whether they read any further.

- **There's no real-time interaction between sender and receiver.** The receiver may have difficulty correctly interpreting the message, because he or she may not be able to ask questions, check inferences, or paraphrase the message in a timely manner. You can try to do these things through subsequent e-mails, but people often lose interest in the process.

- **Communication is limited to the exchange of words.** Other cues to people's messages and feelings that are conveyed by facial expressions, body language, and tone of voice are lost.

- **Misinterpretation of content or intent.** There's a growing dictionary of meanings associated with different modes of expression in e-mail. Unfortunately, people pick up these meanings informally, if at all, and sometimes send e-mails that convey the wrong message.

A client told me of the time when he sent an e-mail to a coworker and, to emphasize a particular message, he typed the message in bold characters. The person to whom he sent the e-mail never responded and appeared to ignore him when they passed each other in the hallways. After several days, my client sought the person out and asked whether there was a problem. My client's coworker said he was upset and insulted that my client yelled at him in his e-mail. My client expressed complete surprise and confusion and asked his coworker how an e-mail message could suggest a person was yelling. Apparently, typing your message in bold face is equivalent to yelling at your recipient. Fortunately for my client, he was able to learn of the misunderstanding and correct it. But one has to wonder how many times such understandings go unnoticed and unaddressed.

## Using e-mail appropriately

E-mail can be an effective component of a comprehensive communication system. Consider using e-mail to do the following:

- **Confirm oral discussions and agreements.** In these instances, you want a written message to stand on its own, with no interactive discussion or explanation. If a person needs to ask questions, the written message hasn't documented the information clearly and accurately.

- **Sharing straightforward factual information that requires little or no clarification.** Share simple messages in straightforward language. Tell people how they can get in touch with you if they have any questions.

Don't, however, use e-mail as the exclusive means of communication to do the following:

- **Support brainstorming to analyze problems and develop new ideas.** Use e-mail to announce the brainstorming session, invite people to attend, identify the topic(s) to be explored, and provide relevant background material for people to review before the session. Use e-mail to share a summary of the results of the meeting and actions being taken. But conduct the actual interchange of ideas in a face-to-face session.

- **Build and sustain team members' trust and commitment.** While you do want to use e-mail to inform people of team members' background and experience, commitments, and accomplishments, be sure to provide sufficient opportunities for face-to-face meetings to help team members become familiar and comfortable with each other.

- **Share an important message.** Perhaps you can share the message initially through e-mail, but follow up with phone calls and in-person meetings to discuss the message and ensure that your recipient has correctly understood its content.

### Getting the most out of your e-mail messages

When sending a message with e-mail, try the following:

- **Be concise.** Use clear, measurable words and avoid technological jargon and acronyms, whenever possible.

- **Read over your e-mail after you compose it and before you send it.** Remember, people's impressions of you, your ideas, and your attitude are strongly affected by what you say and how you say it. Take a moment to read your e-mail message before your send it. Make sure there are no typos.

- **Anticipate.** Put yourself in your audience's shoes. How might they misinterpret your message? What additional information might they want to have? Is it clear what they're supposed to do in response to your message? In other words, try to minimize the need for five e-mails back and forth to raise questions and clarify points when one, well-thought-out e-mail would have been sufficient.

- **Check to be sure it's been received.** If possible, program your system to let you know automatically when your audience has opened e-mail that you send. If that's not possible, ask the person to send you a return e-mail to let you know he or she received your initial e-mail or verify the message has been received with a phone call or a quick face-to-face conversation.

- **Keep a copy of important e-mails.** Keep copies of important e-mails you send to confirm the information that you actually did send to your project audience. (See Chapter 7 for more on project audience.)

# Part V

## The Part of Tens

The 5th Wave    By Rich Tennant

"I think Dick Foster should head up that new project. He's got the vision, the drive, and let's face it, that big white hat doesn't hurt either."

## In this part . . .

It's nice to have hundreds of pages of detailed information to guide you through your project's ups and downs. However, when a crisis hits, you'd like to have a few handy tips that you can use to head off potential disaster.

In this part, I share many hints and tips for dealing effectively with some of the more common and troublesome project management situations.

# Chapter 17

# Ten Questions to Help You Plan Your Project

. . . . . . . . . . . . . . . . . . . . . . . . . . . . . . . . . . . . . . . . . .

*In This Chapter*

▶ Clarifying your project's purpose

▶ Describing outcomes, schedules, and resources

▶ Addressing the uncertainties

. . . . . . . . . . . . . . . . . . . . . . . . . . . . . . . . . . . . . . . . . .

*W*hen you begin a project, you always feel the pressure to jump in and start doing the work to meet the aggressive time schedules. You'd like to be sure it's planned out before you start, but you're not quite sure where to begin, and you're always under pressure to start producing results.

Answer the following questions, to develop a complete, responsive, and achievable plan.

## Why Is Your Project Being Done?

As soon as you're assigned to your project, get a clear and complete picture of why it's being performed. Determine the following:

- ✔ What situation(s) led to your project?
- ✔ Who had the original idea?
- ✔ Who else is looking to benefit from it?
- ✔ What would happen if your project weren't done?

An accurate appreciation of your project's purpose will lead to better plans, a greater sense of team member commitment, and improved performance. See Chapter 2 for a discussion of the background portion of the purpose section in the Statement of Work.

# Who Will You Need to Involve?

Determine who may play a role in your project's success. Identify the following:

- **Drivers:** People looking for your project's results
- **Supporters:** People who'll help your project succeed
- **Observers:** People interested in your project

After you have a comprehensive list, you can decide whom you want to involve and when and how you want to involve them, based on the time and resources you have available. See Chapter 7 for more information on identifying project audiences.

# What Results Will You Produce?

Specify all the outcomes you plan that your project will produce. Be sure you

- Describe clearly each product, service, or impact
- Make sure the outcomes are measurable
- Include performance targets

Confirm that your project's drivers (see Chapter 7) feel that these outcomes will meet their needs and expectations. See Chapter 2 for more discussion about how to frame your project objectives.

# What Constraints Must You Satisfy?

Identify all information, processes, and guidelines that will restrict what you can do on your project and how you can do it. Distinguish between the following:

- **Limitations:** Restrictions set by people outside your project team
- **Needs:** Restrictions that you and your project team members establish

See Chapter 2 for more information on project constraints.

# *What Assumptions Are You Making?*

Identify all information you use to plan your project that may be inaccurate. Add to and document these assumptions as you develop different parts of your project plan. See Chapter 2 for further details about project assumptions.

# *What Work Must Be Done?*

Identify all the activities required to complete your project. For each activity, specify

- ✓ **The work to be done:** The processes and steps to be performed
- ✓ **Inputs:** All people, facilities, equipment, supplies, raw materials, funds, and information required to perform the activity
- ✓ **Results you'll produce:** Products, services, or situations that will be produced during the performance of the activity
- ✓ **Interdependencies:** Activities that must be completed before you can start the current one; activities you can start to perform after you've completed the current one
- ✓ **Duration:** The actual time on the calendar required to perform the activity

See Chapter 3 for how to describe the project work you'll have to perform.

# *When Will You Start and End Each Activity?*

Develop a detailed schedule with clearly defined activities and frequent intermediate milestones. Take the following into account:

- ✓ **Interdependencies:** What you'll have to finish before you can begin your activity
- ✓ **Resource availability:** When you'll need particular resources and when they'll be available

See Chapter 4 for more information on how to develop a project schedule.

# Who'll Perform the Project Work?

Specify the following information for all the people you'll need to work on your project:

- ✔ Identify each person by name, position description or title, or skills and knowledge required to do the assignment.

- ✔ When more than one person will work on the same activity, describe the particular role each person will have and how the people will coordinate their efforts.

- ✔ Specify the level of effort each person will have to invest.

- ✔ If a person will work less than full time on an activity, specify exactly when during the activity she will spend her time.

Consult with the people who'll perform the tasks to develop this information. See Chapter 5 for help with estimating personnel requirements.

# What Other Resources Will You Need?

Identify all equipment, facilities, services, supplies, and funds that you'll need to perform your project work. Specify how much of each resource you'll need and when you'll need it. See Chapter 5 for more discussion on how to identify nonpersonnel resources.

# What Could Go Wrong?

Identify those parts of your project you feel may not go according to your plan. Choose those risks that you think pose the greatest potential dangers to your project's success and develop plans to minimize their negative impact. See Chapter 14 for information on how to manage project risks.

# Chapter 18

# Ten Ways to Hold People Accountable

*In This Chapter*
- ▶ Clarifying the request
- ▶ Emphasizing the importance
- ▶ Telling others about the commitment
- ▶ Tracking performance

*P*roject success requires that you can count on the help promised to you by people over whom you have no direct authority. The tips in this chapter help you increase the chances that people will live up to their commitments.

# Involve People Who Really Have Authority

Confirm with the person's supervisor that the person can spend the necessary time to help you. Getting this agreement at the outset

- ✔ Reduces the chances that the person's supervisor will inadvertently assign work to the person that will make it impossible for him or her to give you your products on time

- ✔ Establishes a relationship with the person's supervisor so that you can ask for help if work isn't being done in a timely manner or express your appreciation when it is

- ✔ Elicits a commitment to perform from someone who does have authority over the resources needed to do the work

Be sure to let the person know you want to bring his or her supervisor into the discussion and why; otherwise it appears that you're bringing in the supervisor because you don't trust the person.

# Be Specific Regarding End Results, Time Frames, and Expected Levels of Effort

Often, when a person doesn't perform according to your expectations, it's because he or she

- ✔ Misunderstood the results you wanted
- ✔ Misunderstood your time frame
- ✔ Underestimated the effort needed to produce those results

Be specific regarding what you want, when you want it, and how much effort you think it will take.

# Get a Commitment!

Get a specific commitment to do the work promised. Beware of platitudes and generalities such as:

- ✔ I'll try.
- ✔ I'll give it my best shot.
- ✔ You can count on me.
- ✔ You know I always work hard.
- ✔ I think your project is great.

# Put It in Writing

Confirming all oral agreements in writing does the following:

- ✔ Clarifies the agreement you reached
- ✔ Serves as a reminder of the promise made

A written confirmation emphasizes the seriousness of the commitment. For some reason, people sometimes feel they can promise things verbally and it's okay if they don't honor their promises. But when it's in writing, it looks official.

# Emphasize the Urgency and Importance of the Assignment

Tell the person where his or her work fits into the overall project plan. People will put in a greater effort if they know that it really makes a difference.

# Tell Others about the Person's Commitment

Don't make this a test of power between you and the person; instead, tell others about the work the person has agreed to perform. Your most precious professional asset is your reputation. The more people know about the work the person has promised to do, the greater the recognition he or she will get when the work is done (or not!).

# Agree on a Plan for Monitoring the Person's Work

Discuss when and how you'll follow up. Following up

- Reinforces that the assignment is important and that you fully expect the person will perform it in the time frame promised
- Helps you identify as soon as possible any problems that may arise
- Gives you confidence that work is proceeding well

When you develop your follow-up schedule

- ✔ Check to see when the person plans to start and to do the different parts of the task.
- ✔ Plan to follow up at times when clearly definable intermediate milestone should have been reached.

# Monitor the Person's Work

Check on progress when you said you would. Following through on your commitment sends a message that you expect the person to follow through on his or hers.

You may find that phone calls, drop-ins, and other verbal follow-up may be sufficient.

When you check with the person, emphasize that you're calling to see if he or she has any questions or if there's anything you can do to help them with the assignment.

# Always Acknowledge Good Performance

When the person gives you the promised work on time:

- ✔ Tell them how much you appreciate their efforts.
- ✔ Tell others, including the team, the person's supervisor, and key project drivers.

# Act As If You Have the Authority

Remember, after a person commits to do some work for you, that person gives you the right to act as if you have authority over him or her.

# Chapter 19

# Ten Steps to Getting Your Project Back on Track

● ● ● ● ● ● ● ● ● ● ● ● ● ● ● ● ● ● ● ● ● ● ● ● ● ● ● ● ● ● ● ● ● ● ● ● ● ● ● ● ● ● ● ● ● ● ● ●

*In This Chapter*

▶ Determining what went wrong

▶ Reaffirming your plan

▶ Refocusing team direction and commitment

● ● ● ● ● ● ● ● ● ● ● ● ● ● ● ● ● ● ● ● ● ● ● ● ● ● ● ● ● ● ● ● ● ● ● ● ● ● ● ● ● ● ● ● ● ● ● ●

**S**ometimes you join a project in progress and you find that things are languishing. Or sometimes, the project on which you're working loses focus. To get back on track, think of the remaining work as a new project: Develop a revised project plan, announce your plan to the organization, and track your performance closely. This chapter helps you get started.

## Determine Why Your Project Got Off Track

The first step toward fixing a problem is understanding it. Describe exactly how your project is off track. Possibilities include that you're

✔ Behind schedule

✔ Overspending your resource budgets

✔ Not producing the desired outcomes

Identify the reasons why your project is off track. Possibilities include

✔ Key people left the team or new ones joined it

✔ Key drivers lost interest or new ones entered the picture

✔ The business environment changed

✔ New technology emerged

✔ Organizational priorities shifted

# Reaffirm Your Key Drivers

Identify the people who stand to benefit from your project. Consider people who originally wanted your project to be performed, as well as others who may have emerged since the project began. Reaffirm the benefits your project will provide them and encourage their active support.

# Reaffirm Your Project Objectives

Reconfirm your project's objectives with your project's drivers. Modify or add to the original objectives if people's needs have changed. Be sure the objectives are specific and measurable and that people believe they're achievable.

# Reaffirm the Activities Remaining to Be Done

Work with team members to reconfirm, modify, or eliminate the activities originally identified or add new ones, as needed. For all activities, clarify resources required, estimated durations, and interdependencies.

# Reaffirm Roles and Responsibilities

Work with team members to clarify people's roles and responsibilities for the remaining project activities. Identify and resolve conflicts that arose during the work performed to date. Eliminate any ambiguities that existed in the original plan.

Encourage all team members to reaffirm their commitments to project success.

# Develop a Viable Schedule

Revise your original schedule, as needed, to allow for all the work remaining to be completed by the required end date. Define meaningful intermediate milestones you'll use to track your ongoing performance.

# Reaffirm Your Personnel Assignments

Clarify who you'll need to perform the remaining work, how much effort they'll have to invest, and when. Get additional team members assigned to the project, if needed. Confirm that all team members understand the effort they'll have to invest and agree to do it.

# Develop a Risk-Management Plan

Chances are you'll now have additional project activities to perform, new members on the team, and a tight schedule to meet. While you may be able to develop a plan that has a chance of meeting your targets, the plan most likely will have risks. Identify, analyze, and plan to minimize the negative impact of those risks.

For those risks you decide to address proactively, consider the following:

- ✔ Trying to minimize the chances they'll occur
- ✔ Developing contingency plans, in case they occur

Continually update your risk-management plan as you proceed through the remainder of your project.

# Hold a Midcourse Kickoff Session

Galvanize the team and reawaken the organization's interest in your newly replanned project by holding a midcourse kickoff session. In addition to announcing your anticipated results and time frames, your aim is to convince people that you have a viable plan, a unified commitment, and a high likelihood of success.

## *Closely Monitor and Control Performance for the Remainder of the Project*

Ensure that your project doesn't get off track again by

- ✔ Frequently tracking performance and comparing actual achievements with those planned
- ✔ Reporting to key audiences on your ongoing progress
- ✔ Promptly dealing with any problems that arise

# Chapter 20

# Ten Tips for Being a Better Project Manager

**S**uccessful project management depends not just on what you do, but on how you do it. Your attitudes and behaviors toward people affect how they respond to you. This chapter can help you successfully win people's support.

## Be a "Why" Person

Look for the reasons behind requests and actions. Understanding why helps ensure you respond appropriately and increases motivation and buy-in. Find out for yourself and share the information with others.

## Be a "Can Do" Person

Look at all problems as challenges and find ways to overcome them. Be creative, flexible, and tenacious. Keep working at the problem until you solve it.

# Don't Assume

Take the time to find out the facts; use assumptions only as a last resort. With every assumption comes a risk that you're wrong. The fewer the assumptions, the more confidence you'll have in your plan.

# Say What You Mean; Mean What You Say

Communicate clearly. Be specific, letting people know exactly what you mean. Tell them what you want them to know, what you want them to do, what you'll do for them. You may think that being vague gives you more leeway. In reality, it just increases the chances for misunderstanding.

# View People as Allies, Not Adversaries

Focus on common goals, not individual agendas. Making people feel comfortable will encourage brainstorming, creative thinking, and the willingness to try something new. Viewing and treating people as adversaries can put them on the defensive and encourage them to become enemies.

# Respect Other People

Focus on people's strengths rather than their weaknesses. Find something in each person that you can respect. People work harder and enjoy it more when they're around others who appreciate them.

# Think "Big Picture"

Keep things in perspective. Understand where you want to wind up and how what you're doing will help you get there. Share your vision with others.

# Think Detail

Be thorough. If you don't think it through, who will?

# Acknowledge Good Performance

Take a moment to acknowledge good performance. Tell the person, tell the person's boss, tell team members, tell the person's peers.

# Be Both a Manager and a Leader

Attend to people, as well as to information, processes, and systems. Create and share a vision and excitement, as well as a sense of order and efficiency. See Chapter 12 for more information about management and leadership.

# Appendix A

# Glossary

**accountability:** Feeding back consequences to people based upon their performance.

**activities plan:** A table listing planned project activities and the dates on which they're supposed to start and end.

**activities report:** A table listing project activities, the dates on which they're supposed to start and end, and the dates on which they actually do.

**activity:** Work required to move from one event to the next in your project.

**activity-on-arrow diagram:** Network diagram format in which circles represent events and arrows represent activities.

**activity-in-the-box diagram:** Network diagram format in which boxes represent both events and activities.

**assumption:** Statement about uncertain information you're taking as fact as you conceive, plan, and perform your project.

**audience:** A person or group that is needed to support, is affected by, or is interested in your project.

**authority:** The ability to make binding decisions about your project's products, schedule, resources, and work packages.

**availability:** The portion of time you're on the job, as opposed to on leave.

**background:** How and why your project was created, by whom, and the organizational and external environmental contexts in which it will be performed; the "why" of your project.

**backing in:** The process of starting at the end of your project and working your way back toward the beginning, identifying activities as you go and estimating durations that will eventually add up to the amount of time you have been told the project can take.

**backward pass:** The process of beginning at the end of your project and moving back along each path toward the start of your project, calculating latest allowable start and finish dates for all activities as you proceed.

**bar chart:** See *Gantt chart.*

**baseline:** The plan you'll use to guide project activities and support project performance assessments.

**budget:** A detailed, time-phased estimate of the costs of all resources required to perform your project.

**business-requirements document:** A description of the business needs to be addressed by a requested product, service, or system.

**centralized-organization structure:** An approach for handling projects in which individual units are established to handle all project work for your organization in particular specialty areas.

**champion:** A person in a high position in the organization who strongly supports your project, will advocate for your project in disputes, planning meetings, and review sessions, and will take whatever actions are necessary to help ensure your project is successfully completed.

**completed, approved project budget:** A detailed project budget that the essential people approve and agree to support.

**confirmation of purchase order:** A reply from a vendor agreeing to provide an item you've requested and reconfirming the price and associated costs.

**constraint:** A restriction that will limit what you're to achieve, how you can do it, when, and for what cost.

**cost-benefit analysis:** A comparative assessment of your project's anticipated benefits with respect to the estimated costs for performing your project and introducing and using the results produced.

**cost report:** A table listing activities, their planned cost, and the expenditures actually made.

**critical path:** A sequence of activities in your project that takes the longest time to complete.

**delegation:** Assigning some or all of your authority to someone else.

**dependency:** A relationship between activities in which one must finish before the other can start.

**dependency diagram:** See *network diagram.*

**detailed budget estimate:** An itemization of the estimated costs for each project activity.

**direct costs:** Expenditures for resources that are used solely to perform project activities.

**distribution list:** List of people who are to receive copies of a written project communication.

**driver:** Person who has some say in defining the results your project is to achieve; a person for whom you're performing your project.

**duration:** The actual calendar time required to perform an activity. Also called *elapsed time* or *span time.*

**earliest start date:** The earliest date you can possibly start an activity.

**earliest finish date:** The earliest date you can possibly finish an activity.

**Earned Value Analysis:** An approach for determining from resource expenditures alone whether you're over or under budget and whether you're ahead of or behind schedule.

**elapsed time:** See *duration.*

**event:** A significant occurrence in the life of your project. Also called a *milestone* or *deliverable.*

**efficiency:** The proportion of time on the job that you spend on project work, as opposed to organizational tasks not related to specific projects.

**fast tracking:** Performing two or more activities at the same time to reduce the overall time to complete a project.

**feasibility study:** A formal investigation to determine the likely success of performing certain work or achieving certain results.

**float:** See *slack time.*

**forward pass:** The process of beginning at the start of your project and moving along each path toward the end of your project, calculating earliest start and finish dates for all activities as you proceed.

**functional manager:** The direct line supervisor of a project team member.

**functional organization structure:** An approach for handling projects in which separate units addressing the same specialty are established in your organization's different functional groups.

**Gantt chart:** A graph, named after Henry Gantt, comprised of bars on a time-line that depict when each activity will start, be performed, and end.

**general and administrative costs:** Expenditures that help keep your organization operational.

**Human Resources Matrix:** A table depicting, for each lowest level project activity, the people who'll work on it and the total effort they'll invest.

**indirect costs:** Expenditures for personnel, materials, equipment, facilities, and services that support your project work.

**initiator:** The person who had the original idea that led to the creation of your project.

**key-events list:** A table listing planned project events and the dates on which they'll be reached.

**key-events report:** A table listing project events, the dates on which they're supposed to be reached, and the dates on which they are reached.

**kickoff meeting:** Formal meeting to announce the start of your project.

**known unknown:** Information related to your project that you don't have but that someone else does. See also *unknown unknown.*

**labor report:** A table listing activities, the work effort planned for them, and the work effort actually invested.

**latest finish date:** The latest date you can possibly finish an activity and still complete your project in the fastest possible time.

**latest start date:** The latest date you can possibly start an activity and still complete your project in the fastest possible time.

**limitation:** Restriction that others place on the results your project is to achieve, the time frames you have to meet, the resources you can use, and the way you can approach your tasks.

**Linear Responsibility Chart:** A matrix depicting the role each project audience will play in the performance of different project activities.

**Market Requirements Document:** A formal request for a product to be developed or modified.

**matrix organization structure:** An approach for handling projects in which people from different parts of the organization are assigned to work on project teams for less than or equal to 100 percent of their time.

**micromanagement:** A person's excessive, inappropriate, and unnecessary involvement in the details of a task he or she asks another to perform.

**need:** Requirement you determine must be met in order to achieve project success.

**network diagram:** A flow chart illustrating the order in which you'll perform your project's activities.

**noncritical path:** A sequence of activities in your project where you can delay by some amount and still finish your project in the shortest possible time.

**objective:** An outcome or result that your project will produce. Comprised of a statement, one or more performance measures or indicators, and performance targets or specifications.

**objective statement:** A brief narrative description of what your project is to achieve.

**observer:** Person who's interested in the activities and results of your project.

**overhead costs:** Expenditures for resources used to perform project activities that are too difficult to subdivide and allocate directly.

**performance measure:** An indictor that you use to assess your achievement of an objective.

**performance period:** Time span for which you monitor project progress.

**performance target:** The value of a performance measure that constitutes success.

**person effort:** The actual amount of time a person spends working on an activity. Also called *work effort*.

**Person Loading Chart:** A table displaying the level of effort you'll spend on project activities each day, week, or month during which the activity is performed.

**Person Loading Graph:** A graph displaying the level of effort you'll spend on project activities each day, week, or month during which the activity is performed; also called a *resource histogram*.

**PERT (program evaluation and review technique):** A network diagram analysis technique using three estimates (optimistic, pessimistic, and most likely) to describe the range of an activity's span time.

**PERT chart:** A network diagram drawn in the activity-on-the-arrow format.

**post-project evaluation:** A meeting to review the experience gained from your project, recognize people for their achievements, take steps to ensure good practices will be repeated on future projects, and develop plans to correct in future projects any performance problems encountered.

**power:** The ability to influence the actions of others.

**precedence diagram:** A network diagram drawn in activity-in-the-box format.

**primary information source:** Place where the original information you're seeking is contained.

**progress Gantt chart:** A Gantt chart on which activity progress is depicted by shading in an appropriate portion of the activity's bar.

**process:** A series of steps by which a particular function is routinely performed.

**productivity:** The results you produce per unit of time you spend working on an activity.

**program:** Ongoing efforts to accomplish a long-range mission; is comprised of a series of projects.

**project:** A work assignment that has specific outcomes, definite start and end dates, and established resource budgets.

**project abstract:** Highlights of key information about a project. Also called a *project summary* or a *project profile.*

**project charter:** A document issued by upper management that spells out the project manager's authority to coordinate personnel in the performance of a project.

**project control:** Process of ensuring that project work is going according to plan and that the desired results are being achieved.

**project director:** See *project manager.*

**project leader:** See *project manager.*

**project leadership:** Process of creating and sharing the project vision and strategy, eliciting people's commitment and support, and sustaining ongoing motivation.

**project management:** Process of guiding your project from its beginning through performance to its closure. Includes planning, organizing, and control.

**project manager:** The person ultimately responsible for the successful completion of a project.

**project planning:** Developing, within a defined environment, a course of action designed to accomplish specified objectives within established constraints.

**project profile:** See *project abstract.*

**project request**: A written request by a group within your organization to perform a project.

**project summary:** See *project abstract.*

**purchase order:** A formal submission from your procurement department to a vendor asking for an item.

**purchase requisition:** A written, approved request for an item that you submit to your procurement department.

**purpose:** Brief statement of what your project will entail and why it was established. The purpose typically addresses background, scope, and strategy.

**resource histogram:** See *Person Loading Graph.*

**responsibility:** The commitment to achieve specific project results.

**risk:** The possibility that you may not achieve your product, schedule, or resource targets because something unexpected occurs or something planned does not occur.

**risk factor:** A situation that may cause one or more project risks to occur.

**risk management:** The process of identifying possible risks, assessing their potential impact on the project, and developing and implementing plans for minimizing their negative impact project.

**rough order of magnitude (ROM) estimate:** An initial estimate of costs based on a general sense of the type of work your project will entail.

**scope:** A high-level description of the work your project will entail (the "what" of the project).

**secondary information source:** Someone else's report of information contained in a primary source.

**Skills Roster:** A table depicting people's skills, knowledge, and interests.

**slack time:** The amount of time you can delay an activity and still finish your project in the shortest possible time. Also called *float*.

**span time:** See *duration.*

**span time estimate:** Your best sense of how long an activity will actually take.

**stakeholder:** A person or group who is needed to support or will be affected by your project.

**Statement of Work (SOW):** A written confirmation of what your project will produce and the terms and conditions under which you'll perform your work.

**strategy:** Your general approach to the major work of your project; the "how" of your project.

**subtask:** Third level of detail in a work-breakdown structure. Also called a *level-3 breakout.*

**supporter:** Person who'll help you perform your project.

**task:** Second level of detail in a Work Breakdown Structure. Also called a *level-2 breakout.*

**unknown unknown:** Information related to your project that you don't have because it doesn't exist yet. See also *known unknown.*

**weighted labor rate:** A combination of a person's hourly salary and associated indirect costs.

**work assignment:** First level of detail in a Work Breakdown Structure. Also called a *level-1 breakout.*

**Work Breakdown Structure (WBS):** An organized, hierarchical representation of all work to be performed in your project.

**Work Breakdown Structure dictionary:** A compilation of key descriptive information about all lowest level work activities in a Work Breakdown Structure.

**work effort:** See *person effort.*

**work-order agreement:** Written description of work to be performed by people or groups within your organization in support of your project.

# Appendix B

# Earned Value Analysis

● ● ● ● ● ● ● ● ● ● ● ● ● ● ● ● ● ● ● ● ● ● ● ● ● ● ● ● ● ● ● ● ● ● ● ● ● ● ● ● ● ● ● ● ●

*1*'m assuming that, because you're reading this, you've decided you want to find out more about an approach used to help you assess your ongoing project performance. *Earned Value Analysis* is a technique that helps you determine whether you're ahead or behind schedule and whether you're over or under your budget, while only tracking your resource expenditures. It's particularly useful on larger projects to identify those areas where you may need to investigate further for potential problems.

## Defining Earned Value Analysis

Monitoring your project's performance entails determining whether you're ahead, behind, or on schedule and whether you're over, under, or on budget. However, just comparing your actual expenditures with those planned normally can't tell you whether you're over or under budget.

Suppose you're three months into your project and you've spent $50,000. According to your plan, you shouldn't have spent $50,000 until the end of the fourth month of your project. It appears that you're over budget at this point, but you can't tell for sure. Either of the following situations could have produced these results:

- ✔ You could've performed all the work planned but paid more for it than you expected — this would mean that you're on schedule and over your budget.

- ✔ You could've performed more work than you planned but paid exactly what you expected for the work you did — this would mean you're on budget and ahead of schedule.

Of course, many other situations could also have produced these results.

*Earned Value Analysis* is a technique by which you can assess your project's schedule and resource expenditure performance from your resource expenditures to date. With Earned Value Analysis, you determine:

- ✔ **Cost variance:** The portion of the difference between what you planned to spend by a certain date and what you really spent that's true cost savings or loss.

- ✔ **Schedule variance:** The difference between what you planned to spend by a certain date and what you really spent that's due to your being ahead of or behind schedule.

- ✔ **Estimate at completion:** The total amount you'd spend to perform this task, if your spending pattern to date continued until the task was finished.

Figure B-1 depicts the key information used and produced in an Earned Value Analysis. As illustrated, the difference between planned and actual expenditures on the date of the report is due to the combined effects of a schedule delay and a cost savings.

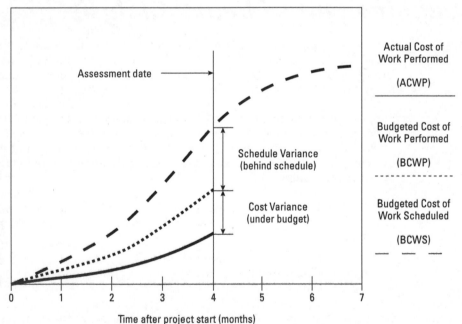

**Figure B-1:** Monitoring using Earned Value Analysis.

Cost and schedule variances and the estimate at completion are calculated from the following information:

- **Budgeted Cost of Work Scheduled (BCWS):** The planned cost for work due to be completed by a specified date.
- **Actual Cost of Work Performed (ACWP):** The amount of funds actually spent for work actually done by the specified date.
- **Budgeted Cost of Work Performed (BCWP):** The planned cost for work actually done by the specified date.

The *earned value* of a piece of work is defined to be equal to the amount you planned to spend to perform it.

Cost and schedule variances are defined in mathematical terms, as follows:

CV = Cost variance

= BCWP − ACWP

In other words, the *cost variance* as of a certain date is the difference between what you planned to spend for the work that you've actually completed and what you really spent.

SV = Schedule variance

= BCWP − BCWS

The *schedule variance* is the difference between your planned expenditures for what you planned to do and your planned expenditures for what you really did.

You can express the cost and schedule variances as percentages, using the following formulas:

CVP = Cost variance percentage

= CV ÷ BCWP × 100

SVP = Schedule variance percentage

= SV ÷ BCWS × 100

Table B-1 illustrates that a positive variance indicates something desirable (that is, either that you're under budget or ahead of schedule), while a negative variance indicates something undesirable (either that you're over budget or behind schedule).

| Table B-1 | Interpretations of Values of Cost and Schedule Variances | | |
|-----------|---------|------|----------|
| *Variance* | *Negative* | *Zero* | *Positive* |
| Cost | Over budget | On budget | Under budget |
| Schedule | Behind schedule | On schedule | Ahead of schedule |

Finally, the estimate at completion is defined as follows:

> EAC = Estimate at completion
>
>    = ACWP ÷ BCWP × total budget

This is a simplistic estimate because it assumes that the spending patterns through the end of the project will be the same as they've been up until now. Of course, circumstances may change the expenditure pattern or you may choose to alter the pattern if you've been overspending and want to get back on track.

These terms and definitions become easier to understand when you consider a simple example. Suppose that you're planning to conduct a series of telephone interviews. Your interview guide is already prepared, and each phone interview is independent of the others. You state the following in your project plan:

- ✔ Your project will last 10 months
- ✔ You plan to conduct 100 interviews each month
- ✔ You plan that each interview will cost $300 to conduct
- ✔ Your total project budget is $300,000

During your first month, you do the following:

- ✔ Conduct 75 interviews
- ✔ Spend a total of $15,000

In reality, this little project is so simple that you don't need Earned Value Analysis to see how you're doing! Because you planned to conduct 100 interviews in the first month and you only conducted 75, you're behind schedule. Because you planned to spend $300 per interview and you only spent $15,000 ÷ 75 interviews = $200 per interview, you're under budget. However, this example gives you a chance to see how you'd calculate the earned value information and what you can learn from it.

1. **Calculate the three information items from which the schedule and cost variances and the estimate at completion are determined:**

   BCWS = What you planned to spend for what you planned to do during the month

   = $300/interview × 100 interviews = $30,000

   ACWP = What you actually spent during the month

   = $15,000

   BCWP = What you planned to spend for what you really did during the month

   = $300/interview × 75 interviews = $22,500

2. **Determine your cost and schedule performance during the month, as follows:**

   Cost variance = budgeted cost of work performed − actual cost of work performed

   = $22,500 − $15,000 = $7,500

   Schedule variance = budgeted cost of work performed − budgeted cost of work scheduled

   = $22,500 − $30,000 = −$7,500

3. **The cost variance and schedule variance percentages are as follows:**

   CVP = CV ÷ BCWP × 100

   = $7,500 ÷ $22,500 × 100 = +33%

   SVP = SV ÷ BCWS × 100

   = −$7,500 ÷ $30,000 × 100 = −25%

The cost variance percentage and schedule variance percentage make sense when you look at the actual numbers for the month. You had originally planned to spend $300 per interview, but in the first month you actually spent $15,000 ÷ 75 = $200 per interview. The difference between your planned per interview cost and your actual is $100, which is 100 ÷ 300 × 100 = 33% less than you planned, meaning that you're 33 percent under budget. You originally planned to conduct 100 interviews in the first month, but you only finished 75. The difference between your planned and actual performance is 25 interviews, which is 25 ÷ 100 × 100 = 25% less than planned, meaning that you're 25% behind schedule.

If your work continues in the same fashion for the remainder of your project, your total project expenditures at completion will be as follows:

$$EAC = ACWP \div BCWP \times total\ budget$$

$$= \$15,000 \div \$22,500 \times \$300,000 = \$200,000$$

In other words, if you continue to perform your interviews for $200 each rather than the planned $300 each, you will spend ⅔ of your total planned budget to complete all of your interviews.

While it makes no sense to do a formal Earned Value Analysis to monitor a project that's this simple, if your project has 50 to 100 activities (or more), an Earned Value Analysis can help you consider jointly the performance on individual activities to identify general trends that may suggest that your entire project will come in over budget or behind schedule. The earlier you identify such trends, the more easily you can take steps to counteract them.

# Determining the Reasons for Observed Variances

Cost and schedule variances suggest project performance isn't going exactly as planned. After you determine that a variance exists, you want to figure out the reason(s) for the variance so that you can take the necessary corrective actions.

Possible reasons for cost variances are as follows:

- ✔ More or less work is required to complete a task than originally planned.
- ✔ The people performing the work are more or less productive than planned.
- ✔ The actual costs of labor and materials are more or less than planned.
- ✔ Actual organization indirect rates are higher or lower than originally planned. (See Chapter 5 for a discussion of indirect rates and how they can affect your project expenditures.)

Possible reasons for schedule variances are as follows:

- ✔ Work scheduled is performed earlier or later than planned.
- ✔ More or less work is required than originally planned.
- ✔ People performing the work are more or less productive than planned.

# *Looking at a Simple Example*

The following example presents a more realistic illustration of how Earned Value Analysis can support insightful analysis of your project's performance.

Suppose the Acme Company has awarded a contract for the production of two specialized and complex corporate brochures to Copies 'R' Us. The contract calls for Copies 'R' Us to produce 500 copies of Brochure A and 1,000 copies of Brochure B. It further states that Copies 'R' Us will produce Brochure A at the rate of 100 per month and Brochure B at the rate of 250 per month. Production of Brochure A is to start on January 1 and production of Brochure B on February 1.

The project plan is depicted in Table B-2.

| Table B-2 | Plan for Copies 'R' Us to Produce Brochures A and B | | | |
|-----------|-------|-------|--------------|------------|
| *Activity* | *Start* | *End* | *Elapsed Time* | *Total Cost* |
| Brochure A | Jan 1 | May 31 | 5 months | $100,000 |
| Brochure B | Feb 1 | May 31 | 4 months | $100,000 |
| Total | | | | $200,000 |

A quick glance suggests that Brochure A will cost $200/copy ($100,000/500 copies) and Brochure B will cost $100/copy ($100,000/1,000 copies).

Suppose it's the end of March, and you're three months into the project. Table B-3 presents a summary of what has happened as of March 31:

| Table B-3 | | Project Status as of March 31 | | |
|-----------|-------|--------------|-----------------|------------|
| *Activity* | *Start* | *Elapsed Time* | *Number Produced* | *Total Cost* |
| Brochure A | Jan 1 | 3 months | 150 | $45,000 |
| Brochure B | Feb 1 | 2 months | 600 | $30,000 |
| Total | | | | $75,000 |

Your job is to figure out your schedule and cost performance to date and what's likely to happen if expenditure patterns stay the same for the remainder of the project.

1. **Determine your cost and schedule performance for the production of Brochure A through March 31.**

    BCWS = $200/brochure $\times$ 100 brochures/month $\times$ 3 months = $60,000

    ACWP = $45,000

    BCWP = $200/brochure $\times$ 150 brochures = $30,000

    Cost variance (CV) = BCWP – ACWP

    CV = $30,000 – $45,000 = –$15,000

    CVP = CV $\div$ BCWP $\times$ 100

    CVP = -$15,000 $\div$ $30,000 $\times$ 100 = –50%

    Schedule variance = BCWP – BCWS

    SV = $30,000 – $60,000 = –$30,000

    SVP = SV $\div$ BCWS $\times$ 100

    SVP = –$30,000 $\div$ $60,000 = –50%

   Your analysis reveals that production of Brochure A is 50 percent behind schedule and 50 percent over budget.

2. **Determine your cost and schedule performance for the production of Brochure B through March 31.**

    BCWS = $100/brochure $\times$ 250 brochures/month $\times$ 2 months = $50,000

    ACWP = $30,000

    BCWP = $100/brochure $\times$ 600 brochures = $60,000

    Cost variance = BCWP – ACWP

    CV = $60,000 – $30,000 = $30,000

    CVP = CV $\div$ BCWP $\times$ 100

    CVP = $30,000 $\div$ $60,000 $\times$ 100 = 50%

    Schedule Variance = BCWP – BCWS

    SV = $60,000 – $50,000 = $10,000

    SVP = SV $\div$ BCWS $\times$ 100

    SVP = $10,000 $\div$ $50,000 $\times$ 100 = 20%

   Your analysis reveals that production of Brochure B is 20 percent ahead of schedule and 50 percent under budget.

3. **Determine the overall status of your project by adding the individual cost and schedule variances for Brochures A and B.**

    Project Cost Variance = –$15,000 + $30,000 = $15,000

    Project Schedule Variance = –$30,000 + $10,000 = –$20,000

**4. Determine your project estimate at completion by adding the individual estimates at completion for Brochures A and B.**

$$\text{EAC for Brochure A} = \text{ACWP} \div \text{BCWP} \times \text{Budget for Brochure A}$$
$$= \$45,000 \div \$30,000 \times \$100,000$$
$$= \$150,000$$

$$\text{EAC for Brochure B} = \text{ACWP} \div \text{BCWP} \times \text{Budget for Brochure B}$$
$$= \$30,000 \div \$60,000 \times \$100,000$$
$$= \$50,000$$

$$\text{EAC for the project} = \$150,000 + \$50,000$$
$$= \$200,000$$

This information is summarized in Table B-4.

| Table B-4 | Performance Analysis Summary | | | | | |
|-----------|------|------|------|------|------|------|
| | **BCWS** | **ACWP** | **BCWP** | **CV** | **SV** | **EAC** |
| Brochure A | $60,000 | $45,000 | $30,000 | −$15,000 | −$30,000 | $150,000 |
| Brochure B | $50,000 | $30,000 | $60,000 | +$30,000 | +$10,000 | $50,000 |
| Total | | | | +$15,000 | −$20,000 | $200,000 |

# Calculating Budgeted Cost of Work Performed

The key to an accurate Earned Value Analysis lies in the accuracy of the budgeted cost of work performed (BCWP). To determine BCWP, you must estimate how much of a task you've completed to date and how much of the task's total budget you planned to spend for the amount of work you've achieved. Usually, you assume that there's a direct relationship between the portion of a task you've completed and the amount of funds you should've spent. In other words, if you've completed 60 percent of the task, you'd figure that you should've spent 60 percent of the total task budget.

For tasks with separate components, like printing brochures or conducting telephone surveys, determining how much of a task you've completed is straightforward. However, if your task entails an integrated work or thought process with no easily segmentable parts, such as designing the brochure, the best you can do is to make an educated guess.

Figure B-2 illustrates three alternate approaches that are typically used to estimate budgeted cost of work performed:

- **Percent-complete method:** BCWP is the product of the fraction of the activity you have completed and the total activity budget.

- **Milestone method:** BCWP is zero until you complete the activity and 100 percent of the total activity budget after you complete it.

- **50/50 method:** BCWP is zero before you start the activity, 50 percent of the total activity budget after you start it but before you finish, and 100 percent of the total activity budget after you finish the activity.

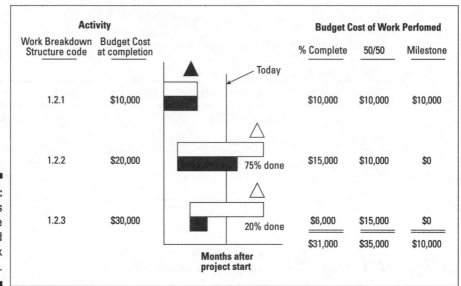

**Figure B-2:** Three ways to define budgeted cost of work performed.

| Activity | | | Budget Cost of Work Perfomed | | |
|---|---|---|---|---|---|
| Work Breakdown Structure code | Budget Cost at completion | | % Complete | 50/50 | Milestone |
| 1.2.1 | $10,000 | Today | $10,000 | $10,000 | $10,000 |
| 1.2.2 | $20,000 | 75% done | $15,000 | $10,000 | $0 |
| 1.2.3 | $30,000 | 20% done | $6,000 | $15,000 | $0 |
| | | | $31,000 | $35,000 | $10,000 |

Months after project start

The milestone method and 50/50 method allow you to approximate BCWP without requiring you to estimate the portion of a task that you've completed.

Figure B-2 compares the accuracy of the three different methods for a simple example. Task 1.2 is comprised of three subtasks: 1.2.1, 1.2.2, and 1.2.3. For this illustration, it's assumed that you know accurately the following amount of work has been done on each subtask:

- Subtask 1.2.1 is complete.

- Subtask 1.2.2 is 75 percent complete.

- Subtask 1.2.3 is 20 percent complete.

The BCWP of Task 1.2 is calculated by adding up the BCWP for each of the three subtasks that comprise Task 1.2. The actual BCWP, as determined with the percent-complete method, should be $31,000. (Again, you can use this method only if you know accurately the percent of the task that you've completed.)

The milestone method is the most conservative and the least accurate. You'd expect that you would spend some money while you're working on the task. However, this method doesn't allow you to declare BCWP greater than $0 until you've completed the activity. Therefore, it'll always appear that you're over budget while you're performing the activity.

The 50/50 method is a closer approximation to reality than the milestone method, because you're allowed to declare a BCWP greater than $0 while you're performing the task. However, it's possible that this approximation could inadvertently mask an overspending situation.

Suppose you'd completed 30 percent of a task with a $10,000 budget. Arguably, you should've spent about 30 percent of your budget, or $3,000, to complete 30 percent of the work on the task. However, the 50/50 method would approximate your BCWP as being $5,000 (50 percent of the total budget for the task). If your actual cost for the work performed was $4,000, you would be over budget. However, the 50/50 method would have you compare your expenditures of $4,000 with your approximated BCWP of $5,000 and it would appear that you were $1,000 *under* budget.

Observe the following guidelines to improve the accuracy of your estimates of BCWP when you use either the 50/50 method or the milestone method:

- Define your activities to be of relatively short duration: Usually 2 weeks or less.
- Define at least seven subelements that you'll sum to give you the BCWP of a higher-level activity.

# Index

## • *Numbers* •

50/50 method, 328–329

## • *A* •

accountability
  behavior messages, 173
  benefits, 174
  defined, 166, 311
  guidelines, 166–167
  lack of, 21
  methods, 299–302
  non-reporting personnel, 172–175
  questions, 172–173
  to teams, 174
accuracy
  BCWP estimate, 329
  defined, 266
  expenditure data, 221–222
  likelihood estimate, 266
  project plan, 17
  schedule performance data, 213
  work effort expenditure data, 217
achieved power, 241–242
activities
  breakdown approaches, 59–61
  breaking down, 53–54
  conditional, 57
  critical-path, 78–79, 92–93
  decomposing, 50–51
  defined, 72, 311
  defining, 74
  dummy, 75
  duration, 68
  example, 56–57
  immediate predecessors/successors, 69
  inputs, 68
  iterative, representing, 57–58

  lowest-level, 110, 208
  with no break points, 58–59
  order of, 65
  outputs, 68
  picnic-at-the-lake project, 86
  plan, 311
  problems with, 212
  project control, 203–204
  project-related, 34–35
  reaffirming, 304
  required resources, 68
  resource estimation, 53
  risk, 67–68, 212
  roles and responsibilities, 68
  simultaneous, 93–97
  start/end time, 297
  subdividing, 98–99
  time estimation, 53
  uncertain, assumptions, 65
  Work Breakdown Structure, identifying, 61
  work detail, 68
  written description of, 191
activities report. *See also* schedules
  defined, 102, 311
  illustrated, 103, 209
  performance data, 209
activities/key-events combined report
  defined, 209
  illustrated, 210
  use of, 211–212
activity performance limitations, 44–45
activity-in-the-box approach. *See also*
    network diagrams
  choosing, 76
  defined, 75, 311
  elements, 75
  illustrated, 76
  using, 75–76

activity-on-the-arrow format. *See also* network diagrams
  choosing, 76
  defined, 74, 311
  dummy activities, 75
  elements, 74
  illustrated, 75
  using, 74–75
actual cost of work performed (ACWP), 321
ad hoc team meetings, 236–237
announcing a project, 200
approaches
  activity breakdown, 59–61
  assumption of, 39
  different, 39
  innovating, 39
approvals
  informing team members of, 188
  Linear Responsibility Chart, 178
  project plan, 17
  required, obtaining, 252
  role, 176, 195
  work-order agreement, 189
  written, 161
ascribed power, 241
asking, 193
assumptions
  defined, 311
  identifying, 297
  not identifying/sharing, 21
  for planned work clarification, 54
  project managers and, 308
  risk factors, 262
  uncertain activity, 65
  writing down, 54
audience list
  adding/removing names from, 155
  creation categories, 150–154
  defined, 150
  developing, 150–151
  development time, 155
  example, 156
  guidelines, 155

illustrated, 154
improving, 154–155
audience list template
  benefits, 157
  defined, 156
  using, 156–157
audiences
  benefits of knowing, 150
  change and, 227
  confirming participation of, 188–191
  defined, 150, 311
  drivers, 158–160
  end user, 153
  external, 151
  groups, 158
  identification, 155
  internal, 151
  involvement methods, 161
  involvement tips, 162
  maintain/support personnel, 153
  observers, 158, 161
  plan, 162
  potential, 152–153
  project-progress report and, 234
  risk factors, 261
  support group, 152–153
  supporters, 158, 160–161
  understanding, 150–157
  What's In It For Me (WIIFM), 162
authority
  acting with, 302
  defined, 162, 165, 311
  defining, 163–164
  direct, 174
  earned, 241
  examples, 165
  getting people with, 162–164
  given, 241
  giving to another person, 171
  involving people with, 299–300
  reconfirming, 164
  responsibility versus, 166
  taking back, 167
  types of, 243

automated impact assessments, 268
availability
  defined, 113, 311
  determining, 113
  efficiency versus, 114
  person-hours, 116–117
  resource, 101

### • B •

background
  defined, 311
  risk factors, 262
backing in, 92, 311
back-to-front approach, 84
backward pass, 312
baselines
  defined, 199, 223, 312
  rebaselining, 223–224
  setting, 199
  using, 199
bottom-up cost estimate, 130, 132
brainstorming approach (Work Breakdown
    Structure), 62–63
breakdown. *See also* Work Breakdown
    Structure
  approaches, 59–61
  by functions, 59–60
  by geographical areas, 60
  method decision factors, 60–61
  by organizational units, 60
  by product components, 59–60
bubble-chart format. *See also* Work
    Breakdown Structure
  benefits, 65
  defined, 64
  illustrated, 64
  interpretation, 64
  uses, 65
budget. *See* project budget
budgeted cost of work performed (BCWP).
    *See also* Earned Value Analysis
  50/50 method, 328–329
  calculating, 327–329
  defined, 321

definition methods, 328
  estimate accuracy, 329
  milestone method, 328–329
  percent-completed method, 328
budgeted cost of work scheduled
    (BCWS), 321
business requirements document, 28, 312

### • C •

capacity
  affect on span time, 72
  resource, 101
career development, 107
centralized structure. *See also*
    organizational environment
  benefits, 138–139
  challenges, 139
  defined, 138, 312
  illustrated, 138
change-control systems, 226
changes
  audience communication and, 227
  impact on Statement of Work, 29
  implementation decision, 226
  implementation instructions, 226
  managing, 226–227
  network diagrams and, 95
  potential impact of, 226
  price of, 226
  in project-progress report, 235
  reflected in schedules, 227
  request, 226
charge
  categories, closing out, 252
  codes, 199
close phase. *See also* phases
  defined, 18
  drivers and, 160
  observers and, 161
  partial completion of, 19
  post-project evaluation and, 275
  risk factors, 261
  supporters and, 161

closing projects
  administrative issues, 252
  announcement, 253–254
  checklist, 250–251
  elements of, 249
  finishing work, 250–251
  planning, 251
  post-project evaluation, 254
  team members and, 252
collaborators, in audience list, 151
commitment(s)
  to common goals, 194
  getting, 175, 300
  lack of, 21
  multiple, juggling, 118–124
  needed, estimating, 109–117
  reconfirming, 205
  for success, 22
  team member, 146
  telling others of, 301
committees, 193
communications
  clear/consistent, 22
  formal, 229
  informal, 229–230
  misunderstandings, 230
  plan, 289
  poor, 21
  procedures, 196
  project manager, 308
  purpose of, 289
  risks and, 269–270
  schedule performance, 213
  team members, 147
  written, 231–232
conceive phase. *See also* phases
  caution, 15
  cost-benefit analysis, 15–16
  defined, 14
  drivers and, 159–160
  example, 15
  observers and, 161
  post-project evaluation and, 274
  questions, 14
  risk factors, 260

rough order-of-magnitude estimate, 129
  supporters and, 160
conditional activities, 57
conflict resolution, 196
constraints
  defined, 312
  risk factor, 262
  satisfying, 296
  time, 92–93
consultation role, 196
contracts
  defined, 28
  office, 192
corrective actions
  delays/variances, 225
  project control, 204
cost report. *See also* expenditures
  defined, 220
  illustrated, 221
  information, 220–221
cost variances
  defined, 320
  formula, 321
  interpretations, 322
  percentage, 323
  reasons for, 324
cost-benefit analysis. *See also* conceive
    phase
  defined, 15, 34, 312
  example, 15–16
  influence factors, 16
  as information source, 34
  results, 34
critical paths. *See also* noncritical paths
  changing, 79
  defined, 78, 312
  determining, 79
  length, 78–80
  length, reducing, 93
critical-path activities
  different strategies for, 93
  monitoring, 78-79
performance period and, 212
  rechecking, 92–93
  removing, 93

**• D •**

decision making, 196
decision trees, 267
decomposition
  defined, 50
  guidelines, 51
define phase. *See also* phases
  defined, 16
  detailed budget estimate in, 129
  drivers and, 160
  observers and, 161
  post-project evaluation and, 274
  project plan, 16–17
  risk factors, 260
  skipping, 19
  supporters and, 160
delays
  causes, identifying, 224–225
  corrective actions, 225
  span time and, 73
  span time estimates and, 100
delegation
  confident, 170
  defined, 312
  degrees of, 170
  determining, 167–169
  situations, 168–169
  support, 168
deliverables. *See* events
denial, 258
dependency
  defined, 312
  diagrams, 74
desirability. *See also* motivation
  clarifying, 244–245
  defined, 244–245
  helping to understand, 245
  personal, 244–245
detailed budget estimate. *See also*
    project budget
  bottom-up, 130, 132
  defined, 128, 313

in definition phase, 129
  developing, 130
  top-down, 130, 132
direct costs. *See also* project costs
  defined, 127, 313
  estimating, 130
  example, 127
discretionary relationships, 84
distribution list, 150, 313
drivers. *See also* supporters
  agreement on objectives, 43
  as audience, 159–160
  confirming participation of, 190–191
  defined, 30, 158, 313
  identifying, 296
  involving, 159–160
  phases and, 160
  project scope confirmation with, 38
  reaffirming, 304
  supporters claim to be, 31, 158
dummy activities, 75
duration. *See* span time

**• E •**

earliest finish dates
  defined, 78, 313
  determining, 80
  in network diagram, 82
earliest start dates
  defined, 78, 313
  determining, 80
  in network diagram, 82
earned value, 321
Earned Value Analysis
  cost variances, 320–324
  defined, 221, 313, 319
  defining, 319–324
  determinations, 320
  example, 325–327
  monitoring with, 320
  schedule variances, 320–324

efficiency
  availability versus, 114
  defined, 112, 313
  factors affecting, 112–113
  failure to consider, 115
  impact of, 116
  in personnel planning, 113
elapsed time. *See* span time
e-mail
  benefits, 290
  copies, keeping, 292
  as documentation, 290
  drawbacks, 290
  improper use example, 290–291
  inappropriate uses, 291
  misinterpretation, 290
  optimizing, 292
  proofreading, 292
  using, 289–292
estimate at completion, 320
events
  defined, 72, 313
  defining, 74
  naming, 90
  as signposts, 72
  simple, 91
expectations
  challenging, facing, 39
  false, eliminating, 24–25
  preset, 44–45
  specifying, 300
expenditures
  analyzing, 220–221
  comparing with plan, 220
  cost report, 220–221
  data accuracy, 221–222
  data collection, 221
  preventing from exceeding budget, 206
  process example, 220
  process leading up to, 219
  tracking, 108, 198, 218–222
  tracking system support, 222
  work effort, 214–217

## • F •

fast tracking, 93, 313
feasibility. *See also* motivation
  defined, 244, 313
  demonstrating, 245–246
  as self-fulfilling prophecy, 246
  as subjective assessment, 246
financial expenditures. *See* expenditures
finishing work. *See also* closing project
  checklist, 250–251
  elements of, 250
  planning, 250–251
  reestablishing team identity/spirit and, 251
  situations/pressures, 250
  smoothly, 251
fixed-group structure
  centralized, 138
  defined, 138
  functional, 140
follow up
  meeting, 174
  post-project evaluation, 277–278
  schedule, 301–302
formal communications, 229
forming stage, 197
forward pass, 313
front-to-back approach, 84
fudge factors
  defined, 101
  as planning compromise, 101–102
functional managers
  in audience list, 155
  defined, 143, 313
  responsibilities, 145
functional structure. *See also*
    organizational environment
  benefits, 140
  challenges, 140–141
  defined, 139–140, 313
  example, 140
  illustrated, 140

## • *G* •

Gantt chart. *See also* schedules
  defined, 102, 314
  illustrated, 104, 119
  progress, 210–211
  resource overload elimination, 121–122
  simultaneous activities and, 119
  using, 118–119
general and administrative costs. *See also*
    indirect costs
  defined, 127, 314
  estimating, 132
goals, team/team member, 194–195
group meetings, 161
groups, 193

## • *H* •

Human Resources Matrix
  defined, 110, 314
  illustrated, 109

## • *I* •

immediate predecessors
  decision methods, 84
  defined, 83
  determining, 83–85
  information, 69
  in initial schedule, 91
  picnic-at-the-lake, 87
  recording, 85
immediate successors, 69
indented-outline format. *See also* Work
    Breakdown Structure
  in combination format, 64
  defined, 63
  illustrated, 64
indirect costs. *See also* project costs
  defined, 127, 314
  estimating, 130–131
  estimation approaches, 132
  examples, 127–128

general and administration, 127, 132
  overhead, 127, 132
  types of, 127
informal communications
  defined, 229
  participation in, 230
informal written correspondence, 161
information
  confirming, 36
  cost-benefit analysis source, 34
  exhaustive search for, 36–37
  network diagrams, 78
  performance, 205
  post-project evaluation, 275
  risks, 269–270
  sharing, 204
  sharing, in writing, 231–232
  sharing, through meetings, 232–234
  similar projects, 65
  supporting, finding, 101
  unknown, 67–68
  Work Breakdown Structure dictionary,
    68–69
  written, 36
initiators
  defined, 314
  identifying, 29–31
  name/position description, 30
  supporters versus, 30
input role, 176
inputs
  identifying, 297
  in PMIS, 207
integrated project-management software.
    *See also* software
  benefits, 286
  caution, 284
  choosing, 285
  defined, 281, 284
  drawbacks, 286
  example, 284–285
  functions, 284
  introducing into operations, 288–289
  reports and, 285

interdependencies, 297
interest. *See also* Skills Roster
  defined, 107
  ratings comparison, 108–109
involvement
  early, 162
  legality, 162
  methods, 161
  plan, 162
  tips, 162
issues
  administrative, at project closure, 252
  dealing with, 177
  identifying, 177
  post-project evaluation, 276
  in project-progress report, 235

• *K* •

key-events list, 314
key-events report. *See also* schedules
  defined, 102, 314
  illustrated, 103, 209
  information, 208
  performance data, 208
kickoff meeting, 314
knowledge. *See also* Skills Roster
  deficiencies, 107–108
  needed, 110
  numerical scale, 107
  productivity and, 112
  ratings comparison, 108–109
  schema, 107
known unknowns, 67–68, 314

• *L* •

labor report
  data, 214
  defined, 314
  illustrated, 215
  information from project plan, 214

latest finish dates
  defined, 78, 314
  determining, 81–82
  in network diagram, 82
latest start dates
  defined, 78, 314
  determining, 81–82
  in network diagram, 82
leadership
  approach to project activities, 240
  defined, 239
  focus, 239
  management versus, 239–240
  project manager, 309
learning, from experience, 242
limitations
  activity performance, 44–45
  defined, 314
  determining, 45
  identifying, 44–46
  including in plan, 46
  resource, 44–45
  result, 44
  schedule, 45
  source, 45
  specific, 45
  types of, 44–45
  vague, 45
Linear Responsibility Charts
  analyzing, 176
  approval, 178
  defined, 175, 314
  developing, 178
  elements, 175–176
  hierarchy, 179
  illustrated, 175, 179
  improving, 179–180
  reviewing, 178, 180
  roles, 176, 196
  situations/issues suggested in, 177
  team involvement in, 180
  in writing, 180

lowest-level activities. *See also* activities
  defined, 110
  start/end dates, 208

## • *M* •

management. *See also* project management
  approach to project activities, 240
  defined, 239
  focus, 239
  leadership versus, 239–240
Market Requirements Document, 28, 314
matrix environment. *See also*
    organizational environment
  benefits, 142
  challenges, 142–143
  defined, 141, 314
  expertise application, 142
  functional managers, 145
  key players in, 143
  problem procedures, 147
  project manager, 143–144
  support, 147
  team assembly, 142
  team identity, 146
  team member buy-in, 146
  team members, 144
  upper management, 145
  working successfully in, 146–147
meetings
  action items, 233
  conduct, 233
  follow-up, 234
  frustrations about, 232
  group, 161
  holding, 238
  improving, 233–234
  kickoff, 314
  one-on-one, 161
  post-project evaluation, 200–201
  preparation for, 233
  productive, 238

  schedules, 199
  sharing information through, 232–234
  starting/ending, on time, 233
  team, ad hoc, 236–237
  team, regularly scheduled, 236–237
  "timekeeper," 233
  upper-management reviews, 236–238
  value of, 233
  view of, 232
micromanagers
  dealing with, 181–183
  defined, 181, 315
  helping gain confidence, 182–183
  interference versus interest, 182
  listening to, 183
  observing, 183
  reasons for, 181
  thanking, 183
  working with, 183
midcourse kickoff session, 305
milestone method, 328–329
milestones. *See* events
mistakes, anticipating, 18–19
monitoring. *See* tracking
motivation
  desirability, 244–245
  factors, 244
  feasibility, 244–246
  as personal choice, 243
  progress, 244, 246–247
  rewards, 240, 244, 247–248

## • *N* •

needs
  defined, 315
  defining, 33
  determining, 46
  examples, 46
  personnel, 109–117
  project addressed, 32–34
  written description of, 191

network diagrams
  activities, 72
  activity-in-the-box approach, 73, 75–76
  activity-on-the arrow approach, 73–75
  analyzing, 76–83
  backward pass, 81–83
  defined, 315
  drawing, 72–73
  elements, 72
  events, 72
  fleshing out, 83–85
  format selection, 76
  formats, 73–76
  forward pass, 79–80
  illustrated example, 77
  information derived from, 78
  in initial schedule, 91
  rules, 77–78
  span time, 72–73
  with stick-on notes, 85
  time changes and, 95
  use example, 85–91
noncritical paths. *See also* critical paths
  defined, 78, 315
  determining, 79
nonpersonnel resources, 124–126
norming stage, 197

**• O •**

objectives
  agreement on, 43
  all, identifying, 42
  anticipating resistance to, 43
  avoiding, 41
  clarifying, 41
  controllable, 42
  creativity and, 43
  defined, 40, 315
  development tips, 42–43
  elements, 40
  example, 40–41
  guarantees and, 43

  measures, 40–41
  performance targets, 40–41
  project success and, 40
  reaffirming, 304
  SMART, 42
  specific, 42–43
  vague, 20
observers
  as audience, 161
  defined, 158, 315
  identifying, 296
  involving, 161
  phases and, 161
off-track projects
  assignment reaffirmation, 305
  determining, 303–304
  key driver reaffirmation, 304
  midcourse kickoff session, 305
  monitoring/controlling performance, 306
  objectives reaffirmation, 304
  remaining activities reaffirmation, 304
  risk-management plan development, 305
  roles and responsibilities
    reaffirmation, 304
  schedule development, 305
one-on-one meetings, 161
organizational environment
  centralized structure, 138–139
  defining, 137–143
  functional structure, 139–141
  matrix structure, 141–147
organization-chart format, 63
organizations
  priorities, 35
  project importance to, 35
  software use, 285
ostrich approach, 258
output role, 176, 196
outputs, in PMIS, 207
overhead costs. *See also* indirect costs
  defined, 127, 315
  estimating, 132

## • *p* •

people. *See also* personnel
  as allies, 308
  benefiting from projects, 31
  implementing project results, 32
  involving, 299–300
  management of, 21
  project success and, 106
  response reasons, 240–241
  skills and knowledge, 106–109
  speaking with, 34, 36
percent-completed method, 328
perform phase. *See also* phases
  defined, 18
  drivers and, 160
  observers and, 161
  post-project evaluation and, 275
  risk factors, 261
  supporters and, 160
performance
  assessment, 204
  comparison, 235
  good, acknowledging, 302, 309
  information, 205
  measure, 315
  off-track project, 306
  periods, 205, 222–223, 315
  in project-progress report, 234
  schedule, 207–214
performance targets. *See also* objectives
  avoiding, 41
  defined, 315
  example, 40–41
person effort. *See* work effort
Person Loading Graph
  defined, 315
  illustrated, 119
  individual, 122
  for planning multiple projects, 124
  resource overload elimination and,
    121–122
  simultaneous activities and, 119
  summary, 123

personnel. *See also* Human Resources
    Matrix; people
  blanks, filling in, 191–192
  identifying, 110
  information specification, 298
  interview/assessment process, 192
  names of, 110, 111
  needs, 109–117
  planning, 106
  position description, 110–111
  risk factors, 263
PERT (program evaluation and review
    technique), 315
phases
  budget-development activity in, 129
  close phase, 18
  completing, 20
  conceive phase, 14–16
  define phase, 16–17
  drivers and, 159–160
  illustrated, 14
  list of, 13, 128
  observers and, 161
  perform phase, 18
  start phase, 17
  supporters and, 160–161
picnic-at-the-lake project
  activities, 86
  activity delays, 89–90
  activity subdivision, 98–99
  constraints, 86
  defined, 85–86
  dependencies, 86–87
  drawing network diagram for, 87–90
  network diagram, 90
  predecessor relationships, 87
  questions, 89
  time reduction, 94–97
planning. *See also* project plans
  audience involvement, 162
  defined, 317
  elements, 12
  initiative, 23
  personnel, 106

planning *(continued)*
  questions for, 295–298
  resource, 105
  time, 96
  unknowns and, 46–47
position description, 110–111
post-project evaluation
  agenda, 277
  close phase, 275
  conceive phase and, 274
  conducting, 254, 276–277
  define phase and, 274
  defined, 200, 273–274, 316
  follow-up, 277–278
  information, 275
  information sources, 276
  invitation to, 276
  issues, 276
  laying groundwork for, 200–201
  perform phase, 275
  preparing for, 273–276
  report, 278
  setting stage for, 275–276
  start phase and, 275
  tips, 276–277
power
  achieved, 241–242
  ascribed, 241
  bases, 243
  defined, 240, 316
  personal, developing, 240–243
prayer approach, 258
precedence diagrams, 74, 316
precision, 266
predecessors
  defined, 83
  immediate, 83–85, 87, 91
  multiple, 91
primary capability, 107
primary responsibility, 176, 195
proactivity, 23
processes
  defined, 12, 316
  management of, 21

in PMIS, 207
  span time estimates and, 100
  team operation, 196
product risk, 264
productivity
  defined, 112, 316
  factors affecting, 112
professional societies, in audience list, 151
programs, 12, 316
progress
  monitoring, inaccurate/late, 21
  as motivation, 244, 246–247
progress Gantt chart. *See also* schedule
    performance
  defined, 210, 316
  illustrated, 210
  reading, 211
project abstract. *See* project profile
project budget. *See also* project costs
  completed, approved, 128, 312
  defined, 126, 312
  detailed, 128
  developing, 126, 128–133
  estimate presentation, 131–133
  example, 131
  exceeding, prevention of, 206
  refining, 128–129
  rough order-of-magnitude estimate, 128
  stages, 128
project champion
  characteristics, 159
  confirming participation of, 190–191
  defined, 32, 159, 190, 312
  obtaining, 147, 159
  recruiting, 32
project charter, 28, 316
project code number, 198
project control
  activities, 203–204
  corrective action, 204
  cyclical nature of, 204
  defined, 203, 316
  elements, 12

information sharing, 204
performance assessment, 204
plan reconfirmation, 203
purpose, 212
project costs. *See also* project budget
    direct, 127
    estimating, 130–133
    general and administrative, 127
    indirect, 127
    overhead, 127
    types of, 126–128
project failure
    causes, 20–21
    risk, 34
project leaders. *See also* leadership
    defined, 144, 316
    successful, 193
project log, 201
project management
    defined, 12, 316
    excuses, 23–24
    failure, 20–21
    false assumptions, 24–25
    mindset, 22–25
    operations, 12
    principles of, 25
    reality, 20
    requirements, 22
    structured, 24
    success, 21
project management information
    systems (PMIS)
    defined, 206
    elements, 207
    illustrated, 207
    inputs, 207
    outputs, 207
    processes, 207
project managers
    assignment of, 146
    assumptions and, 308

"big picture" thinking, 308
as "can do" person, 307
communication, 308
defined, 143, 317
detail thinking, 309
as manager and leader, 309
in matrix environment, 143–144
as number-one career option, 9
performance acknowledgment, 309
project leaders versus, 144
respect, 308
responsibilities, 143–144
role, 22–23
tips for, 307–309
view of people, 308
as "why" person, 307
project plans. *See also* planning
    approval, 17
    clarity/accuracy of, 17
    elements, 16
    reconfirming, 203
    review, 17, 192
    writing, 17
project postmortem. *See* post-project
    evaluation
project profile, 28, 317
project request, 28, 317
project scope
    confirming understanding of, 38
    creep, 227
    defined, 317
    defining, 37–38
    description tips, 37–38
    risk factors, 262
    statement, 37
project strategy
    defined, 38
    examples, 38
    risk factors, 262
    risks, 39
    selecting, 38–39

project success
  areas of, 21
  care/management, 203
  completeness/continuity and, 49
  meeting needs/expectations and, 29
  objectives and, 40
  people and, 106
  proactive, 23
  requirements, 22
project-progress reports
  approved changes, 235
  audiences and, 234
  defined, 234
  frequency, 235
  improving, 235
  information, 234–235
  performance details, 234
  performance highlights, 234
  plans for next period, 235
  problems/issues, 235
  questions, 234
  risk management status, 235
projects
  activities related to, 34–35
  agreements, 11
  announcing, 200
  challenges, 13
  characteristics of, 10–11
  controlling, 203–205
  defined, 9–10, 316
  elements, 10
  external/internal, 11
  importance to organization, 35
  long-term, 59
  multiple, coordinating across, 123–124
  needs addressed by, 32–34
  participants, finalizing, 188–192
  people benefiting from, 31
  phases, 13–18
  planning, 11, 295–298
  processes versus, 12
  programs versus, 12
  purpose, 295
  results implementation, 32
  size, 10
  starting, 187–201
  tracking, 11
proposals
  defined, 219
  request for (RFP), 219
  reviewing, 219
punishment, as motivation, 240
purchase order, 317
purchase requisition, 317
purpose statement, 29

**• R •**

rebaselining. *See also* baselines
  defined, 223
  as last resort, 224
recruiting, 108
regularly scheduled team meetings. *See
  also* team meetings
  defined, 236
  guidelines, 236–237
  schedule, 236
regulators, in audience list, 151
relationships
  discretionary, 84
  illustrating, 175–180
  logical, 84
  required, 83–84
  team member, supporting, 196–197
reports
  activities, 102–103, 209
  activities/key-events, 209–210
  cost, 220–221
  encouraging reading of, 230
  integrated project-management software
    and, 285
  key-events, 102–103, 208–209
  labor, 214–215
  post-project evaluation, 278
  project-progress, 234–235
  schedule performance, 199, 208–211, 213
  written, 231–232
request for proposal (RFP), 219

requester, in audience list, 151
required relationships, 83–84
resource overload elimination
    by changing hour allocation, 121
    by changing start/end dates, 122
    methods, 120–123
resource requirement estimation, 105–133
resources
    activity, 68
    availability, 101, 297
    capacity, 101
    equipment, 124–126
    estimating, 53
    facilities, 124–126
    limitation, 44, 45
    matrix, 125
    nonpersonnel, 124–126
    personnel, 106–124
    planning for, 105
    project work support, 100
    risks, 264
    tracking, 198, 204
    usage charts, 125–126
respect
    achieved, 241
    project manager, 308
    reasons for, 241
responsibilities. *See also* roles
    accountability versus, 166
    activity, 68
    authority versus, 166
    clarifying, 180
    defined, 166, 317
    nonexistent/vague definitions, 21
    primary, 176, 195
    reaffirming, 304
    risk factors, 262–263
    secondary, 176, 195
    sharing, 170–171
    team members, 165–183
    as two-way agreement, 171
results
    cost-benefit analysis, 34
    implementation, 32

limitations, 44
planning, 296
review role, 176
rewards. *See also* motivation
    defined, 244
    example, 247–248
    providing, 247–248
risk factors
    assumptions, 262
    audience, 261
    close phase, 261
    conceive phase, 260
    constraints, 262
    define phase, 260
    defined, 259, 317
    funds, 263
    identifying, 259
    perform phase, 261
    personnel, 263
    potential, eliminating, 264
    project background, 262
    from project evolution, 260–261
    project objectives, 262
    project scope, 262
    project strategy, 262
    recognizing, 259–263
    in risk-management plan, 271
    roles and responsibilities, 262–263
    schedules, 263
    start phase, 260–261
    work packages, 262
risk management
    contingencies, 269
    defined, 258, 317
    insurance and, 269
    poor, strategies, 258
    process, 259, 268–270
    risk selection for, 268
    status, 235
    strategy development, 269
risk-management plan
    defined, 271
    elements, 271
    preparing, 271–272, 305
    sample, 271–272

risks
  activity, 212
  assessment questionnaires, 268
  automated impact assessments and, 268
  category ranking, 265
  choosing, for management, 268
  communicating about, 269–270
  consequences, assessing, 264–268
  dealing with, 257–272
  decision trees and, 267
  defined, 257, 317
  estimation and assessment support,
      267–268
  identifying, 67–68, 259–264
  impact, 267
  increased, 257–258
  likelihood, assessing, 264–266
  monitoring, 259
  not planning for, 21
  ordinal ranking, 265
  potential impact of, 258
  probability of occurrence, 264–265
  product, 264
  relative likelihood of occurrence, 265–266
  resource, 264
  in risk-management plan, 271
  schedule, 264
  strong, 267
  time reduction and, 96
  weak, 267
roles. *See also* responsibilities
  activity, 68
  approval, 176, 195
  assigning, 167–175
  clarifying, 180
  consultation, 196
  defining, 176, 195–196
  input, 176
  Linear Responsibility Chart and, 196
  nonexistent/vague definitions, 21
  output, 176, 196
  primary responsibility, 176, 195
  reaffirming, 304
  review, 176
  risk factors, 262–263

secondary responsibility, 176, 195
team member, 165–183
rough order-of-magnitude estimate. *See
    also* project budget
  in conceive phase, 129
  defined, 128, 317

scapegoating, 167
schedule performance
  activities report for, 209
  analyzing, 208–211
  combined activities/key-events report for,
      209–210
  communication, 213
  data accuracy, 213
  data collection, 211–212
  data definition, 208
  key-event reports for, 208–209
  manual tracking system, 213
  monitoring, 207–214
  monitoring frequency, 212
  percentage-completed measure, 208
  period, 212
  progress Gantt chart for, 210–211
  reports, 199, 208–211, 213
  software, 213–214
  tracking system support, 213–214
schedule variances
  defined, 320
  formula, 321
  interpretations, 322
  percentage, 323
  reasons for, 324
schedules
  in activities report format, 103
  backing into, 92
  change reflected in, 227
  developing, 91–99
  displaying, 102–104
  format decision, 102
  in Gantt chart format, 102, 104
  incomplete/inaccurate, 21
  initial, 91–92

in key-events report format, 102, 103
limitation, 45
meetings, 199
for off-track projects, 305
options, 97
possibility analysis, 71–91
review, 211
risk factors, 263
risks, 264
time constraints, meeting, 92–93
tracking, 198, 204, 207–214
scope creep. *See also* project scope
controlling, 227
defined, 227
secondary capability, 107
secondary responsibility, 176, 195
simple events, 91
skills
deficiencies, 107–108
needed, 110
numerical scale, 107
productivity and, 112
ratings comparison, 108–109
schema, 107
Skills Roster
creating, 108
defined, 106, 318
illustrated, 106
interest, 107
primary capability, 107
for revealing gaps and weaknesses,
107–108
scheme, 107
secondary capability, 107
slack times
associated with sequence of activities, 83
defined, 78, 318
determining, 82–83
tasks, changing start/end times, 122
software
choosing, 283, 286–288
existing organization use of, 285
expenditure tracking system, 222
functions, 286–288
incorrect use of, 281

integrated project-management, 281,
284–286
labor hour tracking system, 218
schedule tracking system, 213–214
stand-alone, specialty, 281–283
supporting, 286–288
types of, 281
use decision, 283
using effectively, 280–289
what it can't do, 280
span time
basis of, 73
cutting, 73
defined, 72, 313
delay and, 73
elements affecting, 72
identifying, 297
rechecking, 92–93
reducing by subdividing activities, 98–99
work effort and, 110
span time estimates, 92
activity components, 100
defined, 99, 318
fudge factor, 101–102
improving, 101–102
negotiating/bartering and, 99–100
unrealistic, 99
stakeholder list, 150
stand-alone, specialty software. *See also*
software
capabilities, 282
concerns, 283
defined, 281
Microsoft, 282
strengths, 283
types of, 282
start phase. *See also* phases
approved budget in, 129
drivers and, 160
jumping into, 19
observers and, 161
post-project evaluation and, 275
requirements, 17
risk factors, 260–261
skipping, 19
supporters and, 160

Statement of Work
approach illustration, 47
as binding agreement, 28
changes impact on, 29
defined, 27, 318
developing, 47–48
document differences from, 28
elements, 28
nonapproval of, 48
steps, 48
terms agreement, 27
storming stage, 197
subdividing activities. *See also* activities
defined, 98
example, 98–99
illustrated, 98
subtasks, 318
supporters. *See also* drivers
agreement on objectives, 43
as audience, 160–161
claim to be drivers, 31, 158
confirming participation of, 190–191
defined, 30, 158, 318
identifying, 296
involving, 160–161
phases and, 160–161
project scope confirmation with, 38

• T •

tasks, 318
team meetings. *See also* meetings
ad hoc, 236–237
regularly scheduled, 236–237
team members
in audience list, 151
buy-in, 146
change and, 227
commitment, 146
communication among, 147
confirmation with, 188–190, 204
contributions,
acknowledging/documenting, 252
defined, 143, 150

explaining team development to, 188
goals, 194–195
informing of approval, 188
lack of commitment, 21
in matrix environment, 144
motivation, 243–248
project closure and, 252
project plan review, 192
relationship development, 196–197
responsibilities, 144, 165–183
roles, defining, 195–196
styles, 146
successful, 193
transitions to new assignments, 252
teams
accountability to, 174
communication, 196
conflict resolution, 196
decision making, 196
defined, 192–193
developing, 192–198
forming stage, 197
functioning of, 146
goals, 194–195
groups/committees versus, 193
guiding, through stages, 198
identity, 194
leadership, poor, 21
norming stage, 197
operating processes, defining, 196
performance assessment, 198
performing stage, 197
procedures, 146
reestablishing identity/spirit, 251
as smooth-functioning unit, 197–198
storming stage, 197
vision, 146
templates
audience list, 156–157
Work Breakdown Structure, 66–67
time
allocating, evenly, 120
constraints, 92–93
delays, 100

log, 216
network diagram and, 95
performing activities at same, 93–97
planning, 96
reducing, 93–99
span, 72–73, 92–93, 98
strategy, devising, 97
time frame limitations, 44
time sheet
collection, 217
data, 215
filling out, 217
illustrated, 216
inaccurate practices, 115
no non-project work category, 114
non-project-specific work categories, 113–114
recording time on, 115
submission, 217
using data from, 115
time-recording system, 218
top down approach (Work Breakdown Structure), 62
top-down cost estimate, 130, 132
tracking
expenditures, 198, 206, 218–222
outcomes, 240
resources, 198, 204
risk status, 259
schedules, 198, 204, 207–214
work effort, 214–218
tracking systems
charge codes, 199
existing, 198–199
expenditure, 222
schedule, 213–214
setting up, 198–199
training, 107

• U •

unknown unknown, 67, 318
unknowns
categories, 67
examples, 47
known, 67–68
in planning process, 46–47
unknown, 67
upper management
in audience list, 151
defined, 143
oversight committee, 147
responsibilities, 145
upper-management reviews. *See also* meetings
defined, 236
running of, 237
tips, 237–238
urgency
assignment, emphasizing, 301
creating, 175
usage charts
computer, 125–126
individual, 125
summary, 125

• V •

vague limitations, 45
variances
causes, identifying, 224–225
cost, 320–324
reasons for, 324
schedule, 320–324

• W •

weighted labor rate, 318
What's In It For Me (WIIFM), 162
Work Breakdown Structure
action verbs and, 54–55
activities with no break points, 58–59
activity breakdown approaches, 59–61
activity order and, 65
brainstorming approach, 62–63
breakdown example, 52–53
breakdown questions, 53–54
bubble-chart format, 64–65
choosing, 70
current, keeping, 65

Work Breakdown Structure *(continued)*
  defined, 52, 318
  detail levels, 52
  developing, 61–63
  different paths, 69–70
  displaying, 63–65
  elements, 52
  entries, identifying, 61
  examples, 55–57, 69–70
  finalizing, 198
  formats, 63–65
  illustrated, 52, 56, 69–70
  indented-outline format, 63–64
  information from similar projects, 65
  iterative activities, 57–58
  for large/small projects, 55
  for long-term projects, 59
  organization-chart format, 63
  people involvement in, 65
  project complexity and, 55
  tips and hints, 65
  top-down approach, 62
  uncertain activity assumptions, 65
  unknowns and, 67–68
Work Breakdown Structure dictionary
  defined, 68, 318
  information, 68–69
Work Breakdown Structure templates
  defined, 66
  developing, 66–67
  improving, 66–67
  as starting points, 67
  updating, 67
  uses, 66
  using, 66
work definition, 49–59
work effort
  defined, 73, 110
  display, 110
  estimates, improving, 117
  estimating, 111–112
  hierarchical estimate, 117
  history and, 111
  proposed, 118, 120

span time and, 110
  tracking, 214–218
work effort expenditures
  data accuracy, 217
  data analysis, 214–215
  data collection, 215–216
  data recording, 217
  labor report, 214–215
  time sheets, 215–216
  tracking system support, 218
work order, 28
work-order agreement
  defined, 189, 318
  identifiers, 189
  illustrated, 189
  information, 189
  information, finding, 190
  start/end dates, 189
  written approvals, 189
written approvals, 161
written confirmation, 300–301
written reports. *See also* reports
  benefits, 231
  drawbacks, 231
  improving chances of people reading, 231
  length, 231–232
  novel approaches to, 231

"yes, but" syndrome, 232

# Notes

# Notes

# Notes

# Notes

# FOR DUMMIES®

## The easy way to get more done and have more fun

---

### PERSONAL FINANCE

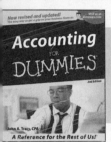

**0-7645-5231-7**

**0-7645-2431-3**

**0-7645-5331-3**

**Also available:**

Estate Planning For Dummies
(0-7645-5501-4)
401(k)s For Dummies
(0-7645-5468-9)
Frugal Living For Dummies
(0-7645-5403-4)
Microsoft Money "X" For
Dummies
(0-7645-1689-2)
Mutual Funds For Dummies
(0-7645-5329-1)

Personal Bankruptcy For
Dummies
(0-7645-5498-0)
Quicken "X" For Dummies
(0-7645-1666-3)
Stock Investing For Dummies
(0-7645-5411-5)
Taxes For Dummies 2003
(0-7645-5475-1)

---

### BUSINESS & CAREERS

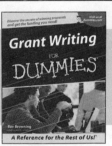

**0-7645-5314-3**

**0-7645-5307-0**

**0-7645-5471-9**

**Also available:**

Business Plans Kit For
Dummies
(0-7645-5365-8)
Consulting For Dummies
(0-7645-5034-9)
Cool Careers For Dummies
(0-7645-5345-3)
Human Resources Kit For
Dummies
(0-7645-5131-0)
Managing For Dummies
(1-5688-4858-7)

QuickBooks All-in-One Desk
Reference For Dummies
(0-7645-1963-8)
Selling For Dummies
(0-7645-5363-1)
Small Business Kit For
Dummies
(0-7645-5093-4)
Starting an eBay Business For
Dummies
(0-7645-1547-0)

---

### HEALTH, SPORTS & FITNESS

**0-7645-5167-1**

**0-7645-5146-9**

**0-7645-5154-X**

**Also available:**

Controlling Cholesterol For
Dummies
(0-7645-5440-9)
Dieting For Dummies
(0-7645-5126-4)
High Blood Pressure For
Dummies
(0-7645-5424-7)
Martial Arts For Dummies
(0-7645-5358-5)
Menopause For Dummies
(0-7645-5458-1)

Nutrition For Dummies
(0-7645-5180-9)
Power Yoga For Dummies
(0-7645-5342-9)
Thyroid For Dummies
(0-7645-5385-2)
Weight Training For Dummies
(0-7645-5168-X)
Yoga For Dummies
(0-7645-5117-5)

---

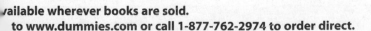

**Available wherever books are sold.**
**to www.dummies.com or call 1-877-762-2974 to order direct.**

# FOR DUMMIES®

## A world of resources to help you grow

---

## HOME, GARDEN & HOBBIES

**Feng Shui For Dummies**

0-7645-5295-3

**Gardening For Dummies** 2nd Edition

0-7645-5130-2

**Guitar For Dummies**

0-7645-5106-X

### Also available:

Auto Repair For Dummies
(0-7645-5089-6)

Chess For Dummies
(0-7645-5003-9)

Home Maintenance For Dummies
(0-7645-5215-5)

Organizing For Dummies
(0-7645-5300-3)

Piano For Dummies
(0-7645-5105-1)

Poker For Dummies
(0-7645-5232-5)

Quilting For Dummies
(0-7645-5118-3)

Rock Guitar For Dummies
(0-7645-5356-9)

Roses For Dummies
(0-7645-5202-3)

Sewing For Dummies
(0-7645-5137-X)

---

## FOOD & WINE

**Cooking For Dummies** 2nd Edition

0-7645-5250-3

**Cookies For Dummies**

0-7645-5390-9

**Wine For Dummies** 2nd Edition

0-7645-5114-0

### Also available:

Bartending For Dummies
(0-7645-5051-9)

Chinese Cooking For Dummies
(0-7645-5247-3)

Christmas Cooking For Dummies
(0-7645-5407-7)

Diabetes Cookbook For Dummies
(0-7645-5230-9)

Grilling For Dummies
(0-7645-5076-4)

Low-Fat Cooking For Dummies
(0-7645-5035-7)

Slow Cookers For Dummies
(0-7645-5240-6)

---

## TRAVEL

**Italy For Dummies** 2nd Edition

0-7645-5453-0

**Hawaii For Dummies** 2nd Edition

0-7645-5438-7

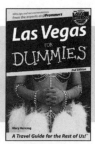

**Las Vegas For Dummies** 2nd Edition

0-7645-5448-4

### Also available:

America's National Parks For Dummies
(0-7645-6204-5)

Caribbean For Dummies
(0-7645-5445-X)

Cruise Vacations For Dummies 2003
(0-7645-5459-X)

Europe For Dummies
(0-7645-5456-5)

Ireland For Dummies
(0-7645-6199-5)

France For Dummies
(0-7645-6292-4)

London For Dummies
(0-7645-5416-6)

Mexico's Beach Resorts For Dummies
(0-7645-6262-2)

Paris For Dummies
(0-7645-5494-8)

RV Vacations For Dummies
(0-7645-5443-3)

Walt Disney World & Orlando For Dummies
(0-7645-5444-1)

---

**Available wherever books are sold. Go to www.dummies.com or call 1-877-762-2974 to order direct.**

# FOR DUMMIES®

## Plain-English solutions for everyday challenges

**OMPUTER BASICS**

**0-7645-0838-5**

**0-7645-1663-9**

**0-7645-1548-9**

**Also available:**

PCs All-in-One Desk Reference For Dummies (0-7645-0791-5)

Pocket PC For Dummies (0-7645-1640-X)

Treo and Visor For Dummies (0-7645-1673-6)

Troubleshooting Your PC For Dummies (0-7645-1669-8)

Upgrading & Fixing PCs For Dummies (0-7645-1665-5)

Windows XP For Dummies (0-7645-0893-8)

Windows XP For Dummies Quick Reference (0-7645-0897-0)

**USINESS SOFTWARE**

**0-7645-0822-9**

**0-7645-0839-3**

**0-7645-0819-9**

**Also available:**

Excel Data Analysis For Dummies (0-7645-1661-2)

Excel 2002 All-in-One Desk Reference For Dummies (0-7645-1794-5)

Excel 2002 For Dummies Quick Reference (0-7645-0829-6)

GoldMine "X" For Dummies (0-7645-0845-8)

Microsoft CRM For Dummies (0-7645-1698-1)

Microsoft Project 2002 For Dummies (0-7645-1628-0)

Office XP For Dummies (0-7645-0830-X)

Outlook 2002 For Dummies (0-7645-0828-8)

## Get smart! Visit www.dummies.com

- **Find listings of even more *For Dummies* titles**
- **Browse online articles**
- **Sign up for Dummies eTips™**
- **Check out *For Dummies* fitness videos and other products**
- **Order from our online bookstore**

**Available wherever books are sold. Go to www.dummies.com or call 1-877-762-2974 to order direct.**

# FOR DUMMIES®

## Helping you expand your horizons and realize your potential

---

### INTERNET

**0-7645-0894-6**

**0-7645-1659-0**

**0-7645-1642-6**

**Also available:**

America Online 7.0 For Dummies
(0-7645-1624-8)

Genealogy Online For Dummies
(0-7645-0807-5)

The Internet All-in-One Desk Reference For Dummies
(0-7645-1659-0)

Internet Explorer 6 For Dummies
(0-7645-1344-3)

The Internet For Dummies Quick Reference
(0-7645-1645-0)

Internet Privacy For Dummies
(0-7645-0846-6)

Researching Online For Dummies
(0-7645-0546-7)

Starting an Online Business For Dummies
(0-7645-1655-8)

---

### DIGITAL MEDIA

**0-7645-1664-7**

**0-7645-1675-2**

**0-7645-0806-7**

**Also available:**

CD and DVD Recording For Dummies
(0-7645-1627-2)

Digital Photography All-in-One Desk Reference For Dummies
(0-7645-1800-3)

Digital Photography For Dummies Quick Reference
(0-7645-0750-8)

Home Recording for Musicians For Dummies
(0-7645-1634-5)

MP3 For Dummies
(0-7645-0858-X)

Paint Shop Pro "X" For Dummies
(0-7645-2440-2)

Photo Retouching & Restoration For Dummies
(0-7645-1662-0)

Scanners For Dummies
(0-7645-0783-4)

---

### GRAPHICS

**0-7645-0817-2**

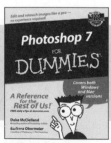

**0-7645-1651-5**

**0-7645-0895-4**

**Also available:**

Adobe Acrobat 5 PDF For Dummies
(0-7645-1652-3)

Fireworks 4 For Dummies
(0-7645-0804-0)

Illustrator 10 For Dummies
(0-7645-3636-2)

QuarkXPress 5 For Dummies
(0-7645-0643-9)

Visio 2000 For Dummies
(0-7645-0635-8)

---

**Available wherever books are sold. Go to www.dummies.com or call 1-877-762-2974 to order direct.**

# FOR DUMMIES®

## The advice and explanations you need to succeed

---

## SELF-HELP, SPIRITUALITY & RELIGION

**Sex For Dummies**
0-7645-5302-X

**Parenting For Dummies**
0-7645-5418-2

**Religion For Dummies**
0-7645-5264-3

### Also available:

The Bible For Dummies
(0-7645-5296-1)

Buddhism For Dummies
(0-7645-5359-3)

Christian Prayer For Dummies
(0-7645-5500-6)

Dating For Dummies
(0-7645-5072-1)

Judaism For Dummies
(0-7645-5299-6)

Potty Training For Dummies
(0-7645-5417-4)

Pregnancy For Dummies
(0-7645-5074-8)

Rekindling Romance For Dummies
(0-7645-5303-8)

Spirituality For Dummies
(0-7645-5298-8)

Weddings For Dummies
(0-7645-5055-1)

---

## PETS

**Puppies For Dummies**
0-7645-5255-4

**Dog Training For Dummies**
0-7645-5286-4

**Cats For Dummies**
0-7645-5275-9

### Also available:

Labrador Retrievers For Dummies
(0-7645-5281-3)

Aquariums For Dummies
(0-7645-5156-6)

Birds For Dummies
(0-7645-5139-6)

Dogs For Dummies
(0-7645-5274-0)

Ferrets For Dummies
(0-7645-5259-7)

German Shepherds For Dummies
(0-7645-5280-5)

Golden Retrievers For Dummies
(0-7645-5267-8)

Horses For Dummies
(0-7645-5138-8)

Jack Russell Terriers For Dummies
(0-7645-5268-6)

Puppies Raising & Training Diary For Dummies
(0-7645-0876-8)

---

## EDUCATION & TEST PREPARATION

**Spanish For Dummies**
0-7645-5194-9

**Algebra For Dummies**
0-7645-5325-9

**The ACT For Dummies**
0-7645-5210-4

### Also available:

Chemistry For Dummies
(0-7645-5430-1)

English Grammar For Dummies
(0-7645-5322-4)

French For Dummies
(0-7645-5193-0)

The GMAT For Dummies
(0-7645-5251-1)

Inglés Para Dummies
(0-7645-5427-1)

Italian For Dummies
(0-7645-5196-5)

Research Papers For Dummies
(0-7645-5426-3)

The SAT I For Dummies
(0-7645-5472-7)

U.S. History For Dummies
(0-7645-5249-X)

World History For Dummies
(0-7645-5242-2)

---

**Available wherever books are sold. Go to www.dummies.com or call 1-877-762-2974 to order direct.**

# FOR DUMMIES®

## We take the mystery out of complicated subjects

## WEB DEVELOPMENT

**0-7645-1643-4**

**0-7645-0723-0**

**0-7645-1630-2**

**Also available:**

ASP.NET For Dummies
(0-7645-0866-0)

Building a Web Site For
Dummies
(0-7645-0720-6)

ColdFusion "MX" For
Dummies (0-7645-1672-8)

Creating Web Pages
All-in-One Desk Reference
For Dummies
(0-7645-1542-X)

FrontPage 2002 For Dummie
(0-7645-0821-0)

HTML 4 For Dummies Quick
Reference
(0-7645-0721-4)

Macromedia Studio "MX"
All-in-One Desk Reference
For Dummies
(0-7645-1799-6)

Web Design For Dummies
(0-7645-0823-7)

## PROGRAMMING & DATABASES

**0-7645-0746-X**

**0-7645-1657-4**

**0-7645-0818-0**

**Also available:**

Beginning Programming For
Dummies
(0-7645-0835-0)

Crystal Reports "X"
For Dummies
(0-7645-1641-8)

Java & XML For Dummies
(0-7645-1658-2)

Java 2 For Dummies
(0-7645-0765-6)

JavaScript For Dummies
(0-7645-0633-1)

Oracle9i For Dummies
(0-7645-0880-6)

Perl For Dummies
(0-7645-0776-1)

PHP and MySQL For
Dummies
(0-7645-1650-7)

SQL For Dummies
(0-7645-0737-0)

VisualBasic .NET For
Dummies
(0-7645-0867-9)

Visual Studio .NET All-in-One
Desk Reference For Dummies
(0-7645-1626-4)

## LINUX, NETWORKING & CERTIFICATION

**0-7645-1545-4**

**0-7645-0772-9**

**0-7645-0812-1**

**Also available:**

CCNP All-in-One Certification
For Dummies
(0-7645-1648-5)

Cisco Networking For
Dummies
(0-7645-1668-X)

CISSP For Dummies
(0-7645-1670-1)

CIW Foundations For
Dummies with CD-ROM
(0-7645-1635-3)

Firewalls For Dummies
(0-7645-0884-9)

Home Networking For
Dummies
(0-7645-0857-1)

Red Hat Linux All-in-One
Desk Reference For Dummies
(0-7645-2442-9)

TCP/IP For Dummies
(0-7645-1760-0)

UNIX For Dummies
(0-7645-0419-3)

**Available wherever books are sold.**
**Go to www.dummies.com or call 1-877-762-2974 to order direct.**

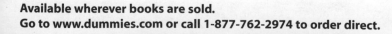

WILEY